Adopting New Medical Technology

MEDICAL INNOVATION AT THE CROSSROADS

VOLUME IV

Annetine C. Gelijns and Holly V. Dawkins, Editors

Committee on Technological Innovation in Medicine
INSTITUTE OF MEDICINE

NATIONAL ACADEMY PRESS
Washington, D.C. 1994

NATIONAL ACADEMY PRESS 2101 Constitution Avenue, N.W. Washington, D.C. 20418

The Institute of Medicine was chartered in 1970 by the National Academy of Sciences to enlist distinguished members of the appropriate professions in the examination of policy matters pertaining to the health of the public. In this the Institute acts under both the Academy's 1863 congressional charter responsibility to be an advisor to the federal government and its own initiative in identifying issues of medical care, research, and education. Dr. Kenneth I. Shine is president of the Institute of Medicine.

The Committee on Technological Innovation in Medicine was established in 1988 by the Institute of Medicine to design a series of workshops that would (a) provide more fundamental knowledge of the process by which biomedical research findings are translated into clinical practice and (b) address opportunities for improving the rationality and efficiency of the process. This volume consists of the proceedings of the fourth workshop in the series, "Examining Coverage and Adoption Decisions About Medical Technologies," held in Washington, D.C., on September 18-19, 1992. This workshop and its proceedings were supported by Abbott Laboratories, AEtna, Blue Cross and Blue Shield Association, the Health Industry Manufacturers Association, the Howard Hughes Medical Institute, and Pfizer. The opinions and conclusions expressed here are those of the authors and do not necessarily represent the views of the National Academy of Sciences, any of its constituent parts, or the organizations providing support.

Library of Congress Cataloging-in-Publication Data

Adopting new medical technology / Committee on Technological Innovation in Medicine, Institute of Medicine; Annetine C. Gelijns and Holly V. Dawkins, editors.

p. cm.—(Medical innovation at the crossroads; v. 4)

"Proceedings of the fourth workshop in the series 'Examining coverage and adoption decisions about medical technologies,' held in Washington, D.C., on September 18-19, 1992"—T.p. verso.

Includes bibliographical references and index.

ISBN 0-309-05035-9

1. Medical innovations—Congresses. 2. Insurance, Health—United States—Congresses. 3. Social medicine—United States—Congresses. 4. Health care reform—United States—Congresses. I. Gelijns, Annetine C. II. Dawkins, Holly V. III. Institute of Medicine (U.S.). Committee on Technological Innovation in Medicine. IV. Series.

[DNLM: 1. Technology Assessment, Biomedical—congresses. 2. Diffusion of Innovation—congresses. 3. Technology, Medical- economics—United States—congresses. 4. Technology, Medical-trends—United States—congresses. 5. Insurance, Health, Reimbursement—United States—congresses. 6. Health Policy—United States—congresses. WI ME342F v.4 1994 / W 74 A239 1994]

R855.2.A36 1994

610—dc20

DNLM/DLC

for Library of Congress

94-7852

CIP

Printed in the United States of America

The serpent has been a symbol of long life, healing, and knowledge among almost all cultures and religions since the beginning of recorded history. The image adopted as a logotype by the Institute of Medicine is based on a relief carving from ancient Greece, now held at the Staatlichemuseen in Berlin.

Committee on Technological Innovation in Medicine

GERALD D. LAUBACH, *Chair,* Former President, Pfizer, Inc.
SUSAN BARTLETT FOOTE, Health Advisor, Office of Senator Dave Durenberger, U.S. Senate
BEN L. HOLMES, Vice President and General Manager, Medical Products Group, Hewlett-Packard Company
WILLIAM N. HUBBARD, JR., Former President, the Upjohn Company
LUCIAN L. LEAPE, Lecturer on Health Policy, Harvard School of Public Health
KENNETH L. MELMON, Professor of Medicine and of Pharmacology, Department of Medicine, Stanford University School of Medicine
H. RICHARD NESSON, President, Brigham and Womens Hospital
UWE E. REINHARDT, James Madison Professor of Political Economy, Woodrow Wilson School of Public and International Affairs, Princeton University
NATHAN ROSENBERG, Professor of Economics, Stanford University MICHAEL R. SOPER, Former National Medical Director, CIGNA
JOHN E. WENNBERG, Professor of Epidemiology, Department of Community and Family Medicine, Dartmouth Medical School

Project Staff

Program on Technological Innovation in Medicine
ANNETINE C. GELIJNS, Program Director (until February, 1993)
HOLLY V. DAWKINS, Research Assistant
HELEN C. ROGERS, Senior Project Assistant

Acknowledgments

The Committee on Technological Innovation in Medicine wishes to acknowledge the many individuals and organizations who contributed to this volume. These papers were originally presented at the Institute of Medicine workshop, "Examining Coverage and Adoption Decisions About Medical Technologies" (see appendix A for the agenda). Undoubtedly first among those to be thanked are the authors of these papers. The committee thanks them profoundly for the sustained effort and time that went into preparing their presentations and writing their chapters. It also acknowledges the significant contributions of the workshop organizing committee and the workshop moderators, discussants, and participants.

The committee notes with appreciation that support for the workshop or the proceedings came from several organizations. This volume would not have been possible without the support of Abbott Laboratories, AEtna, Blue Cross and Blue Shield Association, the Health Industry Manufacturers Association, the Howard Hughes Medical Institute, and Pfizer.

The committee would also like to express its gratitude to the Institute of Medicine staff who facilitated the committee's work. Annetine Gelijns, then director of the program on technological innovation in medicine and now at the College of Physicians and Surgeons, Columbia University, was both the conceptual and editorial foundation of this volume. Holly Dawkins shepherded the volume through innumerable drafts and revisions. Helen Rogers was invaluable as both a keen commentator on substantive aspects and as the logistical maven of all the committee's undertakings. Finally, the committee is deeply appreciative of the support of four individuals: Kathleen N. Lohr, director of the Division of

Health Care Services, Karl D. Yordy, former director of the Division of Health Care Services, Enriqueta Bond, executive officer of the Institute of Medicine, and Kenneth I. Shine, president of the Institute of Medicine.

Gerald D. Laubach

Chair

Committee on Technological Innovation in Medicine

Contents

List of Tables and Figures

TABLES

FIGURES

List of Abbreviations

ACP	American College of Physicians
AHCPR	Agency for Health Care Policy and Research
AZT	zidovudine
BCBSA	Blue Cross and Blue Shield Association
BDMS	Bureau of Data Management and Strategy of the Health Care Financing Administration
CABG	coronary artery bypass graft
CEAP	Clinical Efficacy Assessment Project of the American College of Physicians
CMDs	carrier medical directors
CRD	chronic renal disease
DRG	diagnosis-related group
FDA	Food and Drug Administration
GNP	gross national product
HCFA	Health Care Financing Administration
HDC-ABMT	high dose chemotherapy with autologous bone marrow transplantation
HMO	health maintenance organization
IOM	Institute of Medicine
JCAHCO	Joint Commission on the Accreditation of Health Care Organizations
MRI	magnetic resonance imaging
NCI	National Cancer Institute
NIH	National Institutes of Health
OHTA	Office of Health Technology Assessment

PET	positron emission tomography
PORTs	patient outcomes research teams
PPOs	preferred provider organizations
PPS	prospective payment system
PROs	peer review organizations
QALY	quality-adjusted life year
R&D	research and development
RCT	randomized clinical trial
TEC	Technology, Evaluation, and Coverage Program of Blue Cross and Blue Shield Association
t-PA	tissue plasminogen activator
VA	Department of Veterans Affairs

Adopting New Medical Technology

PART I

Setting the Stage

1

Introduction

GERALD D. LAUBACH, ANNETINE C. GELIJNS, AND HOLLY V. DAWKINS

The proceedings presented here summarize the fourth in a series of Institute of Medicine workshops whose intent is to critically examine medical innovation —that is, the process by which scientific and technological findings are translated into actual benefits in clinical practice. They appear at a time when the United States is engaged in a profound debate about the future of its health care system. President Clinton only recently unveiled his Health Security Plan, the principal objectives of which are to extend access to health care to all Americans, maintain the quality of health care in the United States, and contain the escalating costs of health care (Health Security Act, 1993; The President's Health Security Plan, 1993). Although the specific shape and nature of the reform legislation that will ultimately be enacted are as yet unknown, it will have major implications for the generation and application of new medical technologies.

One can discern three major strategies in the President's proposal that will attempt to shape technological change in a quality-enhancing as well as cost-reducing direction. The first set of policies focuses on changing the demand for medical care through the introduction of such mechanisms as managed competition and global budgets. Volume III in this series (Institute of Medicine, 1992) explored in considerable detail the impact of such structural changes on innovative activities. As Weisbrod also argues in chapter 2 of this volume, such changes are expected to lead to more cost-effective utilization of medical technology; this, in turn, will inevitably exert a strong influence on the rate and direction of subsequent research and development efforts. At the same time, the second major strategy of the reform proposal recognizes that if technological change is to be redirected it is essential to examine the underlying scientific and engineer ing knowledge base and the supply-side policies that stimulate technological expansion. In the current debate, for example, considerable attention is geared toward the level of investment in basic biomedical research and the number and mix of specialists versus generalists. The third set of policies concerns strengthening the information bases about the risks, benefits, and costs of medical interventions and coupling this information more strongly to decisions about the coverage, adoption, and use of medical technologies.

This fourth volume in the *Medical Innovation at the Crossroads* series focuses on that third set of policies. It addresses a critical juncture in the medical innovation process: the transition of a medical technology from "experimental" to "accepted."' These days, the care a patient receives is greatly shaped by a myriad of individual coverage and adoption decisions, which can range from a physician's choice of a diagnostic test, to a hospital drug formulary committee's acceptance of a new biotechnology agent, to the decision by an insurance company or health maintenance organization about whether to cover positron emission tomography scanning or lung transplants. Thus, both providers and payers have become important gatekeepers and determinants of the acceptance and utilization of medical interventions. Despite this importance, previous volumes in this series suggest that the nature of these various coverage and adoption decisions is still very much a mysterious "black box." Moreover, these decisions often appear to be highly variable; for example, a health plan may cover a medical technology in one region but not in another. Taken together, these observations provide a strong stimulus to take a closer look at the "real world" of coverage and adoption decisionmaking: What criteria guide these decisions? On what information are they based? Who supports the underlying assessments?

Luce and Brown (chapter 3), from interviews with both providers and payers, conclude that assessment activities are increasing but that the information about benefits, risks, and costs is often highly inadequate. In the absence of such information, the adoption and use of technology have been shaped by a complex set of social, financial, and regulatory forces (Fendrick and Schwartz, chapter 5). Indeed, these forces often counterbalance the incentives to make decisions on the basis of careful technology assessments. High-technology medicine, for example, is often a source of social and professional prestige. Consequently, hospitals view new technology as a way to attract high-quality specialists and a greater number of patient referrals. Not surprisingly, the degree of competition has been found to fuel the adoption of new technologies. For instance, hospitals in close proximity to other hospitals are much more likely to have open-heart surgery facilities than isolated hospitals (Robinson et al., 1987). Nevertheless, as Anderson and Steinberg argue in chapter 4, hospital managers' incentives to perform technology assessments and to base their acquisition decisions on such assessments have increased recently.

Coverage decisionmaking exhibits a somewhat similar trend. Traditionally, coverage decisionmaking has been based more on administrative procedures than on the results of rigorous evaluations. The chapters in this volume underscore the fact, however, that payers are strengthening the emphasis on medical technology evaluations in their decisionmaking processes. Interestingly, cost is not yet an explicit criterion; for example, Buto refers in chapter 6 to the lengthy, and unsuccessful, history of the proposed regulations to add cost-effectiveness to the Health Care Financing Administration's criteria for coverage. Cost has always, however, been important in selecting those technologies that will be more rigorously screened by payers.

A striking departure from previous practice is described by a number of payers in this volume (see, in particular, Gleeson and McGivney, chapters 7 and 9 respectively). In the past, medical benefit contracts for nearly all payers, public and private, had standard provisions that specifically excluded coverage for "investigational" or "experimental" therapies (see Newcomer, chapter 10). As a result, coverage decisions were generally binary—that is, "yes or no"—decisions. In response, patients often successfully battled payer's decisions not to cover experimental therapies in the courtroom (see Lairson, chapter 8). This in turn prompted the development of provisional coverage, a promising mechanism through which the patient care costs associated with an experimental procedure will be covered if patients are part of a predetermined research protocol. The resulting data are then used by payers to formulate a final coverage decision. In this volume, a variety of payers discuss their recent experience with provisional coverage for autologous bone marrow transplantation for advanced breast cancer.[1]

This new approach for coverage decisionmaking is notable in two ways. First, evaluative research is often too expensive for any single organization to perform well. Collaborative approaches involving government, insurers, hospitals, and manufacturers are needed. Such approaches can be problematic, however. It is worth remembering that, in 1990 and 1991, six insurers put forward a proposal to financially support evaluative research at the federal Agency for Health Care Policy and Research. The antitrust concerns raised about the proposal were, however, perceived as a serious problem by some; in addition, other interests have long been concerned about a centralized focus for technology assessment. The collaboration between payers, individual hospitals, and the National Cancer Institute in the case of autologous bone marrow transplantation is therefore a promising move.

The second noteworthy element of this new approach is that provisional coverage can provide a mechanism for implicitly acknowledging a fundamental

[1] As this volume was being prepared for publication a notice came through the news media of a case where Health Net, the second-largest California HMO, was ordered to pay $89.1 million in punitive and compensatory damages to the family of a patient with breast cancer for whom it had not covered autologous bone marrow transplantation—an experimental technology (*Washington Post,* 1993). We regard this decision as highlighting the critical nature of the coverage and adoption decisions discussed in this volume.

aspect of medical innovation. Innovation takes place not only in industrial and academic laboratories but at the bedside and is often highly incremental in nature. Early assessments and binary coverage decisions are unlikely to accurately capture all the benefits, risks, and costs of a medical technology. The concept of provisional coverage, however, points toward a more flexible process that allows decisions about coverage, reimbursement, and utilization to change as the technology evolves.

The increased demand, from both providers and payers, for better information on the value of new medical interventions is also stimulating manufacturers to invest more heavily in outcomes research and cost-effectiveness analyses (see Marshall, chapter 12). All of these activities put heavier demands on methods of technology assessment. In chapter 11, Leape comprehensively discusses the strengths and weaknesses of both experimental (e.g., randomized controlled trials) and observational (e.g., claims database) methods of assessing medical technologies. The final question that then remains is, Who shall support these assessments? In chapter 13, Garber and Owen review the relative roles and responsibilities of government, payers, and manufacturers. They conclude that the current investment in technology assessment and outcomes research is highly inadequate and discuss several mechanisms for improving this situation.

In sum, the imminence of health care reform should not obscure the considerable changes that have already taken place in the provision and financing of health care (see Foote, chapter 14). The United States has witnessed an impressive degree of growth in the number of people participating in prepaid capitated arrangements, and even traditional indemnity plans have nearly all adopted such managed care tools as utilization management and review. These changes provide much stronger incentives than existed in the past to assess the value of existing, as well as emerging, medical care. The chapters in this volume review the strengths and weaknesses of present coverage and adoption practices, highlight opportunities for improving both decisionmaking processes and the underlying information base, and consider approaches to instituting the much needed increase in financial support for evaluative research. These topics will remain highly relevant in the years to come; for example, the establishment of a minimum benefits package raises questions about how decisions to include or exclude services in that package are best made. It is the committee's hope that the discussions in this volume will contribute some answers to such questions and to the debate about the future health care system in general.

REFERENCES

Institute of Medicine. 1992. *Medical Innovation at the Crossroads.* Vol. 3, *Technology and Health Care in an Era of Limits.* A. C. Gelijns, ed. Washington, D.C.: National Academy Press.

Health Security Act. 1993. Report no. PB93-233625KSV. Springfield, Va.: National Technical Information Service, U.S. Department of Commerce.

The President's Health Security Plan. 1993. Report no. PB93-234979. Springfield, Va.: National Technical Information Service, U.S. Department of Commerce.

Robinson, B., Gamick, D. W., McPhee, S. I. 1987. Market and regulatory influences on the availability of coronary angioplasty and bypass surgery in U.S. hospitals. *New England Journal of Medicine* 317:85-90.

Washington Post. 1993. Family Awarded $89.1 Million From HMO in Cancer Death. December 30, p. A 12.

2

The Nature of Technological Change: Incentives Matter!

BURTON A. WEISBROD[1]

Technological change involves two dimensions—invention and adoption. Much of the recent attention to cost containment in health care has focused on whether newly available technologies should be adopted, that is, whether they pass some form of cost-effectiveness test. It is clearly important to examine the question of whether a new health care procedure, diagnostic test, or drug is worth its cost relative to alternatives. Yet, by concentrating on the assessment of technologies that already exist, one implicitly assumes that inventions of new technologies are generated by exogenous factors over which society has no control.

Are social choices limited to deciding when and whether to utilize newly developed medical advances? Or can society influence what kinds of advances are produced by the research and development process?

In the economy generally, each year brings many new inventions that are simply ignored, temporarily or even permanently. Knowledge about how to produce new or improved products is not tantamount to actual provision; the cost may exceed what buyers are willing to pay. Does this separation of invention from adoption hold in the health care sector?

Probably not! When life itself is at stake, society finds it excruciatingly difficult to withhold access to effective new technologies even when they are extremely costly, as is the case with organ transplants and mechanisms for sustaining life for very low birth weight babies. Having to choose between making

[1] Most of this paper was previously published as "The health care quadrilemma: An essay on technological change, insurance, quality of care, and cost containment" in the *Journal of Economic Literature,* 29:523-552, 1991.

such technologies available to all who can benefit from them, with enormous cost consequences, and restricting availability to persons with the ability to pay, or otherwise rationing access, poses choices with powerfully divisive social and political consequences.

Society needs to recognize that to control these divisive forces society needs to intervene earlier in the process of technological change-at the stage of research and development (R&D). This chapter highlights the means by which the health care insurance system sends signals to the R&D sector and how those signals affect incentives that generate tomorrow's new technologies. Those incentives will determine whether the new technologies drive health care costs upward or downward.

Incentives matter! Public policy can and does provide the R&D sector, where new technologies are developed, with incentives to pay more attention either to enhancing quality or to reducing costs. Depending on which of those is emphasized, tomorrow's health care technology arsenal will provide society with expanded opportunities either to extend life expectancy and enhance quality of life or to reduce costs. Public policy can choose the degree to which society concentrates on each of these social goals; unfortunately, they conflict.

Throughout most of the post-World War II era the incentive signal sent from the health care finance system to the R&D sector has been to enhance quality of care regardless of costs. Over the past decade the incentive signal has been changing, shifting toward an emphasis on costs. It is not my purpose to determine the socially appropriate balance between quality and cost. Rather, it is to emphasize the inevitability of such a choice and the instruments through which the choice can be made.

One of the mechanisms currently being utilized to contain costs in hospitals is the Medicare diagnosis-related group (DRG) system. The effectiveness of such a price control mechanism in a dynamic context of technological change has received little attention; it deserves more, however, since the mechanism, depending on how it is administered, can have a profound effect on the R&D sector.

To see this, consider two alternative scenarios that differ dramatically in their response to technological change; they are polar opposites, and intermediate positions are possible, but they help to clarify social policy alternatives. In one, the DRG classification system is permanent and impervious to technological change; any new technology must fit into one of the existing DRG classes at prices that are not affected by the new technologies. In this case, an invention that would enhance quality of care but at an extremely high cost relative to the DRG price that a hospital would receive would have a weak market; a hospital considering adoption of such a quality-improving innovation would not be able to cover its costs unless it could supplement its resources with revenue from other sources such as gifts. Thus, it would be likely to reject utilization of the quality-enhancing invention. The rigid DRG system would discourage the R&D

sector from developing anything that raised costs, regardless of its effects on quality.

An alternative scenario would posit a quite resilient DRG system. In this case every new invention that enhanced quality would result in either (1) establishment of a new DRG class with an associated price that is high enough to make hospital utilization of the new invention profitable, or (2) a reinterpretation of an existing DRG class to encompass the new invention, together with an increase in the associated price. In this situation the R&D sector would see that anything that raised quality would be greeted with an effective price high enough to make it profitable for hospitals to adopt it. The cost-containment goal of the DRG system would be entirely undermined with respect to new technologies.

Which of these scenarios, or which position between them, is likely to emerge from the political-regulatory process is unclear. The outcome, however, matters a great deal—whether one's concerns are largely with cost containment or with the advance of medicine.

At the Institute of Medicine conference on coverage and adoption decisionmaking about medical technologies, the principal focus was on the rapidly growing area of technology assessment. This chapter, however, concentrates attention on the process that produces the new technologies requiring assessment. It highlights some consequences of attempts by society to gain control over the health care system to achieve multiple goals—encouraging technological change, expanding access to new technologies through insurance, sustaining or improving the quality of health care services, and controlling costs.

INTRODUCTION

During the roughly four decades since the end of World War II, the health care system in the United States has experienced historically unprecedented changes in three dimensions. First, *new technologies* have revolutionized the ways in which health care is capable of being practiced. Almost all of today's armamentarium of disease diagnosis and treatment devices and techniques were unknown 40 years ago. In the case of prescription drugs, for example, about 10 percent of the 200 top-selling drugs are new each year, and only 25 percent of the 200 top-selling drugs in 1972 remained in the group 15 years later (Cleeton et al., 1988).

Second, *the role of health care insurance*—private and public—has expanded dramatically. By 1980, 82.5 percent of the U.S. population had some health care insurance, compared with fewer than 10 percent in 1940.[2]

[2] Throughout the postwar period the expansion of private health care insurance has been spurred by federal tax policy. By making employer-financed health insurance nontaxable income to employees, federal policy distorted worker choice between health insurance and cash wages, encouraging excess health insurance (Feldstein and Allison, 1974; Pauly, 1974; Mitchell and Vogel, 1975; Mitchell and Phelps, 1976; Taylor and Wilensky, 1983; Chernick et al., 1987).

Third, *personal health expenditures* have soared. From $300 per capita in 1950, they leaped to $1,493 in 1987 (all in 1982 dollars). The percentage of the gross national product (GNP) devoted to medical care almost tripled over that period—from 4 to 11 percent (U.S. Bureau of the Census, 1979, p. 97; U.S. Bureau of the Census, 1989, p. 90; Letsch et al., 1988).

This chapter explains how the expansion of health care insurance has paid for the development of cost-increasing technologies and how the new technologies have expanded demand for insurance. My goal is less to review the vast literature on the health care system and the rising level of real expenditures on it than to reflect on the dynamic interplay of incentives for the R&D sector to develop particular kinds of new technologies, the role of the insurance system in that process and, reciprocally, the long-run effects of new technologies (any new knowledge about health care) on the character of the health care insurance system. The broad model outlined here highlights the ways in which the quality of health care that can be supplied in a technically feasible manner at any point in time and the breadth of access to that care influence each other and the aggregate level of health care expenditures; but the model is not fully specified, nor is it tested rigorously. Thus, this chapter should be seen as a personal interpretation —largely positive, rather than normative, in character—of a period of enormous growth and massive change in both the practice and finance of health care.

The central focus on technological change—as an independent variable causing changes in the form and extent of insurance coverage, and as a dependent variable, being influenced by incentives operating through the health insurance system—highlights the impact of incentives; both the pace and types of research and development are functions of rewards that are endogenously variable, as are the comprehensiveness of insurance coverage and the breadth of access to it.[3] The following propositions are set forward: (1) The amount of resources going into the R&D process and its direction during some time interval depend in part on the mechanisms expected to be used to finance the provision of health care in future periods, when the fruits of the research process become marketable. This is simply to say that R&D is influenced by expected utilization, which depends on the insurance system. Reciprocally, (2) the demand for health care insurance depends, in part, on the state of technology, which reflects R&D in prior periods. These relationships help to explain why (3) long-run growth of health care expenditures is a by-product of the interaction of the R&D process with the health care insurance system.[4] I also examine briefly some effects of alternative forms of health care insurance on the quality of care, as distinguished from its quantity,

---

[3] Other effects of health insurance, particularly on incentives for utilization of health services, have received considerable attention. For a recent and valuable review, see Pauly (1986).

[4] Other forces also affect health care expenditures. Rising real income appears to have a positive effect on demand for health care; an income elasticity of +0.2 (or less) has been estimated from the RAND health insurance experiment (Manning et al., 1987).

and long-run changes in the definition of "health care" under insurance, as endogenous R&D alters the menu of technically feasible measures.

To understand the markets in which health care is provided and financed, it is useful to consider ways in which health care differs from most other commodities. First, it sometimes involves the preservation of life or, at least, major effects on the quality of life. Second, it is a technically complex commodity that abounds with informational asymmetries that are adverse to consumers (Arrow, 1963; Akerlof, 1970; Titmuss, 1971). Third, and as a result of these two characteristics, "nonmarket" (government and private nonprofit) suppliers in the health care sector, especially among hospitals, nursing homes, and blood banks, play a large role in influencing the interaction between insurance and R&D.[5]

Because health care affects the length and quality of life, many societies have come to accept the normative proposition that "high-quality" care ought to be made available widely, regardless of an individual's ability to pay. This assignment of property right—the breadth of which is under continuing debate results in pressure on government to finance access to some health care redistributively. In the United States, private market financing of health care, by individuals and employers, has been supplemented by governmental resources particularly through the Medicare and Medicaid programs—and, to a smaller extent, through private charitable activities.

Another reason—in addition to providing widespread access—for society's willingness to intervene in private health care markets is the substantial informational asymmetries, which give rise to economic and political demands for consumer protection (Arrow, 1963; Weisbrod, 1978, 1989; Hansmann, 1980). The claims that physicians "induce" demand (Arrow, 1963; Evans, 1974; Wilensky and Rossiter, 1983; Rossiter and Wilensky, 1984; Reinhardt, 1985; Cromwell and Mitchell, 1986; Stano, 1987), that they engage in "defensive" medicine diagnostic testing and other practices that have no expected benefits for patient health but are defenses in "malpractice" suits (Garg et al., 1978; Zuckerman, 1984; Danzon, 1985)—and that they perform "unnecessary" surgery[6] may or may not be valid; they are plausible, however, only if physicians are better informed than their patients (Pauly, 1979) and do not act as perfect agents.[7] The importance of health care to life and well-being, combined with the limited ability of consumers to make well-informed judgments about quality of care and with

[5] Some readers may prefer the term *nonprofit* to *nonmarket*. Whatever term is used, the point is to distinguish private, profit-oriented organizations from the institutions of either government or the private nonprofit sector. To be sure, government and private nonprofit organizations operate in "markets," in the sense that exchange occurs.

[6] A congressional subcommittee estimated that in 1977 there were 2 million unnecessary operations, at a cost of $4 billion and with a loss of 10,000 lives ("Elective surgery: Cut it out," 1979).

[7] Operationalizing the concepts of "induced" demand, "defensive" medicine, and "unnecessary" surgery—each of which reflects a market failure to the extent that it occurs—poses serious problems. These issues, however, are beyond the scope of this chapter.

imperfect agency relationships with physicians, may help to explain why consumers of health care rely upon public and private nonprofit institutions to an unusual degree.

The remainder of the chapter proceeds as follows: The next section contains a brief outline of the recent history of the health care sector in the United States—its evolving technology, changing insurance/finance system, increasing level of real health care expenditures, and the advent of cost-control measures. Then I show how the constellation of services included in "health care" is endogenous, being affected by the interaction of the insurance system and the R&D process. The subsequent sections focus on the effects of R&D (technological change) on the health care insurance system, the reciprocal effects of the insurance system on the R&D sector, and the effects of alternative insurance systems on quality of care, with the state of technology fixed. I then summarize and point out some possible generalizations beyond health care.

Finally, examining these interdependent relationships may help to explain some of the differences across countries in financing of health care and their roles in health care R&D, for the forces at work are not uniquely North American and the policy implications can be generalized. The United States is unusual, however, in the extent to which its actions as a producing and a consuming country influence the rate and direction of health care R&D. No other country is so major an actor in both the R&D (producing) sector and the health care (consuming) sector. For most other countries, outputs of the R&D sector are essentially exogenous to their methods of financing health care, and their systems of health care finance are also essentially exogenous to their own R&D activities. Switzerland, for instance, is a substantial producer of health care R&D (especially pharmaceuticals), but it is a small consumer; the United Kingdom and Japan, although they are not trivial elements in the R&D sector, are larger consumers of the outputs of that sector.[8] It is the enormous size and, therefore, impact of both the producing and consuming elements in the United States that make it such a fine subject for study.

A BRIEF RECENT HISTORY OF HEALTH CARE IN THE UNITED STATES: TECHNOLOGICAL CHANGE AND THE GROWTH OF INSURANCE COVERAGE

One striking aspect of change in the U.S. health care system since World War II has been the dramatic increase in knowledge of means for diagnosing and treating illness. Fifty years ago, physicians were little more than diagnosticians, their activities being essentially "limited to identification of... illness, the prediction of the likely outcome, and then the guidance of the patient and his family

[8] For a broader, European perspective on health care systems, see Organization for Economic Cooperation and Development (1990).

while the illness ran its full, natural course" (*Report of the President's Biomedical Research Panel*, 1976, Appendix A, p. 3). Today, the scope of effective interventions includes kidney dialysis, organ transplants, polio vaccines, arthroscopic surgical techniques, computed tomography scanners, nuclear magnetic resonators, and in vitro fertilization. As recently as a decade ago, heart and liver transplants were virtually unknown, but their numbers have soared, from 62 and 26, respectively, in 1981 to 1,441 and 1,182, respectively, in 1987 (U.S. Bureau of the Census, 1989, table 166).

At the same time that the technology of health care has been changing so dramatically, the system for financing health care has also been revolutionized. In the quarter century between 1950 and 1973 alone, the share of health care expenditures that was met by insurance more than tripled, from 12 to 41 percent (U.S. Bureau of the Census, 1975, table 105). The mix of insurance between private and government insurance also changed during that period; while total private expenditures on health and medical services were growing almost sixfold, from $8.7 billion to $59.8 billion (current dollars), government expenditures (Medicare and, to some extent, Medicaid) were leaping fourteenfold, from $2.5 billion to over $37 billion (U.S. Bureau of the Census, 1975, table 100). Insurance coverage for "major" or "catastrophic" health care costs has also risen sharply, from 22 percent of the population in 1960 to 73 percent by 1984 (U.S. Bureau of the Census, 1987, tables 1, 2, and 137).

Initially, most health insurance was of one particular type—covering a limited menu of only hospital services, perhaps after a small deductible—and paying ("reimbursing") the hospital for the particular services provided to a patient, the payment being equal to the "actual" average cost of treating that patient with whatever technology was used (Stevens, 1989). Included was an approximation of the average variable cost of any diagnostic or therapeutic procedures performed on the patient's behalf, plus a per diem payment for room, board, and basic nursing services and, in the case of for-profit hospitals, a markup. Thus, the payment received by the hospital was determined retrospectively and was a function of endogenous decisions by the hospital and physician as to the length of stay and the resources deployed in treating each specific patient. With hospital revenue being a function of the cost of services provided, there was little incentive to weigh costs against patient benefits. Any diagnostic or therapeutic resource that had a positive expected value of benefits could be provided in a financially feasible manner, and even when there was great uncertainty about the probability distribution of benefits from a new, more costly technology, the absence of a budget constraint encouraged its adoption.

By the 1970s, however, the growth of real expenditures on medical care—reflected in rising private insurance premiums, Medicare budgets, and the share of GNP devoted to health care—had become matters of growing public concern. Some attributed this "health care cost inflation" to the insurance system and its effect on demand; retrospective payment arrangements, operating through the insurance system, were encouraging "overuse" of medical resources (Feldstein and Friedman, 1977; Pauly, 1986). The result was a spate of reforms designed to force health care providers to consider the cost consequences of their decisions. This was done by making more of providers' revenue "prospective." Health maintenance organizations (HMOs) and, beginning in October 1983, the Medicare DRG system for pricing hospital services are the preeminent examples of this type of reform.

Both HMOs and the Medicare DRG prospective payment system confront suppliers with the incentive to be more cost-conscious, but they differ in the comprehensiveness of that incentive. Under the current DRG system for paying hospitals, the "fixed" payment for a particular patient is supplemented by additional payments to cover capital costs; thus, there is some incentive for hospitals to substitute capital for labor.[9] In addition, under the DRG system, as under the previous retrospective pricing system, a hospital's revenue is a function of its admissions of patients; this produces an incentive to hospitalize rather than to utilize approaches that involve nonhospital inputs such as drugs, broad medical management approaches, and instruction of patients in ways to prevent and alleviate problems through lifestyle and dietary measures. HMOs, which have a contractual responsibility to provide medical services, not simply hospital treatment, and receive a flat annual fee per member, maintain a greater financial incentive to utilize alternatives to hospitalization.

To the extent that cost-based insurance has been at the root of the rising expenditures on health care, however, the causal mechanism is less clear than it seems. The "moral hazard" effect of insurance could cause patients and their physician-agents to utilize more health care resources, and therefore aggregate health care expenditures to be greater than they would otherwise be; yet it does not follow that insurance would cause expenditures on health care to *grow* more rapidly. Something had to be changing. That "something" could have been the state of technology that, as we will see, was expanding in a systematic direction as a consequence, at least in part, of the particular form of insurance that had been adopted. An expanding health care insurance system—more widespread coverage of people and broader coverage of health care resources such as pharmaceuticals and chiropractic services—might also account for the growth of health care expenditures, but this explanation would pose the question of why insurance coverage would be expanding.[10]

The major theme of this chapter is that the demand for health care insurance and the process of technological change are interdependent. A shift away from insurance that paid hospitals and physicians on the basis of endogenously deter

[9] I owe this point to an anonymous reviewer

[10] Even with constant technology, real costs of health care could increase if input prices rose —for example, because of increased unionization of hospital labor—and this could increase the demand for insurance, *ceteris paribus* (that is, other things being equal).

mined "costs incurred" and office visits to insurance that paid amounts that were largely independent of costs incurred on behalf of any particular patient represented a major change. It altered incentives to use existing health care resources (that is, their rate of diffusion and utilization), and it altered earlier incentives for the R&D sector to invest in developing medical care techniques that were of higher quality but more costly.

As noted above, the shift in the nature of health insurance has occurred in two principal forms—expansion of HMOs and adoption of the DRG system of hospital pricing. In the decade of the 1980s alone, enrollments in HMOs more than tripled, from 9.1 million in 1980 to 28.6 million in 1987 (U.S. Bureau of the Census, 1989, table 148). Under the DRG prospective payment system, a hospital receives payment (prices) for treatment (e.g., of appendicitis) based on industry-wide costs for each of the 468 DRG categories. Thus, conditional on admission of a patient with a particular diagnosis, what a hospital faces is a price for treatment that is essentially independent of the actual resource cost it incurs (Hogan, 1988).[11]

Both HMOs and the DRG system of pricing hospital services are potentially revolutionary in their incentive effects on R&D.[12] The fact that the principal objective of each of these forms of prospective pricing was fiscal control is not in doubt (Pauly, 1986). Several related matters, however, are far from clear and deserve more research: Why did the shift in insurance mechanisms, from retrospective to prospective, occur when it did? Why did the United States ever start with insurance based on retrospective and fee-for-service pricing; after all, the incentives that cost-based pricing generated were, or at least should have been, apparent long ago, and the fiscal problem, as manifested in the rising share of GNP devoted to health care, has been growing for decades.

In some current research, Paul Boben (1989) presents a model in which retrospective pricing of hospital services and physician services (through fee-for-service payments to physicians on the basis of "usual and customary" fees) is allocatively efficient when there is little insurance coverage and health care prices are determined in relatively competitive markets, but diminishes as that coverage spreads. In this model the discipline of prices on patient and provider behavior that prevails when few people have insurance gives way to growing price insensitivity (inelasticity) with the expansion of insurance. Thus, a "tipping point" is reached, at which the usefulness of market-determined prices as signals of opportunity costs becomes less than its cost in terms of distorted resource

[11] The pricing system is not entirely rigid. For example, a hospital may collect from Medicare more than the DRG price for a limited number of unusually high-cost "outliers."

[12] The DRG system of hospital service pricing initially applied only to Medicare patients. It has subsequently been expanded, however, through private arrangements, to a growing number of other patients who are not covered by the Social Security Medicare law.

allocations (the moral hazard problem). Such modeling of the social choice of the insurance system is in its infancy.

Many of the issues raised above have received scant attention in the literature. The effect of advancing technology on health care financing arrangements, the incentives for R&D inherent in those financial arrangements, and the implications of those arrangements for the quality of the care provided are each the subject of later sections, where I will also consider the inevitability that health care expenditures would soar in the post-World War II era. But, first, how do I define "health care"? How is it affected by technological change and how does its definition affect insurance coverage?

DEFINING "HEALTH CARE"

Up to this point I have been discussing the market for "health care" without defining that market carefully. The endogeneity of the definition of health care under insurance contracts has received some attention (Goddeeris, 1984a,b). Consider two nonmutually exclusive hypotheses concerning the causes and consequences of the definition of health care under insurance: (1) the operational definition of health care, under insurance contracts, is a function of the state of medical technology; (2) the state of medical technology today is a function of economic and political responses to prior definitions of health care coverage under insurance contracts.

The way health care is defined under insurance contracts is important for a number of reasons, positive and normative. It affects the level of insured expenditures, the incentives to utilize resources that are covered relative to those that are not (Feldstein, 1988), and the incentives for the R&D sector to explore various potential health-promoting technologies. At the operational level, the definition of health care is at issue when coverage for chiropractic care or for "experimental" drugs or other "new" technologies is debated.

The effect of health care insurance on incentives for R&D depends on the operational definition of health care-that is, on the boundaries of the insurance contract. Health insurance contracts do not offer the option of coverage only for particular subsets of technologies, such as those already available at a given point in time (Goddeeris, 1984b; Goddeeris and Weisbrod, 1985; Baumgardner, 1989). A reasonable conjecture, however, is that health care expenditures today would be substantially lower than they would be if health care were being defined, for insurance purposes, as limited to the use of medical technologies available at the time the policy took effect or at some other fixed date. The more broadly health care is interpreted under the contract, and the more responsive it is to changes in technology, the broader the range of activities over which insurance will encourage R&D.

What determines how health care is defined? I suggest that the R&D process causes the definition of what is covered by health insurance to change in systematic ways. Technological advances are not only expanding the range of medical capabilities for extending life and enhancing health status, as the latter term is customarily understood, they are also presenting opportunities to deal with problems not conventionally considered to be "illnesses," in ways not conventionally considered "health care."[13]

An illustration of this causal process is the current debate over whether health insurance should necessarily cover in vitro fertilization. This has become an issue only in the past few years, when advances in medical capabilities made such fertilization technically feasible. An advance in medical technology has led to pressure to expand the traditional definition of insurance coverage, pressure being felt now through the political system; by 1988 such insurance coverage had been mandated in five states (U.S. Congress, 1988),[14] and by the end of 1989, laws requiring insurers to cover such "advanced" treatments for infertility had been enacted in nine states and bills had been introduced in eighteen others (Nazario, 1989).

The effect of technological change on the health insurance market can also be seen with "experimental" drugs. The decision to term a drug *experimental* is often seen as a statement of the degree of professional knowledge about its safety and efficacy. It is, however, also a statement of whether the drug will or will not be deemed "health care" for insurance purposes, since insurance typically does not cover "experimental" technologies. For example, as long as the AIDS drug, zidovudine (AZT), was termed *experimental,* its exclusion from coverage under health insurance involved each patient with costs that, until 1990, were in excess of $8,000 per year, even though conventional hospital-based treatment was covered in the traditional fashion.

The hypothesis that the definition of health care is endogenous to the economic-political system in which health care insurance is defined, provided, and financed has important implications, to the extent that it is valid. If insurance coverage is defined, as it has been, to encompass new technologies regardless of the costs involved and to encompass an ever-widening concept of health care that is, itself, responsive to the development of new technologies, the R&D sector will continue to face incentives that reward costly new measures relative to cost-reducing innovations. Such a reward system may not be incentive compatible;

---

[13] Another example of the need to decide, as a matter of public policy, how to define operationally what is health care involves people with physical disabilities. Surgery and physical therapy illustrate "traditional" health care resources employed to reduce the disabilities. City buses that are wheelchair accessible are unquestionably valuable to the disabled; whether their cost should be regarded as health care expenditures and covered by health care insurance is another matter.

[14] As of May 1988, Arkansas, Hawaii, Maryland, Massachusetts, and Texas had enacted legislation requiring private insurers to provide some coverage for in vitro fertilization procedures. Delaware Blue Cross/Blue Shield began offering coverage voluntarily in response to legislative activity (U.S. Congress, 1988).

new technologies may be developed even though they are welfare decreasing, in the sense that the insured population is not willing to pay the real cost of developing and applying the technology (Goddeeris, 1984b; Baumgardner, 1989).

EFFECTS OF RESEARCH AND DEVELOPMENT (TECHNOLOGICAL CHANGE) ON THE HEALTH CARE INSURANCE SYSTEM

Advances in medical technology—involving both diagnostics and treatment—have been, at least arguably, a driving force behind the rapid growth of health care expenditures (Altman and Blendon, 1979; LaCronique and Sandier, 1981; Showstack et al., 1982; Aaron and Schwartz, 1984; Wilensky, 1987). For example, the announcement for a conference cosponsored by the American Medical Association in October 1988 acknowledged the benefits from new medical technology but also cited the position that the growth of medical technology was a primary cause of the quadrupling of per capita health care costs between 1970 and 1986. Even if this causation occurs, however—and existing research is far from conclusive on the matter—the mechanism through which it works is not well understood. Neither is it apparent that technological advances would necessarily increase health care expenditures rather than decrease them.

One mechanism through which technological change could foster increased expenditures on health care would be through its effect on the health care insurance system. If a previously untreatable condition becomes treatable, a possible outcome is that an individual could encounter a larger, but unpredictable, medical care expense for treatment than was previously the case; thus, both the mean and the variance of an individual's health care expenditures associated with that condition could increase.

Pooling of such risks is a logical response. In addition to the increased expected demand for private insurance, collective demand is also likely to increase; the fact that health care, particularly when it has a major effect on life expectancy or quality of life, is widely viewed as a "merit" good (or "altruistic externality" [Pauly, 1986]) results in public pressure on government to ensure that the care is available to whomever needs it medically, regardless of their ability to pay.

An example of such a merit good is organ transplant technology. Reacting to the lifesaving aspects of the new transplant technology, the federal government's Task Force on Organ Transplantation proposed that government pay for all organ transplant operations that patients cannot afford (Pear, 1986). Somewhat similar legislation, enacted in 1972 in response to the development of kidney dialysis (not transplant) technology, had the clear effect of increasing health care expenditures; no patient was rationed from access to the technology and the technology, while life-extending, was more costly in resource terms (although not necessarily in net benefit terms) than simply allowing the victim to go with out treatment and, hence, to die.[15] The interplay of financial and political forces following the development of the dialysis technology (Rettig, 1980; Rettig and Marks, 1983) and the massive public expenditures that ensued may help to explain why there has been no subsequent U.S. legislation covering such complete treatment for any other disease, and why the British National Health System continues to restrict access to dialysis for persons over age 55.

Life-extending technologies highlight the ambiguity of the concept of a technology being "expenditure increasing." Total health expenditures *over a person's lifetime* are likely to increase if the person lives longer, although that is not necessarily the case. However, expenditures *per year of life* can decrease even if lifetime expenditures increase. A new technology that increases the cost of treating a particular disease but that is successful in increasing life expectancy sufficiently to decrease expected health care costs per year of life could diminish the demand for health care insurance; my conjecture is that it would not, but this deserves more attention.[16] The point is that technological change need not increase demand for insurance, even if the change increases the expected cost of treating a particular illness. It could take forms that decrease either the aggregate expected health care cost for all illnesses or the variance. Demand for insurance would also decline even if a new technology increased the aggregate expected cost of treatment, if the variance decreased sufficiently.[17]

If the focus is on the treatment of specific diseases, one finds that some innovations decrease the demand for insurance by decreasing both the expected cost of treating that illness and the cost variance. Administration of the Salk and Sabin polio vaccines, for instance, is quite inexpensive and by providing immunity to the ravaging effects of polio, they have reduced—indeed, virtually eliminated—the variance in health care expenditures associated with contracting that disease and using costly treatment technologies. The potentially enormous ex

[15] The view that dialysis and organ transplants are cost (or expenditure) increasing, *ceteris paribus,* deserves further comment as to what is embedded in the *ceteris paribus* assumption. One element is the set of probabilities of contracting all other diseases. The assumption that these probabilities are constant with respect to the organ transplant or dialysis decision may not be valid; a person whose life is "saved" through the use of one of these technologies may well face a greater probability of dying from other causes than do people who have not been victims of kidney disease.

[16] The effect of increasing life expectancy on total health care expenditures *as a percentage of GNP* is yet another matter. This depends on the productivity of people whose lives are extended, as well as on longer-run effects on birth rates.

[17] Even if technological change increases demand for insurance, it need not follow that the amount of insurance purchased would increase. Insofar as the technological changes were cost increasing, the price of insurance coverage would increase, which would diminish insurance purchases. In fact, the negative price effect of an increasing price for health care insurance appears not to have offset the positive demand-shift effect of technological change, judging from the growth in the fraction of the population with insurance; to be sure, however, much of the growth of insurance coverage over the last two decades has been through government rather than direct consumer purchases in private markets.

penditures that have been eliminated, which include those associated with decades of use of an iron lung and the lifelong costs associated with being crippled, exceed the cost of providing the vaccinations (Weisbrod, 1971). Thus, the polio vaccines, like many other vaccines, have the effect of reducing an individual's expected level of expenditures for treating the disease, as well as the variance around that mean. In the process they reduce the demand for health care insurance.

Organ transplant technology, on the other hand, is a technological advance that has increased both the mean and the variance of desired individual expenditures conditional on medical need. Before the new technology a person with serious liver malfunction, for example, simply died, with comparatively little health care expenditure.[18] With the new technology it has become possible to spend vast sums on effective treatment. A single liver transplant operation can cost $200,000 or more, and subsequent medical attention and medication to prevent organ rejection typically total $10,000-$20,000 annually for life (Hudis, 1986). Thus, a healthy person with some probability of developing liver disease faced a larger expected financial cost of treatment once the new technology was developed and a greater variance in cost; conditional on remaining healthy, the person would spend zero on treatment of his or her liver under either technological state—with or without the transplant capability. Conditional on contracting liver disease, however, the person would spend a great deal more on treatment once the new technology became available. As a result, the development of transplant technology increased private demand for health care insurance, *ceteris paribus.* This is distinct from the increase in demand associated with the merit good-related desire to provide access to lifesaving technology to everyone regardless of ability to pay.[19]

These two cases of technological change—polio vaccines and organ transplants—illustrate several points: (1) some new technologies increase the *expected* health care expenditures for victims of a given disease, *ceteris paribus,* while others decrease them; (2) some new technologies increase the *variance* of health care expenditures for victims of a given disease, *ceteris paribus,* while others decrease it; (3) a technology that increases the mean and variance of health care expenditures for a particular disease would tend to increase the demand for health care insurance, while one that decreased them would tend to reduce the demand for insurance. This latter proposition suggests the following conjecture: since

[18] In fact, however, little is known systematically about the amount of health care expenditures associated with attempts to cope with the debilitating effects of liver dysfunction (or other terminal illnesses), even when life is not prolonged.

[19] Positive income effects associated with rising income could also account for an increase in the demand for health care insurance. One might expect, however, that the income elasticity would be negative, not positive; increased income, *ceteris paribus,* would increase the person's ability to self-insure (Mossin, 1968).

we observe growth in insurance coverage, private and public, the preponderance of technological change in recent decades has apparently increased the means and variances of health care expenditures associated with various diseases rather than reduced them. Society has tended to develop a growing number of new technologies that permit higher levels of health care expenditures.[20]

Vaccines and transplants also illustrate stages in technical progress. Biologist Lewis Thomas (1975) distinguishes among three levels of technology in medicine. "Nontechnology" tides patients over diseases that are poorly understood. It largely involves reassuring patients, providing hospitalization and nursing, but with little hope; "[i]t is what physicians must do now for patients with intractable cancer, severe rheumatoid arthritis, multiple sclerosis, stroke, and advanced cirrhosis" (p. 37).

At a higher level is "halfway technology." This includes dealing, after the fact, with the incapacitating effects of diseases "whose course one is unable to do very much about" (p. 37). It is a technology that adjusts to disease or postpones death. Examples include organ transplantations, the use of artificial organs, and treatment of cancer through surgery, irradiation, and chemotherapy. The cancer measures are halfway technologies because they are directed at "already established cancer cells, but not at the mechanisms by which cells become neoplastic" (p. 39).

Finally "high technology," exemplified by immunization, antibiotics for bacterial infections, and prevention of nutritional disorders, "comes as a result of a genuine understanding of disease mechanisms, and when it becomes available, it is relatively inexpensive ... to deliver" (p. 40).

Thomas described the state of technology at a point in time—not the process of change. If, however, one thinks of a dynamic process, in which knowledge tends to grow from the first of the three levels to the second and then the third, the cost function associated with any particular disease might be an inverted U shape; it is plausible, although certainly not verified, that health care costs are highest for the halfway technologies. In the extreme case of a nontechnology, when the knowledge base is so weak that there is nothing useful to be done, costs are likely to be low, as they are when the high-technology state of knowledge is reached.

The evolution of knowledge about polio is a useful example. Two generations and more ago, the nontechnology stage prevailed. Many victims of the disease died quickly as a result of paralysis; for them, the effects were disastrous, but the attendant health care costs were small. Development of the halfway (iron lung) technology prolonged life but at substantial cost. The high-technology

---

[20] Treatment of heart attacks is another illustration. One study showed that between 1972 and 1982, treatment of myocardial infarction involving more complex technologies such as cardiac imaging, angiography, and coronary bypass graft surgery was associated with a tripling of physician costs per case (Sawitz et al., 1988).

polio vaccines (Sabin and Salk vaccines) dramatically reduced the costs associated with polio, virtually eliminating it in the United States—there were five cases in 1985, compared with over 38,000 in 1954, before the vaccines were developed.[21]

Insofar as the inverted U-shape relationship holds between the state of technology and the resource cost per case, there is an interesting implication. The aggregate effect of technological change on health care costs will depend on the relative degree to which halfway technologies are replacing lower, less costly technologies or are being replaced by new, higher technologies. The development of halfway technologies was implicitly encouraged by the cost-reimbursement insurance system that has dominated hospital and medical care until recently, because there was little or no incentive for medical care providers to avoid costly technologies that were even marginally effective.[22] Empirical research on how, and how much, the medical R&D process is now being affected by the shift to a prospective-pricing incentive system for cost control is in its infancy; there would seem to be an incentive for R&D to shift toward mechanisms that would bypass the high-cost, halfway states of technology.

Depending on whether technological change is predominantly from nontechnology to halfway, rather than from halfway to high or from nontechnology to high, the demand for insurance is likely to differ. With the demand for insurance being a function of uncertainty of loss, demand should tend to increase most rapidly when changes in technology are of the expenditure-increasing, halfway type. Costly new surgical techniques such as organ transplants and the use of artificial body parts spur the demand for insurance; low-cost vaccines diminish it.[23]

Why has there been relatively more development of technologies like organ transplantation than like the polio vaccines? Why, that is, has technological change in health care been "expenditure increasing"? Is it more than chance? To begin examining this issue, I turn to the effects of various kinds of insurance arrangements on incentives for the R&D sector to develop alternative types of technologies. For just as the forms of technological change affect the insurance system, so, too, does the insurance system affect the direction and pace of technological change. Depending on the type of insurance available to consumers, the R&D sector faces differing incentives to search for cost-reducing, "process" innovations relative to quality-increasing but cost-increasing, "product" innovations.

---

[21] Vaccines appear to be more cost reducing than they really are. If vaccination cost is, say, $5 per person, and if the incidence of the disease is 1 in 40,000, then the vaccine cost per case *prevented* is $200,000. That may or may not be resource-cost saving, at least with respect to health care costs.

[22] Halfway technologies are not the only type of R&D encouraged by cost-based, retrospective insurance. Any technology with positive expected benefits is encouraged.

[23] Thomas' typology applies to technologies used for prevention and treatment. While Thomas does not deal explicitly with technologies used for diagnosis, we can think of those as complements to treatment; that is, costs of treatment include costs of determining which treatment mode to use.

EFFECTS OF THE INSURANCE/FINANCE SYSTEM ON RESEARCH AND DEVELOPMENT

Theory suggests the probable direction of the health care finance system's effects on R&D. Depending on hospitals' and physicians' incentives to adopt new technologies (which are contingent on the insurance system through which providers are paid), the R&D sector can face quite different financial incentives for both the level and direction of research. Fiscal pressure on health care providers to contain costs will affect the market for adoption of innovations, and by so doing will alter R&D in predictable ways.

The effects of insurance on R&D are not simply based on the existing insurance system, but on the system expected to exist in the future. The process of developing new medical technologies involves years of planning and research and, when drugs and medical devices are involved, more years of clinical trials to obtain approval by the Food and Drug Administration; in the case of pharmaceuticals, a period lasting 12-15 years is typical between the initiation of a research process and the marketability of a drug. As a result of this lengthy process, the R&D process depends on forecasts of the health insurance system, for the form of expected insurance coverage will determine the strength of the market for new products. If, for example, decisionmakers in the R&D sector believed that development of a particular technology that was costly yet effective would cause government to expand insurance to cover it—as was done with kidney dialysis there could be an incentive to develop the product even though it was not covered under existing insurance.

By directing attention to the effect of health care insurance on R&D, I do not imply that insurance is the only force affecting R&D. Among other forces are the state of scientific knowledge, which affects the probability of scientific success from additional research; demographic variables, which affect the size of potential markets for new products; and political influences on the budget of the National Institutes of Health (NIH), which finances basic research. With respect to NIH, it would be useful to learn more about the way the size and allocation of its scientific research budget are influenced, perhaps quite indirectly, by the health insurance system through its impact on the eventual market for new technologies of various types.

Hospitals, physicians, and other health care providers select the resources used to treat any particular patient from those that are technologically feasible and subject to revenue constraints. These constraints depend partly on the insurance system, which influences both the diffusion of existing technologies and the expected profitability of potential new technologies (Newhouse, 1981, 1988; Goddeeris, 1987). Thus, the following proposition requires testing: the insurance/finance system affects the incentives facing the R&D sector to develop new health care technologies of various "types." Since the demand confronting the health care R&D sector is derived from the demand facing health care providers, alternative insurance/finance systems will have different long-run effects on the demand for innovations. In particular, insurance mechanisms can differ in the incentives they imply for reducing costs relative to enhancing quality.

The two types of insurance payment mechanisms-"retrospective," which pays a provider on the basis of "costs" incurred, and "prospective," which pays sums that are independent of those costs incurred[24]—imply profoundly different incentives for both the development and diffusion of new technologies.

The claim that hospitals operate according to some "technological imperative" that determines medical choices (Fuchs, 1986) and that drives hospitals to adopt the latest technology regardless of cost may well have been correct, but the reason may have been less mystical than the term suggests. The economic incentives explaining the "rapid and indiscriminate adoption of [medical] innovations" (Fuchs, 1986, p. 29) and "the proclivity of doctors and hospitals to adopt almost any plausible new thing—drugs, surgical methods, equipment—that increases capability in any dimension . . . without regard to cost" (Nelson, 1972, p. 56) have been documented for such technologies as intensive care units, cobalt therapy, and the electroencephalograph (Russell, 1979). One "explanation" offered for the insensitivity to cost is an alleged lack of training of physicians and hospital administrators in weighing marginal benefits against marginal costs (Battistella, 1984). Even if this is valid, the impact of insurance-based incentives may well be powerful; "methods of third party payment. .. [do] not give [decisionmakers] any inducement to acquire that ability" (Fuchs, 1986, p. 30).

Analyses of the effect of insurance on the adoption or diffusion of technologies have tended to concentrate on technologies that have already been developed. Less attention has been given to the implicit incentives for the R&D sector to develop various types of innovations. Retrospective pricing sends a clear signal to the R&D sector: *develop new technologies that enhance the quality of care, regardless of the effects on cost.* Careful analysis remains to be done to distinguish causation from spurious correlation, but it appears that in the post-World War II era this signal produced the two results that could be expected: historically unequaled improvements in medical care technology—drugs, devices, diagnostics, clinical procedures, and so forth—and unprecedented growth in health care expenditures.[25]

Transplantation of natural organs has already been mentioned as an example of a high-cost medical innovation made more likely by retrospective insurance.

[24] Arrow (1963) identifies three types of insurance, the third being "indemnity." This type, however, is a special case of prospective coverage in the sense that the insurer pays a fixed amount, conditional on a loss, but independent of the magnitude of the health care costs actually incurred. The indemnity might take the form of a fixed dollar payment for the loss of a limb or for a given illness. If it took the form of a fixed dollar payment per day of hospitalization, it would have the character of retrospective-type insurance.

[25] Such increased costs might or might not pass a full benefit-cost test. The point, however, is that they contributed substantially to the accelerated growth of health care expenditures.

Another example is development of a wide range of implantable artificial joints and artificial organs. The human body has become increasingly like an automobile, with replacements available for an ever-growing number of parts—an arm or a leg, at about $2,000, an elbow at $1,200, an ear at $10,000, and a heart at $50,000-$80,000. They are even available in small, medium, large, and extra large sizes (Kleinfield, 1983). "Installation," of course, is extra and, as with auto parts, is typically many times greater than the price of the part.

Technological advances in recent decades have given us spectacular innovations, but with scant attention to the resource costs of utilizing them. Open heart surgery can replace clogged arteries (coronary artery bypass graft surgery) but at a cost averaging $46,000 (National Center for Health Services Research and Health Care Technology, 1988). A baby born 2.5 months prematurely and weighing well under 2 pounds (907 grams) can be kept alive, but at a cost of $90,000 and with a 10 percent survival rate (French, 1989). Ultrasound technology, computed tomography scanners, positron emission tomography (PET) scanners, and other diagnostic tools aid in disease detection but often at costs of tens of thousands of dollars per case detected—not counting the subsequent costs of surgery or other treatment. The PET scan, which aids in detecting heart disease at a cost of about $1,800 per test—many times this for each case of heart disease detected—has been argued to be only "slightly" better than single emission computed tomography, which costs less than half of a PET scan (Schiffman, 1989). Under retrospective, cost-based financing, even small improvements have been adopted by physicians, hospitals, and other institutions that have had little or no incentive to balance social benefits against costs.

Consider, now, the reward structure implicit in an alternative insurance/ finance *system—prospective payment,* in which payment to a service provider is exogenous to provider decisions, conditional on admission of a patient. The particular version that is being applied to hospitals' Medicare patients and, increasingly, to other patients as well, confronts a hospital (but not the patient's physician) with an exogenously determined set of prices, one for each of 468 diagnoses made at the time of admission.[26] No longer is gross revenue for treating a particular patient a function of the hospital's decisions on use of resources.

Financial incentives for hospitals under such a prospective payment arrangement differ diametrically from the incentives under a retrospective payment arrangement. With a hospital's revenue being exogenous for a given patient once admitted, and an HMO's revenue being exogenous for a member for the given year, the organization's financial health depends on its ability to control costs of

[26] In some instances diagnostic categories can be altered after admission, on the basis of information not available at admission. This produces some degree of revenue endogeneity, because the hospital and physician can decide on the amount of exploratory effort.

treatment.[27] Thus, under a prospective payment finance mechanism, the health care delivery system sends a vastly different signal to the R&D sector, with priorities the reverse of those under retrospective payment. The new signal is, *develop new technologies that reduce costs, provided that quality does not suffer "too much."* (The meaning of "too much" will be examined below.)

When a ceiling was placed on government payment for kidney dialysis, the direction of technical change was affected; large surface dialyzers were developed that cut the time required per session nearly in half, from 6-8 hours down to 3.5-4.5 hours. This led to substantial savings in professional labor costs, which are a major cost component (Rettig, 1980).

The shift to a prospective payment system (PPS) under Medicare appears to have brought about some of the expected changes in utilization of health services. PPS has not diminished use of intensive care units, but it has apparently decreased use of such diagnostic procedures as chest X-rays; in the three years prior to PPS, 1980-1983, the mean annual change in the number of chest X-rays per Medicare patient discharge was zero, whereas for the 1983-1985 period it decreased by 8 percent (Sloan et al., 1988).

HMOs also present providers with an incentive to increase attention to costs relative to medical benefits. HMOs—which are, in effect, mergers of health care providers and insurers—can be expected to adopt more slowly any new technology that is cost increasing, even if it is more effective, than would a provider facing a retrospective pricing system. HMO members have been found to have lower costs per patient-year than do nonmembers whose insurance was based on retrospective costs, largely attributable to a 30 percent lower rate of hospitalization (Luft, 1981); but the rate of introduction of new technologies does not appear to differ, at least as that is reflected in rates of change of per capita costs. The growth rate in total costs per person (including out-of-pocket costs) in the 1960s and 1970s appears to have been about the same (Newhouse et al., 1985) or "only slightly lower" (Luft, 1980) for people in, and those not in, HMOs, after making some adjustments for selection bias.

[27] While hospital revenue is largely exogenous once the patient is admitted, a hospital can influence both its gross and net (of cost) revenues through a variety of mechanisms for controlling admissions. A nongovernmental hospital may, for example, choose not to provide particular services such as an emergency room; it can decide which physicians may serve on its medical staff and, hence, which may admit patients; and it can provide its affiliated physicians with subtle but clear signals to "encourage" patients with complex problems to utilize governmental hospitals. Recent research is disclosing that, with the advent of prospective pricing for Medicare patients at most nongovernmental hospitals in 1983, there has been an increase in admissions to Veterans Affairs hospitals, which are not included in the prospective DRG pricing system; therefore, we might expect them to receive more of the patients with illnesses likely to constitute financial "losers" to for-profit and voluntary nonprofit hospitals (Wolfe, 1989). In the long run, when the location of a hospital is variable, there is additional discretion for nongovernmental hospitals to locate in areas that are less likely to generate unprofitable cases.

The longer-term effects of PPS and HMOs on the R&D sector are more difficult to discern. There has been no formal modeling of the long-run effects on technical change of alternative payment systems for hospitals and physicians. Early literature attempting to explain the rising level of health care expenditures did not identify an important role for technological change. Subsequent literature sometimes directed attention to the effect of technological change on health care costs (Altman and Blendon, 1979), but that change in "quality and style of hospital care" was assumed implicitly to be exogenous—captured econometrically, perhaps, by a time trend (Feldstein, 1971).

The rate of diffusion of a number of existing technologies has been found to be responsive to insurance-related incentives (Russell, 1979; Romeo et al., 1984; Lee and Waldman, 1985; Sloan et al., 1986). There has been little study, however, of the effects of insurance on the R&D sector—private, governmental, and nonprofit—where new technologies are developed, although the linkage between the insurance system and incentives for the R&D sector has been noted (Joskow, 1981; Goddeeris, 1984a,b; Goddeeris and Weisbrod, 1985; U.S. Congress, 1985). The effect of prospective payment insurance on R&D is illustrated by experience in the late 1980s with the cochlear implant for hearing-impaired individuals; scientifically promising research was discontinued as a consequence of its expected unprofitability, which resulted from application of the DRG pricing system. The 3M Company, the manufacturer of the first Food and Drug Administration approved single-channel cochlear implant model, halted research on a multichannel device because of hospitals' financial disincentives (Kane and Manoukian, 1989). Similarly, R&D on assistive communication devices for speech-impaired individuals appears to have been retarded by the lack of insurance coverage; Medicare's payment policy favors inpatient over outpatient care, and there was "an administrative decision that the [communication] devices are not prosthetic devices needed for the functioning of a malformed body member" (U.S. Congress, 1984b, p. 30).

The current climate and incentives facing the R&D sector are not conducive to the development of costly new technologies. Another example is the newly emerging diagnostic procedure PET, which produces three-dimensional images that portray the metabolic and chemical action of tissue. PET is in clinical trial, but the General Electric Company, its developer, "isn't making the kind of investment it did to rush CT (computerized tomography scanners) and MRI (magnetic resonance imaging devices) to market" (Schiffman, 1989). According to a General Electric official, "The government is very cautious about approving reimbursement for PET. In the past, if a technology improved patient care, it would be approved. Now it must also be cost-effective" (Naj, 1990, p. B4).

There are some further implications of the new incentives for hospitals to reduce costs rather than to increase quality. In the new era of prospective pricing of hospital services, there will likely be a diversion of R&D resources away from new surgical techniques and toward lower-cost substitutes, frequently pharma ceuticals. Surgical advances can be cost-reducing, especially when they substitute for other halfway technologies; angioplasty, for example, substitutes for more costly coronary bypass graft surgery, and kidney transplantation substitutes for years of dialysis. When surgical advances substitute, however, for nontreatment, they are likely to increase the cost of treating the specific illness; since life expectancy may increase, though, the effect on mean annual health care costs per capita is less clear. Surgery is costly, relative to nonsurgical interventions, because it is labor-intensive, "custom" production performed on a single patient; as such it has limited capacity for taking advantage of scale economies.[28] Increased use of surgery over the 1972-1982 period, during which retrospective pricing of hospital services dominated, was the primary source of rising treatment costs for patients admitted to a teaching hospital for acute myocardial infarction, respiratory distress syndrome of the newborn, and other intensive treatments for the critically ill (Showstack, et al., 1985).[29] New surgical interventions are likely to be less attractive in a cost-containment environment.

By contrast with surgery, research on those pharmaceuticals that decrease expenditures, relative to those that increase quality but increase expenditures, is more attractive under prospective pricing. This is because demand patterns by hospitals (and HMOs) reflect the search for cost-reducing modes of treatment, including substitutes for costly surgical interventions; in particular, the advent of prospective pricing has increased the expected profitability of R&D on drugs than can prevent the onset of costly treatments—vaccines, for example (Huston and Weisbrod, 1988)—and of R&D on drugs that substitute for surgery—examples are beta-blockers, which can substitute partially for coronary bypass surgery, and cimetidine, which substitutes for ulcer surgery (Geweke and Weisbrod, 1982).

The effects of PPS insurance on the pharmaceutical industry will not, however, be entirely favorable. Pharmaceuticals are not always substitutes for surgery; they are sometimes complements. Development of a new drug that complements surgery can increase the efficacy of surgery and thereby increase the demand for surgery—with major cost implications. In a cost-containment insurance/finance environment, pharmaceutical industry R&D faces an incentive to develop drugs that substitute for surgery rather than enhance its efficacy.

[28] Cost reductions are likely to result, however, from experience—learning by doing—which is a function of total accumulated volume, even if not a function of the rate of surgery per unit of time. In a study of six surgical procedures, including coronary artery bypass and hip replacement, between 1984 and 1986, it was found that mortality declined with volume for five of the six procedures, but current cost per case declined with volume for only two of the procedures. Data covered between 646 and 4,738 hospitals, depending on the procedure (Project Hope, 1988)

[29] Much of the medical literature reports findings for a single hospital. Whether the findings are generalizable to the entire hospital system is not clear.

Organ transplants illustrate the issue. Liver transplantation, a surgical technique, is effective today largely because of a recent technological advance in pharmaceuticals. The drug cyclosporine is crucial because it suppresses the body's immune system reaction to the transplanted organ; yet, unlike earlier immunosuppressant drugs, it does not stop the body from fighting off infections.

The good news about this technological breakthrough is that cyclosporine permits people with liver, kidney, and heart failure to be kept alive, living essentially normal lives. The bad news is that the resulting increase in the efficacy of organ transplant surgery has brought sharp increases in the usage of these very costly procedures. Only 26 liver transplants were performed in 1981 and, while increasing to nearly 1,200 by 1987, some 4,000—4,700 people per year could benefit from the procedure. At a cost of about $200,000 each, plus annual maintenance costs, meeting all the medical needs implies an annual cost of $1 billion for this one procedure (*National Organ Transplant Act,* 1983; Pear, 1986; "Cyclosporine turns five," 1988). Heart, kidney, and other organ transplants suggest many times this level of potential expenditures as a consequence of the pharmaceutical breakthrough. It has also produced political pressure to ensure access to this lifesaving technology, regardless of a patient's ability to pay—pressure that is still being suppressed in part by the expedient of terming the procedures *experimental.* The enormous expenditure potential of technological advances in drugs is currently highlighted by the drug AZT for patients with AIDS. In 1990 it was estimated that some 600,000 people might benefit from this drug, which, even with reductions in price and dosage at that time, costs about $3,000 per year of treatment (Lublin, 1990), for a total potential cost of nearly $2 billion.

Given the current financing environment, why are cost-increasing drugs such as AZT, cyclosporine, and tissue plasminogen activator (t-PA) being developed? Cyclosporine came onto the market prior to the advent of PPS, and given the lengthy research and regulatory process in pharmaceutical research, it is reasonably clear that work related to AZT and t-PA was well under way by the time prospective-type insurance incentives became powerful in the 1980s. Today, the fiscal pressures operating through Medicare, HMOs, and state Medicaid "formularies"—lists of drugs that will be paid for—are reducing drug company incentives to develop drugs for which "high" prices would be required to make the R&D effort profitable.

The form of insurance affects the direction of R&D not only in terms of quality relative to cost. It also affects the incentive to search for methods to treat the ill rather than to prevent their illnesses.[30] In general, health insurance has primarily covered treatment in hospitals, with preventive measures having quite

[30] In the long run, the price of private health insurance depends on the state of the technology. Even so, risk-spreading over all the insured may make it privately profitable for the R&D sector to develop technologies for which the value (willingness to pay) is less than the social cost (Goddeeris, 1984a,b; Baumgardner, 1989).

limited coverage. As a result, the R&D sector has had less incentive to focus effort on prevention than on treatment, with the exception, perhaps, of vaccinations, for which government subsidization is common. Insofar as preventive measures are covered by insurance, they tend to involve technologies that utilize the "health care sector"—especially physicians and hospitals—even though other measures, such as better diet and exercise, might improve health at lower cost.[31]

I do not intend to imply that a reallocation of resources toward prevention would necessarily be efficient, given the existing state of knowledge (Russell, 1986, 1987). Indeed, the concept of efficiency is itself controversial; it certainly can be defined in terms of either patient willingness to pay or some measure of health status and in either private or social terms.[32] The point is that today's state of knowledge about measures for preventing illness and for treating it reflects the historical incentives for R&D of both types, and those incentives have been shaped by the insurance system.

A number of the relationships discussed above may be summarized in the following five diagrams. Figure 2-1 shows that the state of technology, which determines what is possible for the health care system to do, interacts with the health care insurance system, which determines the prices and other incentives that providers and consumers confront, to determine the level of health care expenditures. Figure 2-2 portrays the interaction between the scientific knowledge base and the incentive structure that operates through the health insurance system to affect "tomorrow's" technological base.

Figure 2-3 shows that the technological base that exists at one point in time affects the insurance system, since the more that base presents opportunities to spend large sums of money on health care, the greater will be the demand for insurance. Relatedly, Figure 2-4 points up the likelihood that actual increases in health care expenditures will increase the demand for insurance.

Finally, Figure 2-5 summarizes the relationships shown in Figures 2-1 through 2-4. Even at this simplified level it portrays a complex system of interdependent relationships. Society cannot expect to manipulate any one of the variables—for example, by altering the health care insurance system, incentives for developing new technologies, or the level of aggregate health care expendi

[31] Thus, prevention has its halfway technologies, too (as pointed out by an anonymous referee). For many forms of prevention, insurance is inappropriate because there is little uncertainty about the financial expenditure involved (thanks to Mark Satterthwaite for noting this).

[32] Aaron and Schwartz (1984) define efficiency in medical terms but using a Pareto-like approach: "Medical resources are efficiently used when a given total expenditure cannot be reallocated to alternative kinds of care to achieve an improved medical outcome. .... [Thus] it would not be possible to increase total medical benefits by taking some money away from one service, for example cancer chemotherapy, and spending it on another, say x-ray" (pp. 79, 89). Ellis and McGuire (1986) define efficient supply of care as existing when the physician acts as a perfect agent, weighing a dollar of hospital profit equally with a dollar of benefit to the patient.

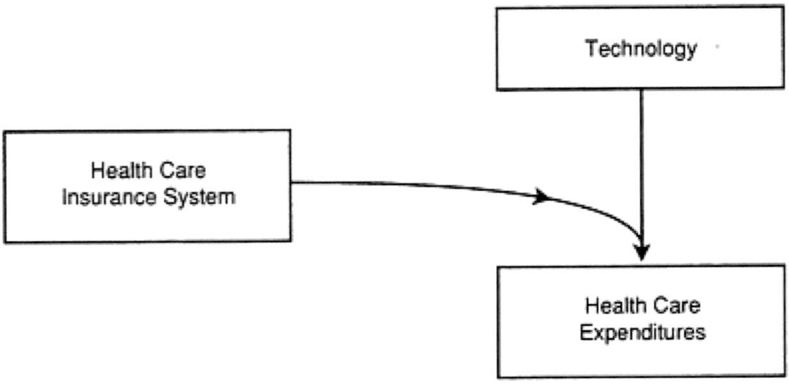

FIGURE 2-1 The state of technology and the incentives to use the technology determine total expenditures: The short run.

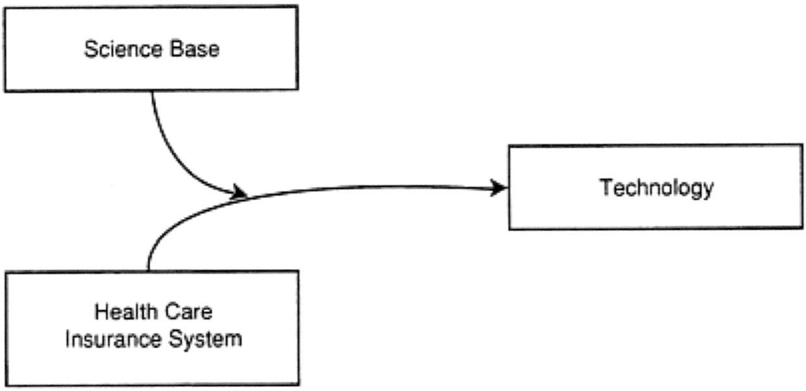

FIGURE 2-2 The health care insurance system establishes incentives for the R&D sector.

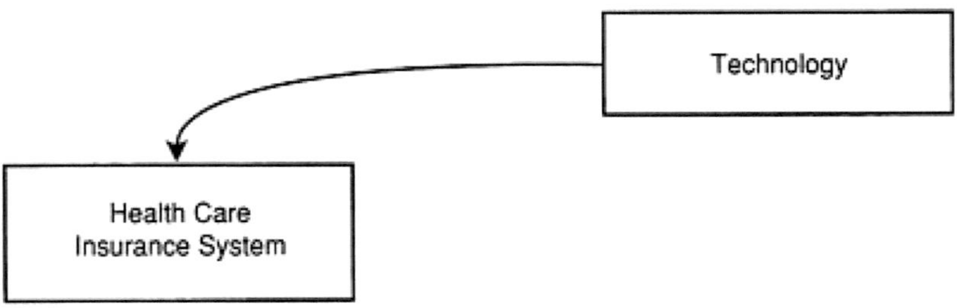

FIGURE 2-3 The technical capability for delivering health care affects the form and coverage of the health care insurance system.

tures—without altering other variables and, ultimately, without affecting outcomes of the system in perhaps quite unexpected ways.

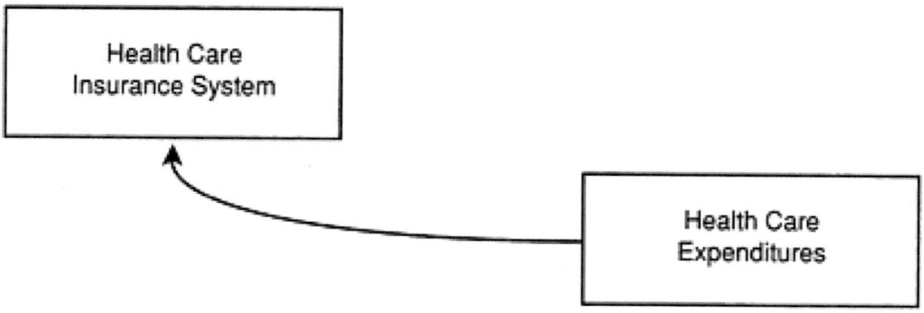

FIGURE 2-4 The level of health care expenditures affects the demand for insurance.

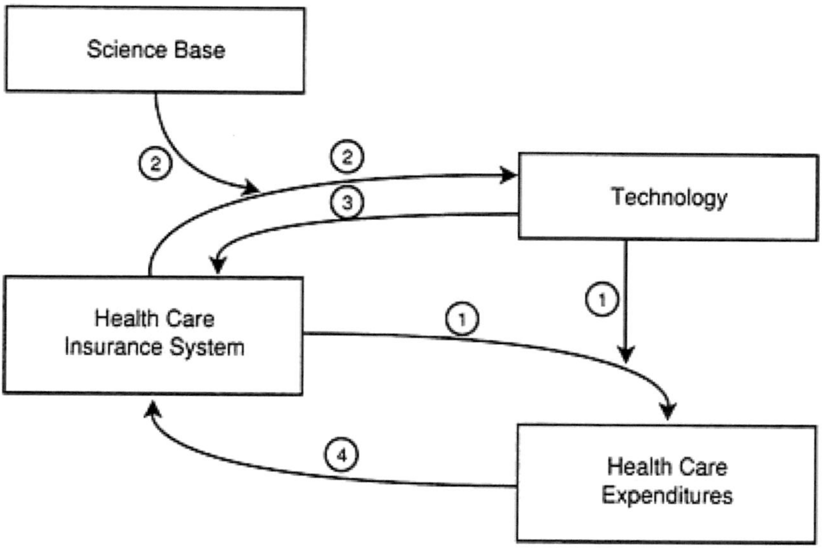

FIGURE 2-5 The dynamic system of interaction of the health care insurance system, technological change, and health care expenditures. Circled numbers 1 to 4 refer to Figures 2-1 to 2-4, respectively.

EFFECTS OF INSURANCE ON CHOICE OF TECHNOLOGY AND QUALITY OF HEALTH CARE IN THE SHORT RUN, WITH TECHNOLOGY GIVEN

In addition to its potential to influence R&D, the health insurance incentive structure also influences the deployment of existing medical technology, with implications for quality and access to care. A retrospective, cost-based reward structure and a prospective reward structure such as a DRG system and an HMO[33] offer very different incentives for provider choice between increasing quality and decreasing costs (Morrisey et al., 1984).

For a given state of technological knowledge, a prospective payment insurance system provides encouragement, at the margin, to use production processes that reduce cost rather than improve quality. This is particularly so when quality is affected in dimensions that are costly for consumers (or regulators or insurers) to observe. The central point is that in a world of asymmetrically high information costs to consumers relative to service providers (e.g., hospitals and HMOs),[34] it is harder to detect reductions in quality in some forms than in others, and the finance system can influence provider incentives to choose among input combinations that differ in the relative importance of effects that are more and less costly for nonproviders to monitor.

Every commodity—health care or anything else—can be thought of as a bundle of attributes that vary in the cost of monitoring them as well as in their importance to buyers. To simplify, consider two classes of attributes—type I, which are costless to monitor, and type II, which are costly to monitor. If consumers respond largely to the observable, type I attributes, then sellers will find price to be essentially independent of quality in the type II dimensions, and quality in the latter forms will be low (Weisbrod, 1988). Price will be a poor gauge of overall quality.

A prospective payment reward structure such as a DRG system is a price control mechanism. It poses the problem of how to ensure that real prices are not raised through the expedient of reducing service quality, especially in the type II dimensions.[35]

The potential effects of price-setting by a governmental agency or private insurer, when quality is asymmetrically costly to monitor, can be seen by comparing the setting of prices for electricity and for care in a hospital or nursing home. A kilowatt-hour of electricity is far more homogeneous and easier to monitor than is a day of care (or any number of other potential measures of output) in a hospital or nursing home.[36] Thus, regulating price does not pose a

[33] There are important differences between an HMO- and a DRG-type payment system—at least as these operate now. For example, the DRG system applies currently only to hospital services, while HMOs cover a wider range of medical services. HMOs may operate their own hospitals, but they typically subcontract with independent hospitals for treatment of HMO members; such subcontracts can take many forms, and with either retrospective or prospective pricing.

[34] An HMO, which vertically integrates a provider group with an insurer, reduces the informational asymmetry between the two, though not between either of them and consumer-patients or regulators.

[35] Throughout this discussion the role of physicians as agents for patients has great importance. I assume that physicians act as imperfect agents, which leaves patients asymmetrically underinformed.

[36] There are other elements of the electric power regulatory process—for example, the "appropriate" levels of inputs—that involve asymmetric costs. The literature on the Averch-Johnson effect focuses, in effect, on the difficulty regulators have in determining the degree of overcapitalization of public utilities under rate-of-return regulation (Averch and Johnson, 1962; Baumol and Klevorick, 1970).

serious risk that quality of output will be compromised in unobservable ways by the regulatory process. Because of the more complex attributes of the health care system, opportunities are greater for providers to reduce output quality in dimensions that, being costly to monitor, are difficult to embody in a performance contract.

The Joint Commission on Accreditation of Health Care Organizations (JCAHCO) recognizes implicitly the distinction between type I and type II characteristics for assessing the quality of a hospital. In his testimony at the 1973 Senate hearings, the executive director of JCAHCO said it was concerned with whether a hospital had the physical environment to permit high-quality medicine to be provided—for example, an operative sprinkler system (a type I attribute)not with the actual clinical practices—that is, how carefully surgery is performed (a type II attribute) (Lohr et al., 1988).[37]

I remarked earlier that under a prospective payment system, financial incentives are to cut costs, provided quality does not suffer "too much."[38] There are consequences, of course, of cutting quality, and they constrain health care providers: tort law liability for medical malpractice, loss of patients to competitors (Hirschman, 1970), loss of donations and volunteer labor, penalties for violating regulatory rules (Weisbrod and Schlesinger, 1986) and professional ethics codes, and, in the case of HMOs, possibly greater costs of treating member-patients in the future.[39] Thus, the financial incentive to reduce costs by cutting quality is presumably equated at the margin with the effects of reduced quality on these revenue and cost variables (Woodward and Warren-Boulton, 1984; Ellis and McGuire, 1986).[40] Little is known about the quantitative importance of each of these constraints, but because of them a prospective payment price control system implicitly encourages health care providers to cut resource use in the type II dimensions—which would minimize revenue losses and other penalties—not in ways that would be socially efficient.[41]

Consumer-patients and donors cannot respond to changes in quality they cannot observe. Thus, given the imperfections in agency relationships (Ellis and

[37] John Porterfield, the JCAHCO executive director, reportedly said that a hospital reviewer would observe whether the hospital's sprinkler system worked and whether certain medical committees functioned and kept adequate records, but if a surgeon on the staff decided that good-quality care required taking out the appendix of all blue-eyed males over age 16, that was none of the JCAHCO reviewer's business.

[38] Morrisey and colleagues (1984) model the effects on quality of care in a hospital confronted by downward price pressure.

[39] For HMOs, the latter effect is attenuated by the uncertainty that the person will remain a member.

[40] Because HMOs involve a prospective payment to cover all "needed" care for the stipulated period, the incentives facing HMOs are analytically very similar to those facing hospitals under DRG pricing; thus, in general, propositions in this section referring to hospitals will also apply to HMOs, *mutatis mutandis* (that is, the necessary changes having been made).

[41] This is analogous to "skimming" and "creaming" of program participants.

McGuire, 1986), the shift to a DRG-type prospective payment insurance system can be expected to cause reductions in quality in precisely those forms that are difficult for insurers to monitor (Weisbrod, 1989). This prediction requires testing, which needs to recognize that in a competitive market there can be simultaneous decreases in type II dimensions of quality and increases in type I dimensions. For example, increased "quality" in easily observed forms such as hospital candlelight dinners for maternity patients and their spouses can attract patients to a hospital, and free dental or eye checkups can attract members to an HMO, even while quality of medical care is being reduced in more subtle, hard-to-detect forms (Weisbrod, 1988, chapters 2, 3, 8).

The reuse of "disposable" items by hospitals illustrates the potential for cutting quality in ways that are difficult for consumers to monitor and an effect of prospective pricing on the choice of production technology. Until the late 1940s, hospitals reused most medical devices; tubing, syringes, needles, etc., were made to be used, sterilized, and used again. When the new technology of disposables was introduced after World War II, it was quickly adopted by a health care finance system that encouraged the greater convenience and safety of disposables and that deemphasized the cost consequences. The expanding system of retrospective-pay health insurance that covered all "reasonable" hospital costs spurred both the development and the adoption of disposable items along with any other technology that was arguably quality enhancing.

Today, with the shift to prospective pricing, sterilization and reuse is returning. This change may or may not be efficient—allocatively or medically. What is striking is that hospitals are reusing items that are labeled by the manufacturers for "one-time-use only" (Otten, 1984). Even "disposable" filters for kidney dialysis machines are being reprocessed and reused (U.S. Congress, 1984a).

These practices reduce hospital costs. They may have no effect on revenues, for they are difficult for consumers (but presumably not their physician-agents) to observe. Thus, the financial consequences are relatively unambiguous. At the same time, the effect on health risks of reusing disposables is not currently known (Chu et al., 1986; National Center for Health Services Research and Health Care Technology, 1986). While the safety debate proceeds, the dispute is being resolved in favor of the cost-reducing technology. This is in sharp contrast to the situation in the 1950s, when the incentive structure was reversed; at that time, single-use disposables replaced the prior use-sterilize-reuse technology, despite the absence of strong evidence of favorable health effects.

In general, the switch to prospective payment can be expected to bring changes in the technology of health care of just that type: they have clearly favorable effects on costs, but subtle or uncertain, yet presumptively nonpositive effects on the quality of care. I say "presumptively" nonpositive because, given the state of technical knowledge, any change in resource use that is made after a change in incentives could have been made before; disposables could have been reused earlier.

Another quality-related dimension of hospital behavior likely to be affected by a shift to prospective pricing for hospitals is the length of a patient's stay. Confronted, under a DRG pricing system, by a fixed price for treating each patient, hospitals have a financial incentive to discharge patients earlier (Lave et al., 1988). Even if they do so, however, it is difficult for a patient to determine whether he or she has been discharged "quicker but sicker" (Heinz, 1986). Here, once again, a crucial question is how well asymmetrically underinformed patients are represented by physician-agents.

A reduction in use of hospital inputs is not necessarily inefficient, in economic or medical terms; the cost savings may exceed the loss in benefits (although placing a value on the benefits is difficult), and in some situations there might be no medical benefits at all from, say, a longer hospital stay. Neither, though, is a reduction in inputs necessarily efficient. Input substitutions and cost reductions that may result from the shift from cost-based to prospective insurance cannot be assumed to be efficient or inefficient in a world of asymmetrically underinformed patient-consumers who confront prices that often bear little relationship to real marginal costs. Public policy, if it is to increase allocative efficiency, clearly demands understanding of the effects of pricing and other interventions on both quality and cost, not simply on costs. In particular, there should be attention to the tendency of a prospective payment insurance pricing system to cause input substitutions that overvalue reductions in easily observed expenditures and undervalue attention to reductions in quality that are more costly to observe.

The response of the health care sector to financial incentives may not be the same for its various institutional elements—private enterprise, government, and private nonprofit. In the hospital industry, 65 percent of all short-term beds are in private nonprofit hospitals; 26 percent are in government hospitals. Thirty percent of nursing home beds are in nonprofit (22 percent) or government (8 percent) facilities. Of kidney dialysis centers, 48 percent are nonprofit and an additional 12 percent are governmental (Weisbrod, 1988). The key question is this: In response to a public policy shift from cost-based to prospective payment to providers, is there a different response, quantitatively or qualitatively, depending on the institutional ownership mix of the industry?[42] Confronted by the incentives that prospective payment provides to discharge patients earlier and to engage in other forms of quality-shaving actions in the type II dimensions, do for-profit, nonprofit, and government organizations respond differently?[43] Does institutional form matter?

[42] A related issue is how competition among organizations of various ownership types affects long-run equilibrium, and whether one form of institution can be expected to drive out the others (Schiff and Weisbrod, 1987).

[43] Whether earlier discharge of a hospital patient is a type I or a type II attribute is debatable. I regard it as type II. While the length of stay for any patient is easily observable, what is difficult for the patient to observe is whether the length of stay was lower than it would have been if the physician and hospital were not responding to the altered financial incentive of PPS.

Finding the answers to these questions requires modeling the behavior of each form of organization and the process of competition among them. There has been some attention to the conditions of equilibrium in institutionally mixed industries (Schiff, 1986; Marmor et al., 1986; Phelps and Sened, 1989), but strong conclusions have not been reached.

Economic behavior may differ across ownership forms because of differences in objective functions, constraints, or both. Profit maximization is typically assumed for the private enterprise components of the health care sector, but a variety of objective functions have been suggested for the nonprofit sector (Newhouse, 1970; Davis, 1973; Pauly and Redisch, 1973; James, 1983; Young, 1983), as have various constraints on the distribution of profit[44] and access to public subsidies and private donations of money and time (Hansmann, 1980; RoseAckerman, 1982; Easley and O'Hara, 1983; Holtmann, 1983; Clotfelter, 1985; Steinberg, 1986; Weisbrod and Dominguez, 1986).[45]

DRG pricing provides the same financial incentive for all hospitals to discharge patients earlier than would a retrospective pricing system, but because of differences in objective functions and constraints, the behavioral responses may differ among institutional forms. There have been studies, for example, of the effect of prospective payment on the condition, at discharge, of elderly patients with hip fractures (Palmer et al., 1989; Fitzgerald et al., 1988) in two nonprofit hospitals, but they have not examined differences across ownership forms.[46]

More generally, neither theory nor empirical tests have resolved the question of whether there are systematic differences among institutional forms. Econometric evidence, while mixed, is growing that when for-profit, nonprofit, and government organizations coexist in a given industry—as they do in hospitals and nursing homes, for example—they do behave differently. Differences have

[44] Nonprofit organizations are not legally restricted from engaging in profitable activities; they are, however, restricted in what they may do with the profits. Little explicit attention has been devoted, however, to the enforceability of this constraint (Weisbrod, 1988). This is relevant to the "managerial discretion" models of Williamson (1967), Alchian and Demsetz (1972), and Migué and Bélanger (1974).

[45] All organizations, regardless of ownership, confront the same technological constraints, but they face different financial constraints in such forms as nonprofits' exemptions from property and sales taxes and eligibility for postal subsidies. Charitable contributions of time and money to a nonprofit hospital (but not to a proprietary hospital) might respond positively to the amount of unprofitable services it provides to low-income, uninsured, or other "deserving" people. The relationship between donations to nonprofit organizations and the tax and expenditure behaviors of government—the "crowding out" effect—has also received attention in the public finance literature. At the theoretical level, see Warr (1982); Roberts (1984), Bergstrom et al. (1986), and Andreoni (1988); for empirical studies, see Abrams and Schmitz (1978, 1984) and Schiff (1985).

[46] Palmer and colleagues (1989) found no change in ambulation status, comparing patients discharged from one nonprofit hospital in the several years before and after the change in price incentives. Fitzgerald and colleagues (1988), studying a single "community" hospital (presumably also a nonprofit), found significantly reduced mobility.

been examined in four principal dimensions: (1) access to care, as reflected by admission of uninsured patients (e.g., provision of "uncompensated" care) and the use of waiting lists rather than prices, (2) quality of care, (3) cost-efficiency, and (4) extent of opportunistic behavior toward asymmetrically underinformed consumers.

Systematic behavioral differences between private firms and nonprofit organizations have been found in some studies (Gray, 1986 [which summarizes a number of studies]; Herzlinger and Krasker, 1987; Lewin et al., 1988; Weisbrod, 1988; Selden, 1989), but not in others (Clark, 1980; Sloan and Vraciu, 1983; Gaumer, 1986). Nonprofit providers of health care, especially the church-affiliated nonprofits, appear to utilize a somewhat greater proportion of their resources to care for the indigent; they provide a wider range of services (and in this sense, higher quality); and they take less advantage of their informational advantages over patients.

Neither the underlying theory nor the available, nonexperimental data, however, are yet strong enough to justify confident generalizations about differences in institutional behavior. Measuring quality of service in a hospital (Shortell and Hughes, 1988), controlling for differences in patient conditions, and distinguishing care of the indigent from "bad debts" associated with poor management all remain subjects for future research, as does any differential responsiveness to the development of new technologies.[47] There is also a question of the appropriate estimation modeling; many econometric efforts to detect differential behavior across institutional forms may have misspecified their models, controlling erroneously for variables such as organization size, which are endogenous to the choice of institutional form (Weisbrod and Mauser, 1990).

CONCLUDING REMARKS

Economists' concerns about skyrocketing health care expenditures have focused heavily on insurance and its encouragement of inefficiently great utilization. Yet it is clear that much of the growth in health care expenditures during the post-World War II period has resulted not from increased prices for existing technologies but from the price for new technologies. Newly developed technologies have driven up both costs of care and the demand for insurance, while also expanding the range of services for which consumers demanded insurance. At the same time, expanding insurance coverage, which includes more people as well as a growing array of health care inputs, has provided an increased incentive to the R&D sector to develop new technologies and a growing incentive for subsets of consumers, who could benefit from particular new technologies, to

[47] In a related study of rapidity of introduction of new technologies in HMOs relative to fee-for-service providers, the RAND Corporation health insurance experiment found an apparently slower rate of introduction in HMOs (Newhouse et al., 1985).

seek a wider definition of what would be covered by insurance. Both the resource costs of health care and the technical ability to prolong life and enhance its quality have risen sharply. The interactive process involving insurance and R&D is still evolving. It is increasingly being influenced by the recent change in incentives associated with the shift from retrospective, cost-based insurance coverage to prospective, exogenously determined pricing.

Although this chapter has focused on the health care sector, the kinds of incentive effects it has examined are quite general. As an example of the potential effect of insurance on incentives facing the R&D sector, consider another major area of public policy and expenditure—education. Unlike health care, which has been financed for decades by a retrospective, cost-based finance system, elementary and secondary education has been financed traditionally through what amounts to a prospective payment system; roughly speaking, state and local governments have given the schools a fixed grant per child. This is roughly analogous to a DRG system with a single DRG, so that every patient (child) entering a hospital (school) brings a fixed sum of revenue to the provider. A school district can also be thought of as, like an HMO, providing "comprehensive" services to all "members" (students) in return for a fixed annual fee. By examining how the interaction of finance mechanisms and R&D incentives have operated in the health and education areas, one can gain insight into what the health care system would be like today, had the country taken an alternate route for financing it, as well as how a change in school finance would be likely to have an impact on the education system.

Assume that public schools had been financed differently—in the way hospitals have been financed until recently: (1) school revenue was determined through a retrospective (cost-based) pricing system, in which (2) teachers were empowered to decide what resources should be used (a) to diagnose a particular child's educational "needs" and (b) to meet those needs, and (3) a bill for the cost of the resources used for each child was sent to government or a private insurer and subsequently paid to the school district.

Two questions arise: If such a system had been adopted after World War II for schools, what would have happened over the subsequent 40 years to the level of education expenditures? What would have happened to the pace of technological change in education? The lessons from health care suggest conjectures: if schooling had been "insured" on the basis of retrospective costs, expenditures would have increased far more rapidly than they did and the pace of technological innovation in schools would have been far greater than it was.

Since education actually utilized a prospective pricing system, while health care utilized a retrospective pricing system, it is interesting to compare the two programs in terms of expenditure growth and technological change. First, with respect to expenditures, the share of GNP devoted to public elementary and secondary education has changed little over several decades (in which enrollments have remained relatively constant); between 1960 and 1985, for example, years of virtually identical school enrollments (36.7 million and 36.6 million, respectively) public school expenditures increased from 3.03 percent of GNP to 3.42 percent (U.S. Bureau of the Census, 1987, tables 186, 190 and 698); meanwhile, health care expenditures were rising from 4.6 to 10.7 percent of GNP (U.S. Bureau of the Census, 1975 and 1987).

Second, with respect to the pace and nature of technological change that might have occurred in education had retrospective pricing prevailed, one can do some informed speculating. To begin, compare, impressionistically, the technological change that has occurred in health care and in education. The typical hospital, for example, is barely comparable to its counterpart several decades ago, with entirely new techniques and facilities for diagnosis and treatment. The typical school, however, differs far less from its post-World War II counterpart, utilizing similar classrooms, teachers trained in similar ways, and instructional techniques that, despite some computerization in recent years, employ capital labor ratios that have changed relatively little.

One can predict that if retrospective reimbursement had prevailed for schools, the private sector would have devoted more resources to development of "improved" educational diagnostic and learning technologies; had that been the case, society would probably find now that education, like health care, had improved dramatically, but that society was paying a great deal more for it.

Today, the public policy "problems" in health care and education are perceived to be sharply different, and in ways that correspond to the differences in finance mechanisms (although other forces are doubtless also at work). In health care, the central policy focus is on control of expenditures, with quality of care not generally being seen as a problem.[48] In education, it is the reverse—the policy focus is on "low" quality of education, with control of school expenditures receiving relatively less attention.

The ideas presented above are a mixture of solid knowledge, soft knowledge, and hypotheses requiring testing. In order to expand knowledge about health care and provide financial access to it, society needs to understand more fully the dynamic process through which the health insurance sector, private and public, interacts with the R&D sector. This area offers a rich research agenda with enormous potential, for the policy implications extend far beyond health care and across geographical boundaries.

REFERENCES

Aaron, H. J., and Schwartz, W. B. 1984. *The Painful Prescription: Rationing Health Care.* Washington, D.C.: Brookings Institution.

[48] Problems of the uninsured are serious, but are receiving less attention than is the general problem of cost containment.

Abrams, B. A., and Schmitz, M. D. 1978. The crowding-out effect of governmental transfers on private charitable contributions. *Public Choice* 33(1):29-37.

Abrams, B. A., and Schmitz, M. D. 1984. The crowding-out effect of governmental transfers on private charitable contributions: Cross-section evidence. *National Tax Journal* 37 (4):563-568.

Akerlof, G. 1970. The market for lemons: Qualitative uncertainty and the market mechanism. *Quarterly Journal of Economics* 84(3):488-500.

Alchian, A., and Demsetz, H. 1972. Production, information costs and economic organization. *American Economic Review* 62(5):777-795.

Altman, S. H., and Blendon, R., eds. 1979. *Medical Technology: The Culprit Behind Health Care Costs?* DHEW Publication PHS 79-3216. Washington, D.C.: U.S. Government Printing Office.

Andreoni, J. 1988. Privately provided public goods in a large economy: The limits of altruism. *Journal of Public Economics* 35(1):57-73.

Arrow, K. 1963. Uncertainty and the welfare economics of medical care. *American Economic Review* 53(5):941-973.

Averch, H., and Johnson, L. 1962. Behavior of the firm under regulatory constraint. *American Economic Review* 52(5): 1053-1069.

Battistella, R. 1984. Review of *The Public/Private Mix for Health,* by Gordon McLachlan and Alan Maynard, eds. *Inquiry* 21(1):98-99.

Baumgardner, J. R. 1989. Forms of Insurance and the Pattern of Aggregate Technical Change in Medical Care. Working Paper, Duke University, Department of Economics.

Baumol, W. J., and Klevorick, A. K. 1970. Input choices and rate of return regulation: An overview of the discussion. *Bell Journal of Economics and Management Science* 1(2):162-190.

Bergstrom, T., Blume, L., and Varian, H. 1986. On the private provision of public goods. *Journal of Public Economics* 29(1):25-49.

Boben, P. 1989. Modeling the Shift from Retrospective to Prospective Pricing of Health Care. Discussion Paper, University of Wisconsin-Madison, Center for Health Economics and Law.

Chernick, H. A., Holmer, M. R., and Weinberg, D. H. 1987. Tax policy toward health insurance and the demand for medical services. *Journal of Health Economics* 6(1): 125.

Chu, F., Novak, N., Radany, M. H., and Perry, S. 1986. Reuse and reprocessing of disposable medical devices: Legal liability issues. *Journal of Health Care Technology* 3(1):5-12.

Clark, R. C. 1980. Does the nonprofit form fit the hospital industry? *Harvard Law Review* 93 (7):1416-1489.

Cleeton, D., Goepfrich, V. T., and Weisbrod, B. A. 1988. The Consumer Price Index for Prescription Drugs: Dealing with Technological Change. Working Paper, University of Wisconsin-Madison, Center for Health Economics and Law.

Clotfelter, C. T. 1985. *Federal Tax Policy and Charitable Giving.* Chicago, Ill.: University of Chicago Press.

Cromwell, J., and Mitchell, J. B. 1986. Physician-induced demand for surgery. *Journal of Health Economics* 5(4):293-313.

Cyclosporine turns five. 1988. *Science* 242(4876):198.

Danzon, P. M. 1985. *Medical Malpractice.* Cambridge, Mass.: Harvard University Press.

Davis, K. 1973. Theories of hospital inflation: Some empirical evidence. *Journal of Human Resources* 8(2):181-201.

Easley, D., and O'Hara, M. 1983. The economic role of the nonprofit firm. *Bell Journal of Economics* 14(2):531-538.

Elective surgery: Cut it out. 1979. *Science News* 115(1):9.

Ellis, R., and McGuire, T. 1986. Provider behavior under prospective reimbursement, *Journal of Health Economics* 5(2): 129-151.

Evans, R. G. 1974. Supplier induced demand: Some empirical evidence and implications. In: M. Perlman, ed. *The Economics of Health and Medical Care.* London: Macmillan.

Feldstein, M. S. 1971. Hospital cost inflation: A study of non-profit dynamics. *American Economic Review* 61(5):853-872.

Feldstein, M. S. and Allison, E. 1974. "Tax Subsidies of Private Health Insurance" in *The Economics of Federal Subsidy Programs. Part 8.* Papers submitted to the Subcommittee on Priorities and Economy in Government, Joint Economic Committee, 93rd Congress, 2nd session, July.

Feldstein, M. S., and Friedman, B. 1977. Tax subsidies, the rational demand for insurance, and the health care crisis. *Journal of Public Economics* 7(2):155-178.

Feldstein, P. J. 1988. *The Politics of Health Legislation: An Economic Perspective.* Ann Arbor, Mich.: Health Administration Press.

Fitzgerald, J. F., Moore, P. S., and Dittus, R. S. 1988. The care of elderly patients with hip fracture: Changes since implementation of the prospective payment system. *New England Journal of Medicine* 319(21): 1392-1397.

French, H. W. 1989. Tiny miracles become huge public health problem. *New York Times,* Feb. 19, pp. 1, 22.

Fuchs, V. R. 1986. *The Health Economy.* Cambridge, Mass.: Harvard University Press.

Garg, M. L., Gliebe, W. A., and Elkhatib, M. B. 1978. The extent of defensive medicine: Some empirical evidence. *Legal Aspects of Medical Practice* 6(1):25-29.

Gaumer, G. L. 1986. Medicare patient outcomes and hospital organization mission. In: B. Gray, ed. *For-Profit Enterprise in Health Care.* Washington, D.C.: National Academy Press.

Geweke, J., and Weisbrod, B. A. 1982. Clinical evaluation of a new drug. *Medical Care* 20 (8):821-830.

Goddeeris, J. H. 1984a. Insurance and incentives for innovation in medical care. *Southern Economic Journal 51(2):530-539.*

Goddeeris, J. H. 1984b. Medical insurance, technological change, and welfare. *Economic Inquiry* 22 (1):56-67.

Goddeeris, J. H. 1987. Economic forces on hospital technology: Lessons from the U.S. experience. *International Journal of Technology Assessment in Health Care* 3(2): 223-240.

Goddeeris, J. H., and Weisbrod, B. A. 1985. What we don't know about why health care expenditures have soared: Interaction of insurance and technology. *Mount Sinai Journal of Medicine* 52 (9):685-691.

Gray, B., ed. 1986. *For-Profit Enterprise in Health Care.* Washington, D.C.: National Academy Press.

Hansmann, H. 1980. The role of non-profit enterprise. *Yale Law Journal* 89(5):835-901.

Heinz, J. 1986. The effects of DRG's on patients. *Business and Health* 3(8):17-20.

Herzlinger, R., and Krasker, W. 1987. Who benefits from nonprofits? *Harvard Business Review* 65 (1):93-106.

Hirschman, A. O. 1970. *Exit, Voice, and Loyalty.* Cambridge, Mass.: Harvard University Press.

Hogan, C. 1988. *Urban and Rural Hospital Costs: 1981-85.* DHHS Publication (PHS) 88-3419. Hospital Studies Program Research Note 12, National Center for Health Services Research and Health Care Technology Assessment . Rockville, Md.: Public Health Service.

Holtmann, A. G. 1983. A theory of non-profit firms. *Economica* 50(200):439-449.

Hudis, J. 1986. The organ game. *Health* 18(10):61-66.

Huston, J., and Weisbrod, B. A. 1988. Benefits and Costs of Human Vaccines. Working Paper, University of Wisconsin-Madison, Center for Health Economics and Law.

James, E. 1983. How nonprofits grow: A model. Journal of Policy Analysis and Management 2 (3):350-365.

Joskow, P. 1981. Controlling Hospital Costs: The Role of Government Regulation. Cambridge, Mass.: MIT Press.

Kane, N. M., and Manoukian, P. D. 1989. The effect of the Medicare prospective payment system on the adoption of new technology: The case of cochlear implants. *New England Journal of Medicine* 321(20): 1378-1383.

Kleinfield, N. R. 1983. Companies in search of bionic man. *New York Times,* Nov. 20, Section 3, pp. 1, 26-27.

LaCronique, J. F., and Sandier, S. 1981. Technological innovation: Cause or effect of increasing health expenditures. In: C. Altenstetter, ed. *Innovation in Health Policy and Service Delivery.* Cambridge, Mass.: Oelgeschlaher, Gunn, and Hain.

Lave, J. R., Frank, R. G., Taube, C., Goldman, H., and Rupp, A. 1988. The early effects of Medicare's prospective payment system on psychiatry. *Inquiry* 25(3):354-363.

Lee, R. H., and Waldman, D. M. 1985. The diffusion of innovations in hospitals. *Journal of Health Economics* 4(4):373-380.

Letsch, S., Levit, K. R., and Waldo, D. R. 1988. National health expenditures, 1987. *Health Care Financing Review* 10(2):109-122.

Lewin, L. S., Eckels, T. J., and Miller, L. B. 1988. Setting the record straight: The provision of uncompensated care by not-for-profit hospitals. *New England Journal of Medicine* 318 (18):1212-1215.

Lohr, K. N., Yordy, K. D., and Thier, S. O. 1988. Current issues in quality of care. *Health Affairs* 7 (1):5-18.

Lublin, J. S. 1990. 1990. FDA lets Wellcome cut dosage of drug for AIDS, easing pressure for price cut. *Wall Street Journal,* Jan. 17, p. B2.

Luft, H. S. 1980. Trends in medical care costs: Do HMOs lower the rate of growth? *Medical Care* 18 (1): 1-16.

Luft, H. S. 1981. Health Maintenance Organizations: Dimensions of Performance. New York, N.Y.: John Wiley & Sons.

Manning, W. G., Newhouse, J. P., Duan, N., Keeler, E. B., Leibowitz, A., and Marquis, M. S. 1987. Health insurance and the demand for medical care: Evidence from a randomized experiment. *American Economic Review* 77(3):251-277.

Marmor, T., Schlesinger, M., and Smithey, R. W. 1986. A new look at nonprofits: Health care policy in a competitive age. *Yale Journal on Regulation* 3(1):313-349.

Migué, J.-L., and Bélanger, G. 1974. Toward a general theory of managerial discretion. *Public Choice* 17(4):27-47.

Mitchell, B. M., and Phelps, C. E. 1976. National health insurance: Some costs and effects of mandated employee coverage. *Journal of Political Economy 84(3):553*571.

Mitchell, B. M., and Vogel, R. J. 1975. Health and taxes: An assessment of the medical deduction. *Southern Economic Journal* 41(4):660-672.

Morrisey, M. A., Conrad, D. A., Shortell, S. M., and Cook, K. S. 1984. Hospital rate review: A theory and an empirical review. *Journal of Health Economics* 3(1):2547.

Mossin, J. 1968. Aspects of rational insurance purchasing. *Journal of Political Economy* 76 (4):553-568.

Naj, A. K. 1990. Diagnostic equipment field in squeeze. *Wall Street Journal,* September 6, pp. B1, B4.

National Center for Health Services Research and Health Care Technology. 1986. *The Reuse of Hemodialysis Devices Labeled for Single Use Only.* Washington, D.C.: National Center for Health Services Research and Health Care Technology.

National Center for Health Services Research and Health Care Technology. 1988. New technologies result in increased physician services and costs. In: *Research Activities.* Washington, D.C.: National Center for Health Services Research and Health Care Technology.

National Organ Transplant Act. Hearings before the Subcommittee on Health and the Environment, July 29, Oct. 17, 31, 1983. Washington, D.C.: U.S. Government Printing Office.

Nazario, S. L. 1989. Infertility insurance gains backing. *Wall Street Journal,* December 5, pp. B1, B5.

Nelson, R. R. 1972. Issues and suggestions for the study of industrial organizations in a regime of rapid technical change. In: V. R. Fuchs, ed. *Policy Issues and Research Opportunities in Industrial Organization.* New York, N.Y.: National Bureau of Economic Research and Columbia University Press.

Newhouse, J. 1970. Toward a theory of nonprofit institutions: An economic model of a hospital. *American Economic Review* 60(1):64-75.

Newhouse, J. 1981. Erosion of the medical marketplace. *Advances in Health Economics and Health Services Research* 2:1-34.

Newhouse, J. 1988. Has the erosion of the medical marketplace ended? *Journal of Health, Politics, Policy, and Law* 13(2):263-279.

Newhouse, J. P., Schwartz, W. P., Williams, A. P., and Witsberger, C. 1985. Are fee-for service costs increasing faster than HMO costs? *Medical Care* 23(8):960-966.

Organization for Economic Cooperation and Development. 1990. *Health Care Systems in Transition.* Paris: OECD.

Otten, A. L. 1984. Reuse of devices by hospitals and doctors stirs debate over cost savings and safety. *Wall Street Journal,* Sept. 14, p. 27.

Palmer, R. M., Saywell, R. M., Zollinger, T. W., et al. 1989. The impact of the prospective payment system on the treatment of hip fractures in the elderly. *Archives of Internal Medicine* 149 (10):2237-2241.

Pauly, M. V. 1974. Overinsurance and public provision of insurance: The roles of moral hazard and adverse selection. *Quarterly Journal of Economics* 88(1):44 62.

Pauly, M. V. 1979. What is unnecessary surgery? *Milbank Memorial Fund Quarterly* 57:95-117.

Pauly, M. V. 1986. Taxation, health insurance, and market failure in the medical economy. *Journal of Economic Literature* 24(2):629-675.

Pauly, M. V., and Redisch, M. 1973. The not-for-profit hospital as a physicians' cooperative. *American Economic Review* 63(1):87-100.

Pear, R. 1986. Federal payment for transplants for poor studied. *New York Times,* May 18, Section 1, p. 31.

Phelps, C. E., and Sened, I. 1989. Market Equilibria with Not-For-Profit Firms. Working Paper 191, University of Rochester, Department of Political Science.

Project Hope. 1988. Trends in the Concentration of Six Surgical Procedures Under PPS and Their Implications for Patient Mortality and Medicare Costs. Chevy Chase, Md.: Project Hope, Center for Health Affairs.

Reinhardt, U. 1985. The theory of physician induced demand: Reflections after a decade. *Journal of Health Economics* 4(2):187-193.

Report of the President's Biomedical Research Panel. Washington, D.C.: U.S. Government Printing Office, 1976.

Rettig, R. A. 1980. The politics of health cost containment: End-stage renal disease. *Bulletin of the New York Academy of Medicine* 56(1): 115-138.

Rettig, R. A., and Marks, E. 1983. The Federal Government and Social Planning for End-Stage Renal Disease: Past, Present, and Future. Santa Monica, Calif.: RAND Corporation.

Roberts, R. D. 1984. A positive model of private charity and public transfers. *Journal of Political Economy* 92(1):136-148.

Romeo, A. A., Wagner, J. L., and Lee, R. H. 1984. Prospective reimbursement and the diffusion of new technologies. *Journal of Health Economics* 3(1): 1-24.

Rose-Ackerman, S. 1982. Charitable giving and "excessive" fundraising. *Quarterly Journal of Economics* 97(2): 193-212.

Rossiter, L. F., and Wilensky, G. R. 1984. Identification of physician-induced demand. *Journal of Human Resources* 19(2):231-244.

Russell, L. B. 1979. *Technology in Hospitals.* Washington, D.C.: Brookings Institution.

Russell, L. B. 1986. *Is Prevention Better Than Cure?* Washington, D.C.: Brookings Institution.

Russell, L. B., ed. 1987. *Evaluating Preventive Care: Report on a Workshop.* Washington, D.C.: Brookings Institution.

Sawitz, E., Showstack, J. A., Chow, J., and Shroeder, S. A. 1988. The use of in-hospital physician services for acute myocardial infarction: Changes in volume and complexity over time. *Journal of the American Medical Association* 259(16):2419-2422.

Schiff, J. 1985. Does government spending crowd out charitable contributions? *National Tax Journal* 38(4):536-546.

Schiff, J. 1986. Nonprofit Behavior in the Long Run. Working Paper, Tulane University, Department of Economics.

Schiff, J., and Weisbrod, B. A. 1987. Competition Between For-Profit and Nonprofit Organizations. Working Paper, University of Wisconsin-Madison, Department of Economics .

Schiffman, J. R. 1989. Debate grows over clinics pushing costly PET scans. *Wall Street Journal,* Apr. 3, p. B 1.

Selden, T. M. 1989. Does Institutional Form Matter? Economic Behavior in the Inpatient Mental Health Care Industry. Research Paper 6, University of Wisconsin-Madison, Mental Health Research Center.

Shortell, S. M., and Hughes, E. F. 1988. The effects of regulation, competition, and ownership on mortality rates among hospital inpatients. *New England Journal of Medicine* 318 (17):1100-1106.

Showstack, J. A., Shroeder, S. A., and Matsumoto, M. F. 1982. Changes in the use of medical technologies, 1972-1977: A study of 10 inpatient diagnoses. *New England Journal of Medicine* 306(12):706-712.

Showstack, J. A., Stone, M. H., and Shroeder, S. A. 1985. The role of changing clinical practices in the rising costs of hospital care. *The New England Journal of Medicine* 313(19):1201-1207.

Sloan, F. A., and Vraciu, R. A. 1983. Investor-owned and not-for-profit hospitals: Addressing some issues. *Health Affairs* 2(1):25-37.

Sloan, F. A., Valvona, J., Perrin, J. R., and Adamache, K. W. 1986. Diffusion of surgical technology: An exploratory study. *Journal of Health Economics* 5(1):31-62.

Sloan, F. A., Morrisey, M. A., and Valvona, J. 1988. Medicare prospective payment and the use of medical technologies in hospitals. *Medical Care* 26(9):837-853.

Stano, M. 1987. A clarification of theories and evidence on supplier-induced demand for physician services. *Journal of Human Resources* 22(4):611-620.

Steinberg, R. 1986. Should donors care about fundraising? In: S. Rose-Ackerman, ed. *The Economics of Nonprofit Institutions.* New York: Oxford University Press.

Stevens, R. 1989. In Sickness and in Wealth: American Hospitals in the Twentieth Century. New York, N.Y.: Basic Books.

Taylor, A. K., and Wilensky, G. R. 1983. The effect of tax policies on expenditures for private health insurance. In: J. A. Meyer, ed. *Market Reforms in Health Care.* Washington, D.C.: American Enterprise Institute.

Thomas, L. 1975. *The Lives of a Cell.* New York: Bantam Books.

Titmuss, R. M. 1971. The Gift Relationship: From Human Blood to Social Policy. New York: Pantheon Books.

U.S. Bureau of the Census. 1975. *Statistical Abstract of the United States, 1975.* Washington, D.C.: U.S. Government Printing Office.

U.S. Bureau of the Census. 1979. *Statistical Abstract of the United States, 1979.* Washington, D.C.: U.S. Government Printing Office.

U.S. Bureau of the Census. 1987. *Statistical Abstract of the United States, 1987.* Washington, D.C.: U.S. Government Printing Office.

U.S. Bureau of the Census. 1989. *Statistical Abstract of the United States, 1989.* Washington, D.C.: U.S. Government Printing Office.

U.S. Congress, Office of Technology Assessment. 1984a. *The Hemodialysis Equipment and Disposables Industry.* Washington, D.C.: U.S. Government Printing Office.

U.S. Congress, Office of Technology Assessment. 1984b. *Medical Technology and Costs of the Medicare Program.* Washington, D.C.: U.S. Government Printing Office.

U.S. Congress, Office of Technology Assessment. 1985. Medicare's Prospective Payment System: Strategies for Evaluating Cost, Quality, and Medical Technology. Washington, D.C.: U.S. Government Printing Office.

U.S. Congress, Office of Technology Assessment. 1988. *Infertility: Medical and Social Choices.* Washington, D.C.: U.S. Government Printing Office.

Warr, P. G. 1982. Pareto optimal redistribution and private charity. *Journal of Public Economics* 18 (1):131-138.

Weisbrod, B. A. 1971. Costs and benefits of medical research: The case of poliomyelitis. *Journal of Political Economy* 79(3):527-544.

Weisbrod, B. A. 1978. The Private Nonprofit Sector: Facts in Search of Theory. Discussion Paper 501, University of Wisconsin-Madison, Institute for Research on Poverty.

Weisbrod, B. A. 1988. *The Nonprofit Economy.* Cambridge, Mass.: Harvard University Press.

Weisbrod, B. A. 1989. Rewarding performance that is hard to measure: The role of nonprofit organizations. *Science* 244(4904):541-546.

Weisbrod, B. A. 1991. The health care quadrilemma: An essay on technological change, insurance, quality of care, and cost containment. *Journal of Economic Literature* 29:523-552.

Weisbrod, B. A., and Dominguez, N. O. 1986. Demand for collective goods in private nonprofit markets: Can fundraising expenditures help overcome free-rider behavior? *Journal of Public Economics* 30(1):83-95.

Weisbrod, B. A., and Mauser, E. 1990. Partial vs. Total Effects of Institutional Form: Disentangling Endogenous from Exogenous Variables. Working Paper, Northwestern University, Center for Urban Affairs and Policy Research.

Weisbrod, B. A., and Schlesinger, M. 1986. Public, private, nonprofit ownership and the response to asymmetric information: The case of nursing homes . In: S. RoseAckerman, ed. *The Economics of Nonprofit Institutions.* New York: Oxford University Press.

Wilensky, G. R. 1987. Technology as Culprit and Benefactor. Paper presented at a conference on health care policy, November 12-14, The College of William and Mary.

Wilensky, G. R., and Rossiter, L. F. 1983. A re-examination of the use of physician services: The role of physician initiated demand. *Inquiry* 20(2): 162-172.

Williamson, O. 1967. *The Economics of Discretionary Behavior.* Chicago, Ill.: Markham Press.

Wolfe, B. 1989. Assessment of the Effect of Medicare's PPS on the Demand for V.A. Inpatient Services: An Examination of Externalities of a Public Policy. Paper presented at the meetings of the Association for Public Policy and Management, Washington, D.C.

Woodward, R. S., and Warren-Boulton, F. 1984. Considering the effects of financial incentives and professional ethics on "appropriate" medical care. *Journal of Health Economics* 3 (3):223-237.

Young, D. 1983. *If Not for Profit, for What?* Lexington, Mass.: Lexington Books, D.C. Heath.

Zuckerman, S. 1984. Medical malpractice: Claims, legal costs, and the practice of defensive medicine. *Health Affairs* 3(3): 128-133.

3

The Impact of Technology Assessment on Decisions by Health Care Providers and Payers

BRYAN R. LUCE AND RUTH E. BROWN

Medical technology capabilities are growing at a fantastic rate. Genetically engineered treatment modalities, increasingly sophisticated lasers, diagnostic imaging, and other biotechnical advances are expanding the means of detecting and treating many diseases. There appears to be no limit to what technology might accomplish, given infinite resources. Concurrent with technological advances, however, the health care system is under pressure to provide services to the country's growing elderly population, to extend health care services to the uninsured and the underinsured, and to contain costs. Thus, providers and insurers are caught between constrained budgets and the demand that they pay for the use of expensive new technologies. Tough decisions must be made. In making these decisions, providers and payers increasingly turn to technology assessment as a tool to help set priorities and provide a rationale for their decisions.

Technology assessment is defined as "a comprehensive form of policy research that examines the technical, economic, and social consequences of technological applications" (U.S. Congress, Office of Technology Assessment, 1982) and as the "careful evaluation of a medical technology for evidence of its safety, efficacy, cost, cost-effectiveness and ethical and legal implications, both in absolute terms and in comparison with other competing technologies" (Perry, 1988). Included under the rubric of primary technology assessment are economic, quality-of-life, efficacy, and patient outcome studies. Many organizations in the government and private sectors conduct technology assessments, and the volume of studies in the literature has increased dramatically over the past decade.

As we report in this chapter, however, many providers and insurers generally consider these terms in a much narrower sense. To providers, medical technology means costly devices and diagnostics, whereas technology assessments primarily consist of a net financial impact assessment (combining acquisition cost with expected revenue) or a synthesis of existing data. To insurers, technology assessments are means of distinguishing experimental from state-of-the-art procedures in an effort to determine whether to cover them.

OBJECTIVE

Although it has long been suspected that technology assessment plays a role in the purchase and coverage decisions of health care providers and third-party payers, little supportive evidence for this exists in the literature besides the sheer number of assessments that have been conducted.

Nevertheless, the demand for medical technology assessment has been growing considerably over the past decade as health care providers and payers grapple with escalating health care expenditures. Hospitals and health maintenance organizations (HMOs) are being held more financially responsible than in the past and need to provide services efficiently if they are not to exceed allowed reimbursement levels (Sorian, 1988). As a result, purchase decisions are made under greater scrutiny. Insurers (including self-insured employers) are focusing on the appropriate use of expensive procedures to combat rising health care expenditures and premiums. In 1989, the Health Care Financing Administration proposed a rule that would explicitly allow the federal government to consider cost-effectiveness in making Medicare coverage decisions (*Federal Register,* 1989). Such a major change in the conduct of Medicare-related decisionmaking would likely be the first of similar steps by other third-party payers. Other countries have already made similar moves—Australia and Ontario, Canada, are proceeding toward using cost-effectiveness data in the benefits approval process, primarily for the drug formularies.[1]

The analysis described in this chapter was undertaken to discover how providers and payers use technology assessments in their decisionmaking and it focuses on the implications for the medical products industry. A better understanding of these decisionmaking processes will assist the medical products industry—and, for example, medical specialty societies—in preparing to meet current and future demands for technology assessment research. Industry can thus help to ensure that decisions regarding new technology are made responsibly, with full knowledge of the value that products bring to patients and the institutions serving them.

[1] "A formulary is a list of drugs carried by a given institutional provider. Large organizations use formularies to buy drugs in bulk, as well as to limit the number of different drugs that are covered and/or that must be kept in stock. Choices about which drugs are carried usually are made by a hospital, HMO, or Medicaid pharmacy and therapeutics advisory committee. Decisions often are based upon assessments by committees of the relative safety, effectiveness, and cost-effectiveness compared to other formulary pharmaceuticals" (Halm and Gelijns, 1991, p. 17, n.7).

METHODOLOGY

We used a case-study design employing semistructured, in-depth telephone interviews with selected individuals from hospitals, HMOs, third-party payers, self-insured employers, and government health programs to determine the following:

- how the organizations make purchase, coverage, and utilization decisions;
- what information is sought about medical technologies;
- what difficulties are experienced in using available technology assessment information; and
- what the future holds for technology assessment.

We selected a nonrandom sample of institutions to be interviewed, including four hospital systems, two community hospitals, one university hospital, one university-affiliated hospital, two HMO-affiliated hospitals, one national and three regional HMOs, and two purchasing groups. The institutions were located across the United States and were of various sizes. We also interviewed five third-party payers, two third-party administrators, two case management companies, Medicaid and Medicare administrators, and four large self-insured employers.

Although we interviewed a small number of individuals relative to the total number of providers and third-party payers in the country, we received similar comments from people with similar perspectives. We believe that the general picture would not be changed by interviewing additional individuals.

RESULTS

A summary of our findings is presented in Table 3-1. All of the organizations interviewed are actively engaged in technology assessment activities at some level and use technology assessments in their decisionmaking process. Their interest in technology assessment is based on the perceived need to be cost conscious in purchase decisions and to determine treatment efficacy before making coverage policy decisions. All respondents expected that technology assessment will continue to increase in importance and will become one of the several *required* pieces of information used in the decisionmaking process.

We found that most institutions and organizations have committees responsible for assessing new technology before purchase or coverage policy decisions are made. The level of training and the experience of committee members vary widely. Hospital staffs are generally less sophisticated and have other duties in addition to their assessment activities. HMO and third-party-payer committees are likely to have more training in assessment methods and to concentrate on technology assessment activities.

Most providers identified a threshold cost ($100,000 to $250,000) above which formal assessments are required (for example, computed tomography scan

TABLE 3-1 Summary of Findings by Type of Organization

Hospitals	HMOs	Third-Party Payers
Why are assessments conducted?		
• To help control costs • To make prudent purchaser decisions • To hunt for new technology	• To help make purchase decisions • To provide basis for coverage decisions	• To provide rationale for coverage decisions • To separate experimental from state-of-the-art procedures
Who conducts assessments?		
• Formal muitidisciplinary committees • Formulary committees • Department chiefs	• Formal multidisciplinary committees for broad policy decisions • Multidisciplinary device committees • Formulary committees • Department chiefs	• Formal multidisciplinary committees
What technology is assessed?		
• All devices/diagnostics over a threshold ranging between $100,000 and $250,000 • Less costly items at the discretion of the requesting department • Pharmaceuticals	• Costly procedures for coverage decisions • Costly technology for purchase decisions • Less costly items at the discretion of the requesting department • Pharmaceuticals	• Costly procedures • Controversial procedures
What technology assessment information is used?		
• Peer-reviewed journals • Manufacturers' literature • Meetings/seminars • ECRI, AHA • In-house financial analyses	• Peer-reviewed journals • OHTA, OTA assessments • Recommendations from medical specialty associations and AMA • Cost-effectiveness data not used in coverage decisions	• Peer-reviewed journals • OHTA, OTA, HIAA assessments • Recommendations from medical specialty associations and AMA • Cost-effectiveness data not used

ABBREVIATIONS: OHTA, Office of Health Technology Assessment; OTA, Office of Technology Assessment of the U.S. Congress; HIAA, Health Insurers Association of America; ECRI, (formerly) the Emergency Care Research Institute; AHA, American Hospitals Association; AMA, American Medical Association.

ners and yttrium aluminum garnet lasers are above the threshold, whereas pacemakers and disposable endoscopes are not). Those technologies not meeting the threshold are typically assessed more informally at the department level in hospitals or HMOs. The assessments conducted by hospitals are primarily financial analyses of costs and investment "payback" so that purchasers can make prudent decisions or are a hunt for new technologies that might promote the hospital. Pharmacy formulary assessment committees are separate from other technology assessment committees.

Third-party payers and HMOs as payers conduct assessments that focus on both costly and controversial technologies and procedures. Patient outcomes are included when possible for HMO purchase and coverage assessments and are always considered (if available) in insurers' coverage decisions. Long-term outcomes (e.g., survival over a year, rather than the immediate outcome of the procedure) are considered by insurers if appropriate data are available. In contrast to the providers, who focus on costs, the insurers maintain that the cost of a procedure is not considered in their coverage decisions.

The primary sources of technology assessment information used by providers and payers are peer-reviewed journals and information from manufacturers. HMO and third-party-payer respondents are more likely to include information from such sources as the Office of Health Technology Assessment, the Office of Technology Assessment, medical specialty organizations, and professional organizations such as the Health Insurance Association of America. Occasionally, providers or payers conduct or commission technology assessment research. Each individual we surveyed commented that his or her institution or organization will rely on technology assessment even more in the future and will require a centralized repository for technology assessment information.

DISCUSSION

Generally, our findings conform to what might be expected by knowledgeable observers and suggest important lessons. All the payers and providers we contacted use technology assessment information to aid in their coverage and purchase decisionmaking processes. The quality, scope, and future of payer and provider technology assessment activities vary depending on who conducts the analysis, whether the decision is related to purchase or coverage, and whether the technology assessed is a drug, a medical procedure, or a device.

Quality Issues

The quality of the technology assessments conducted by providers and payers is often less than ideal and generally does not conform to the larger definition of technology assessment established within the research community. Nonetheless, the state of the art has advanced significantly in recent years. In the past, hospitals usually provided whatever physicians requested with little, if any, evaluation effort. Medical directors of HMOs and insurers had very little scientific information on which they could rely to make coverage decisions. Now payers and providers are establishing multidisciplinary committees that are becoming increasingly knowledgeable consumers of technology assessment research. We expect improved levels of sophistication to become the norm and to affect the demand for more comprehensive and rigorously achieved technology assessment information.

To date, three major factors have limited the optimal use of technology assessment information in decisionmaking.

Individual Skill Levels in Technology Assessment Vary Widely

Individuals on drug formulary assessment committees are generally familiar with and understand technology assessment methods, primarily through exposure to the relatively abundant pharmaceutical clinical trial literature. By contrast, most other individuals involved in hospital technology purchase decisionmaking have not been trained in the conduct or analysis of technology assessment, nor are they experienced in adapting technology assessment data to their decisionmaking. HMOs and third-party payers are more likely to employ individuals trained in biostatistics or health services research and who have had experience in conducting and interpreting technology assessments. It is not surprising, therefore, to find different levels of sophistication and rigor of assessment activities in different settings.

Technology Assessment Research is Expensive

Major technology assessments that use existing data generally cost between $40,000 and $50,000. Prospective research (e.g., controlled, random clinical trials) is considerably more expensive and can cost upward of $500,000. Thus, providers and payers are usually limited to conducting assessments based on existing data—and even then assessments are limited to high-cost or controversial technologies. Payers and providers almost always rely on manufacturers, academe, and government for high-quality prospective research. Thus, core expertise in technology assessment research rarely resides within the organizations that actually *use* the results of such research in their decisionmaking.

Timely Technology Assessment Information is Scarce

Nearly all of the respondents commented that currently available technology assessment data are insufficient or appear too late to be of help in their assessments. Drug formulary assessment committees have a richer supply of peer reviewed clinical trial data on which to base their decisions. However, the paucity of technology assessment information in other areas leads many inexperienced users to accept whatever is available without much discrimination.

Scope Issues

Costs clearly play a major role in the technology assessment process. Since assessments in hospitals are often financial analyses for purchase decisions, costs play a dominant role. This is not merely due to tight budgets; regulation also plays a role. For example, the state of Minnesota has passed legislation requiring hospitals to obtain prior approval before making major capital equipment purchases. Approval is granted only if the expenditure meets standards established by a commission established to keep down spending on health care (*Medicine and Health,* April 20, 1992).

HMOs and insurers do not conduct assessments on all new technologies but primarily limit assessments to expensive procedures. Yet, these decisionmakers uniformly assert that costs do not play a role in making coverage and reimbursement decisions. Most analysts would question this assertion, particularly in light of the fact that high costs are one of the major reasons that payers are conducting assessments of new technologies. We can only surmise that HMOs and insurers feel societal and constituent pressures to base decisions on health benefit issues and to avoid being perceived as rationing health care on the basis of costs.

We note several developments that counter the denial that costs play a role in coverage decisions.

- Every year since the mid-1960s, the scientific health literature has had a rapidly increasing number of cost-benefit and cost-effectiveness studies (Elixhauser et al., 1993), indicating that economics generally plays a key role in medical technology assessment.
- The Health Care Financing Administration proposed regulations to permit consideration of cost-effectiveness analyses in its coverage decisionmaking (*Federal Register,* 1989).
- The Oregon Medicaid program made an explicit decision to ration health care on the basis of cost-effectiveness analyses (Fox and Leichter, 1991).
- Australia is the first country to require new drug approval to include cost-effectiveness analyses (Drummond, 1992). Ontario, Canada, is preparing a similar policy to include cost-effectiveness criteria in evaluating drugs (Ontario Drug Program Branch, 1991) and, in Europe, drug pricing authorities are encouraging and accepting industry's submission of cost-effectiveness data.
- Battelle's and other researchers' experiences in the pharmaceutical area in the United States, Canada, and Europe suggest that market pressures and pricing authorities have led to cost-effectiveness assessments in the research and development of most breakthrough, and often expensive, drugs.

- Companies often think of these assessments as "price justification" activities, which is exactly what coverage decisionmakers are implicitly asking.

Thus, notwithstanding our respondents' statements, economics clearly plays a major role in the reasons they engage in technology assessment and even in the assessments themselves. One problem with explicitly excluding economic considerations from the analysis is that decisionmakers may miss the impact that a new technology might have on patient management pathways, laboratory test expenditures, number and length of hospital stays, and other factors that affect the total costs of a medical technology. The resulting technology assessments may therefore undervalue the impacts of important innovations.

Future Issues

Providers will continue to conduct assessments for major capital expenditures from an institutional point of view and be very oriented toward "prudent purchases." However, they will become more sophisticated in reviewing data and information in the literature; they will communicate better among themselves; and as they continue to evolve into larger hospital and managed care systems, their expertise will grow commensurately and their viewpoints will become less narrow. We expect that future medical device assessment committees will follow the lead of formulary committees and will include cost-effectiveness as one of the key criteria for the adoption of a new technology.

HMOs and insurers will continue their technology assessment efforts. Their coordination of assessments will likely intensify to the extent allowed by law, not only in terms of more efficient information transfer but also in the pooling of resources so that they can assess more technologies better. The private-public efforts—first by the Institute of Medicine's Council on Health Care Technology and, second, by the Technology Assessment Collaboration Proposal (*Medicine and Health,* January 20, 1992), although both stalled—are indicators that there is intense interest in technology assessment and a need to pool funding and coordinate assessment efforts.

Other indicators of the continued increase in assessments are the expansion of both the Agency for Health Care Policy and Research's outcomes research agenda and that agency's recent pharmaceutical outcomes research initiative. The trends toward increasing outcomes research come in an environment of cost constraints that is leading to greater consolidation of providers and insurers, including more managed care. These enlarged organizations will have more motivation and may have greater clout to require or demand information from medical device and pharmaceutical manufacturers.

The findings of the study described in this chapter reveal that many decisionmakers, especially those at hospitals, are not well prepared to assess the available technology assessment information and do not have the resources to conduct technology assessment studies on a routine basis on their own. Overall, we are left with the impression that decisionmakers are inundated with new (and usually very expensive) technologies and that physicians and patients are demanding the latest innovations. At the same time, decisionmakers are under intense budgetary pressures and have a very poor information base to assist them in making their decisions. Thus, these decisionmakers are eager for timely, relevant, and credible information to help them make decisions concerning technology purchase, adoption, and coverage policy. Government, the medical products industry, and medical societies have the opportunity—and perhaps the obligation—to support decisionmaking by educating customers, targeting information to meet real-world needs, making information more accessible, and providing more and better technology assessment studies. Efforts could be divided so that the medical drugs and devices industries assess their products, the federal government assesses medical and surgical procedures, and the medical specialty societies focus on guiding the efforts in all areas.

Education

Government, industry, and medical societies can assert leadership in educating insurers and providers about technology assessment so that responsible decisions can be made. They already actively sponsor educational activities for medical professionals. The provision of materials and programs on how to use patient outcomes and cost-effectiveness data would be a natural extension of these efforts.

Financial Support

Government and industry can also contribute toward the costs of technology assessments. For example, better systems for tracking patient outcomes are needed. This requires both technical and financial investments that could be supplied in part by both government and the medical products industry. Industry and government could also team up to support public-private efforts to finance technology assessments. These efforts could be similar to those attempted in the past (for example, the Institute of Medicine's Council on Health Care Technology and the recent technology assessment collaboration proposal spearheaded by the insurance industry). Financial support for clearinghouse activities, development of data-tracking systems, and methodology research are all necessary to meet future demands for information.

Information

Most important, government, industry, and possibly medical specialty societies have the opportunity to fill the information vacuum we have identified in this chapter. The health care community is currently making technology decisions with insufficient data. As a result, some of these decisions may be suboptimal. Not only can they increase the knowledge base by supporting patient outcomes and cost-effectiveness research, but they can also target information to specific decisionmakers' needs. Appropriate studies can be sponsored early in the technology development process so that decisionmakers have the information they need when they need it.

Finally, whether industry, government, and medical specialty societies capitalize on the opportunities identified above, the demand for technology assessment information will continue. The respondents in the present study have identified needs in education, resources, and research; they uniformly predict that technology assessment activities will become increasingly important in making their technology purchase and coverage decisions. Indeed, both the health care market and public policy makers are already beginning to require considerably expanded technology assessment information from manufacturers.

REFERENCES

Drummond, M. 1992. Australian guidelines for cost-effectiveness studies of pharmaceuticals. *Pharmacoeconomics* 1(Suppl.):61-69.

Elixhauser, A. E., Luce, B. R., Taylor, W. R., and Reblando, J. 1993. Health care CBA/ CEA: An update on the growth and composition of the literature. *Medical Care* 31(7 Suppl.):JS1-JS1 1, JS 18-JS149.

Federal Register. Medicare Program: Criteria and procedures for making medical services coverage decisions that relate to health care technology. January 30, 1989. 54(18).

Fox, D. M., and Leicher, H. M. 1991. Rationing care in Oregon: The new accountability. *Health Affairs* 10:7-27.

Halm, E. A., and Gelijns, A. C. 1991. An introduction to the changing economics of technological innovation in medicine. In: Institute of Medicine. *Medical Innovation at the Crossroads.* Vol. 2, *The Changing Economics of Medical Technology.* A. C. Gelijns and E. A. Halm, eds. Washington, D.C.: National Academy Press.

Medicine and Health, January 20, 1992. AHCPR rejects assessment gift. 46(3).

Medicine and Health, April 20, 1992. Minnesota passes health reform bill. 46(16).

U.S. Congress, Office of Technology Assessment. 1982. *Strategies for Medical Technology Assessment.* Washington, D.C.: U.S. Government Printing Office.

Ontario Drug Program Branch. October 1991. Guidelines for drugs benefit formulary/ comparative drug index. Draft paper. Ontario Drug Program Branch.

Perry, S. 1988. Technology assessment in health care: The U.S. perspective. *Health Policy* 9:317-324.

Sorian, R. 1988. The Bitter Pill: Tough Choices in America's Health Policy. New York: McGraw-Hill.

PART II

Provider Decisionmaking

4

Role of the Hospital in the Acquisition of Technology

GERARD F. ANDERSON AND EARL P. STEINBERG

Hospitals are major consumers of both new and established medical technologies. In 1991, for example, hospitals spent $30 billion on capital projects and had to choose which drugs and devices to purchase from among 750,000 different options (Lumsdon, 1992). Hospitals need to make decisions regarding the purchase of "big-ticket" items—such as automated labs, radiography and fluoroscopy equipment, patient monitors, magnetic resonance imagers, and computed tomography scanners (Anderson, 1990)—as well as "little-ticket" items—such as tissue plasminogen activator versus streptokinase and high- versus low-osmolality contrast media. In addition, hospital managers are confronted with decisions regarding whether their hospitals should perform procedures considered by insurers to be experimental and for which reimbursement is uncertain, such as autologous bone marrow transplantation for women with metastatic breast cancer (Hall and Anderson, 1992).

In addition to their role as consumers of medical technology, hospitals influence the diffusion of technology in other ways. For example, since hospitals are generally the earliest adopters of new technologies, their reactions to those technologies have a major impact on the subsequent acquisition decisions made by other types of providers. In addition, hospitals are the sites for many clinical trials of drugs and devices and for the clinical training of most physicians.

In this chapter we discuss how recent public policy decisions have provided hospital managers greater incentives to conduct technology assessments. We then contrast the likely characteristics of technology assessments performed from a societal perspective with those of technology assessments performed from a hospital perspective. Our major conclusions are that technology assessments conducted from the perspective of the hospital could result in the greater and more rapid diffusion of technology, with less emphasis placed on controlling total health care costs or improving the long-run health status of the population, than assessments conducted from a societal perspective. The difference between a hospital's perspective and society's perspective should be kept in mind when regulations and payment systems are designed.

THE CHANGING FINANCIAL ENVIRONMENT

Until recently, hospital managers had little financial incentive to critically evaluate new or established technologies (Anderson and Steinberg, 1984). Hospitals were paid under a cost- and charge-based reimbursement system that essentially gave them a "blank check" to purchase equipment without the need to monitor the medical practices of their physicians (Davis et al., 1990). For pharmaceuticals in particular, full cost would be paid for virtually any new product that was approved by the Food and Drug Administration and not considered experimental by insurers because public and private insurers were not aggressively pursuing utilization review (Hall and Anderson, 1992).

Recent changes, however, have provided hospital managers with a stronger incentive to become involved in both medical practice evaluation and technology assessment. The change from cost- and charge-based reimbursement to prospective payment has changed technology-intensive departments, such as radiology, from being "profit centers" to being "cost centers." In addition, with the inclusion of capital expenditures under the Medicare prospective payment system, hospital managers have become more concerned about their capital budgets, since hospitals can no longer pass higher capital costs on to the Medicare program. Instead, they must now finance capital expenditures from internal funds, venture capital, partnerships, retained earnings, philanthropy, leasing, rental, borrowing, or, in the case of not-for-profit hospitals, equity financing. In addition, the increased level of enrollment in health maintenance organizations and other managed care programs has forced hospitals to scrutinize technology acquisitions more closely. Finally, the judicial system has made hospitals legally responsible for the medical care delivered by the physicians on their staffs (*Darling v. Charleston Community Memorial Hospital,* 1965).

Although government and private payers have given hospital managers a stronger financial incentive to become prudent purchasers of medical technology and to monitor medical practices more closely, several other legal and organizational forces are counterbalancing the financial incentives of hospital managers to become more prudent purchasers of new technologies. For example, hospital managers are confronted with the threat of antitrust violations if they purchase equipment jointly with other hospitals and the threat of violations of the safe harbor regulations if they become joint partners with physicians (Anderson, 1992). Certificate-of-need regulations may prevent some hospitals from pur chasing equipment that would increase their productivity. Malpractice concerns could arise if a hospital deviates from the trends that are prevailing at the moment and does not purchase certain equipment or use certain drugs. Moreover, academic medical center hospitals may choose to adopt technologies that are not cost-effective to remain in the forefront of research and education (Anderson et al., 1989).

Probably the most important constraint on the hospital manager's discretion with respect to technology acquisition decisions is imposed by the medical staff, a body that is crucial for attracting patients to the hospital. In most cases, the clinical and financial incentives of a physician are to do everything possible for a patient rather than to pay close attention to cost and cost-effectiveness (see chapter 5, this volume). In addition, in the case of new technologies that have high public visibility, such as magnetic resonance imaging, a hospital may conclude that it is in its overall economic interest to acquire the technology to protect or enhance its market share of patients, even if it thinks reimbursement for the technology may fall short of its cost (Steinberg et al., 1988).

Thus, although a number of new forces that increase hospitals' incentives to perform technology assessments and monitor medical practices have emerged over the past decade, other incentives cut against these new forces. As a result, it is unclear how extensively hospital managers have actually altered their behaviors. For example, only 20 percent of hospitals had established a formal technology assessment committee by 1992 (up from 18 percent in 1990), and only an additional 11 percent were considering the formation of such a committee in 1992 (Johnsson et al., 1991; Lumsdon, 1992).

MODELS OF HOSPITAL BEHAVIOR

Economists have developed several theories to explain the behavior of hospital managers (Feldstein, 1988). We present three models of hospital behavior—models of price, technology, and utility competition—and propose that these theories be used to consider how different types of technology assessments could influence the scope of technology diffusion and the nature of medical practice.

The price competition model uses traditional economic theory to explain hospital behavior. This model assumes that the hospital manager faces a downward-sloping demand curve and evaluates technologies from the perspective of profitability. From that perspective, new technologies are acquired when the expected revenue stream exceeds the expected cost over the useful life of the product. In making these financial calculations, the hospital manager takes into account the fact that each service contributes to the financial viability of the entire hospital; therefore, the purchase of certain "loss leaders" that benefit the entire hospital may be permitted (Steinberg et al., 1988). Examples of such "loss leaders" are helicopter services, which are money-losing operations in nearly every circumstance, but that can bring visibility to the hospital and attract "profitable" patients for other parts of the hospital (Anderson, 1990).

The technology competition model derives from three different theories of hospital behavior: the sales maximization theory (hospitals want to be the largest); the conspicuous consumption theory (hospitals want to show that they are the most technologically advanced); and the physician cooperative theory (hospitals will acquire technology that maximizes physician income). In the technology competition model, physicians and potential patients are assumed to be attracted to new technologies and innovative medical practices. To obtain a competitive advantage over other hospitals, it is desirable to be the first hospital in a geographic area to acquire a new technology or to demonstrate a proficiency with a new medical procedure. Even for hospitals that do not strive to be trendsetters, it is still important to maintain technological parity with other hospitals.

The third model of hospital behavior is the utility maximization model. Under this model, the hospital manager invests in technology, subject to a budget constraint, to enhance the quality or quantity of services that are provided. In this model, technology competes against other services, such as nursing, for a share of the hospital's budget, and new and established technologies are evaluated within this context.

All three of these models may explain hospital managers' behavior to some extent. To assess how accurately these theoretical models predict hospital managers' actual behavior, it is useful to examine the factors that hospital managers profess to consider when making acquisition and utilization decisions. In chapter 3 of this volume, Luce and Brown reported on the results of their survey of factors that influence hospital managers. In an earlier volume in this series, Paul Griner, general director of the Strong Memorial Hospital, identified eight factors that influence the adoption of new technology: capital financing, hospital payment methods, degree of regulation, degree of competition, hospital capacity, evidence of effectiveness, organizational arrangements, and the decisionmaking process (Griner, 1992).

Other hospital managers have conceptualized the technology acquisition process from more of a strategic planning perspective. In making technology acquisition and utilization decisions, they consider the need to improve existing clinical strengths, provide synergy with existing technologies, be consistent with the hospital's overall mission, minimize financial risk, and recognize the life span of a product. According to a survey of 524 health care managers in 1990, the following criteria were rated as "very important" by more than half of them: the ability to establish or expand services (85 percent), receipt of a return on investment (71 percent), and the ability to reduce operating costs (67 percent). The enhanced image of the hospital (47 percent) and medical staff pressures (43 percent) were also cited frequently (Anderson, 1990).

A comparison of the economist's and manager's perspectives of what motivates the hospital manager suggests a number of commonalities. The profitability of the investment is an important consideration, although it must be viewed from the perspective of the entire institution. Hospitals compete to be the first to acquire new technologies to enhance their market share, satisfy the medical staff, and improve the image of the hospital. Increasingly, it is necessary for hospital managers to make trade-offs between the acquisition of new technology and other competing demands for constrained resources. All of these considerations will affect a hospital manager's perspective when he or she evaluates a new technology.

TECHNOLOGY ASSESSMENT: SOCIETAL VERSUS HOSPITAL PERSPECTIVE

Several factors should be considered when performing any technology assessment (Fuchs and Garber, 1990). These include not only clinical considerations, such as safety, efficacy, and effectiveness, but also economic, legal, and ethical considerations as well as patient satisfaction and preferences. Tools capable of measuring these endpoints have become increasingly sophisticated. Even so, it is critically important to keep in mind the fact that the weight placed on some of these dimensions may depend on the perspective from which the assessment is being conducted.

In the past most technology assessments in the United States were conducted by government entities or academicians, who have tended to perform the assessment from the perspective of society. (In most other countries, the national government continues to sponsor technology assessments that are performed from the perspective of society.) These assessments tended to be performed long after the technologies had diffused widely.

As we have discussed, however, recent public policy in the United States has attempted to induce hospitals to take greater responsibility for conducting technology assessments from their own perspective. The Medicare prospective payment system, for example, uses diagnosis-related groups (DRGs) to pay hospitals and, with few exceptions, DRG payments do not vary by type of technology used. As a result, the hospital is given the financial incentive to conduct technology assessments and evaluate practice patterns with the knowledge that the payment they receive for hospitalization will not vary according to the types of technology that are used.

If more technology assessments are to be conducted from the hospital's perspective, it is important to examine the potential implications of changing the assessment perspective from what benefits society generally to what benefits a specific hospital. In discussing these potential implications, our intention is not to imply that hospital managers do not consider society in making their decisions; rather, our objective is to point out how adoption of the hospital's perspective might affect technological assessment and diffusion at the margin. Our views regarding the effect of changing the perspective from which a technology assessment is performed from a societal to a hospital perspective are as follows. Technology assessments conducted from the hospital perspective will:

- be performed earlier in the diffusion process,
- be more responsive to changes in medical knowledge and practice,
- be more sensitive to local medical conditions,
- place less emphasis on long-term outcomes and total health care costs,
- place more emphasis on legal liability, and
- give less consideration to impacts on other providers.

First, a shift to a hospital perspective is likely to result in the performance of technology assessments at an earlier point in the technology's development. To maintain a competitive advantage over other hospitals, hospital managers need to conduct their technology assessments at as early a stage as possible in the development of a new technology. As a result, they may feel compelled to perform technology assessments while the drug or device is still in clinical trials. In contrast, government is prone to wait until more "complete" information is available before conducting an assessment.

Second, assessments performed from a hospital perspective are more likely to be responsive to ongoing changes in medical knowledge and practice patterns. In part, this is because a hospital's process for performing an assessment is more streamlined and less bureaucratic; it can therefore respond to new information as soon as it becomes available. The capacity to respond quickly may determine whether a hospital succeeds or fails in attracting a substantial share of patients in a competitive market. Government, in contrast, will be more likely to wait until a general consensus has been reached before performing or revising an assessment.

Third, in performing a technology assessment a hospital is more likely than government to consider the implications of local medical conditions, such as the strengths of the physicians on their staff, the institution's mission, the characteristics of the patients in the hospital's catchment area, and the behaviors of other hospitals in the geographic area. An assessment performed from a societal perspective, in contrast, must consider issues from a more aggregated geographic perspective.

Fourth, whereas an assessment from a societal perspective will tend to consider both long-term and short-term outcomes, hospital managers are likely to place greater emphasis on short-term outcomes than on long-term outcomes. For example, a hospital will tend to consider costs incurred during a hospital stay as opposed to the costs incurred over the long term. In addition, they will be less concerned about technologies that prevent readmissions, because under most payment systems readmissions offer the hospital an opportunity for a second payment. The hospital perspective thus could increase long-term health care costs as hospital managers focus on short-term cost implications.

The outcomes emphasized in assessments performed from a societal perspective may differ from those emphasized in technology assessments conducted from a hospital perspective in other ways as well. For example, a hospital may pay more attention to the impact of a technology on patient satisfaction and quality of life than on long-run mortality or morbidity. A hospital is also more likely to consider carefully the malpractice and liability implications of adopting versus not adopting a new technology. In addition, indirect costs associated with morbidity, costs incurred by a patient outside the hospital setting, and intangible costs of suffering are more likely to be considered in an assessment from a societal perspective.

Finally, hospital managers also may tend to be less concerned than society about the impact of their decisions on other providers. For example, one of hospitals' responses to the incentives created by the Medicare prospective payment system was to shorten the length of stay. This increased the number and complexity of patients who were discharged to nursing homes and other providers. Except to the extent that this may have affected hospitals' ability to discharge patients, the changes were of less concern to hospitals than they would be for an assessment conducted from a societal perspective.

In addition, we believe the total cost of multiple hospitals performing independent technology assessments is likely to be greater than the cost of a single assessment conducted by a single entity. Although individual hospitals are unlikely to devote considerable resources to any single assessment, the effect of many hospitals performing assessments on the same technology could result in more total resources being devoted to technology assessment. In view of the cost of performing technology assessments, hospital managers are forming technology assessment consortia.

Societal Versus Hospital Perspective: Some Examples

What is the aggregate effect of these differences in perspective? Because no single technology assessment is likely to illustrate how all of these differences in perspective might manifest themselves, we believe there is value in considering how assessments of a couple of technologies might differ when performed from a hospital versus a societal perspective.

The use of high-dose chemotherapy with bone marrow transplant for treatment of various types of malignancies, such as metastatic breast cancer, is a good example. Although few data are available and one cannot yet determine whether this treatment is effective in patients with metastatic breast cancer, many hospitals already offer this treatment. Their decision to offer the treatment is presumably based on their own consideration of the potential value of establishing themselves as a leader in the adoption of new cancer treatments. When paid for, this treatment also generates substantial revenue, although little is known about the short- or long-term cost-effectiveness of this treatment. Even though sufficient data to evaluate this technology from a societal perspective are clearly not available, some hospitals have made a decision, on the basis of what few data are available, to adopt this treatment. Their views regarding the appropriateness of continuing to offer this treatment may be revised several times as new data be come available, well before an assessment performed from a societal perspective is ever undertaken.

The case of laparoscopic cholecystectomy is also illustrative. Early data have suggested that the short-term outcomes associated with this procedure are quite favorable compared with those associated with traditional cholecystectomy. Patients' lengths of hospital stay are shorter, short-term morbidity is lower, and return to work is reported to be earlier after laparoscopic cholecystectomy compared with that after traditional cholecystectomy. As a result, surgeons and hospitals have rushed to adopt this new procedure.

Data regarding longer-term clinical outcomes and the costs associated with laporoscopic cholecystectomy are just now becoming available. These data suggest that the total costs associated with laparoscopic cholecystectomy, that is, payments to hospitals and physicians, may be higher than those associated with conventional cholecystectomy (Legorreta, 1993). In addition, there is some indication that rates of readmission for procedural complications were initially higher with laparoscopic cholecystectomy than with traditional cholecystectomy, perhaps as a result of the learning curve involved. Even though the latter data may decrease the attractiveness of this technology from a societal perspective, it may not lessen the attractiveness of the technology from a hospital's perspective.

POLICY CONSIDERATIONS

What, then, is the aggregate effect of these differences in assessment perspective on the overall rate of diffusion of medical technology? We believe the answer is "very little to date." Prior to the implementation of prospective payment, hospitals were rapid adopters of new technologies, primarily because several forces promoted the early adoption of new technology and the cost of using those technologies could be recovered easily. Few hospitals deferred acquisition decisions until a technology was mature and an assessment of it had been performed from a societal perspective. Although several changes in regulatory, legal, and payment policies that increase hospital managers' incentives to perform technology assessments have been implemented over the past decade, we believe hospitals continue to be early adopters of new technologies, largely because several forces promoting the early adoption of technology counterbalance the incentives to perform careful technology assessments. If policies that resulted in the performance of more technology assessments from a societal perspective were implemented, with acquisition decisions made on the basis of those assessments, then we believe the rate of adoption of new technology could slow substantially.

If technology assessment conducted from a societal perspective is considered to be the "gold standard," then it is worthwhile to consider various strategies to encourage the use of this perspective. One option is to alter the perspective of hospitals to give them more of an incentive to adopt a societal perspective. For example, the Health Care Financing Administration's 30-day mortality index is an attempt to measure the impact of the hospital visit over a time period longer than most hospital stays. Similarly, the emphasis of peer review organizations on readmission rates requires hospitals to take a longer-term perspective. Increased use of payment for a bundle of services or use of a capitated payment for a year could give hospitals more of an incentive to consider the impacts of their decisions on long-term outcomes, total health care costs, and other providers. Increased competition between hospitals on the basis of data regarding their long-term outcomes or a focus on such outcomes by the Joint Commission on the Accreditation of Health Care Organizations might have similar effects.

CONCLUSION

Recent changes in health care financing have given hospitals more of an incentive to evaluate new technologies from their own perspective. In light of this trend, it is important to consider how this perspective might affect the diffusion of technology. We believe that technology assessment conducted from a hospital perspective instead of a societal perspective promotes the more rapid diffusion of medical technology, gives less weight to long-term outcomes and long-run health care costs, and increases the overall cost of conducting technology assessments. Public policy could mitigate some of these effects by establishing payment systems that emphasize total health care costs and information systems that emphasize the longer-term impacts of different treatment modalities.

REFERENCES

Anderson, G. 1992. The courts and health policy: Strengths and limitations. *Health Affairs* 11:95-110.

Anderson, G., and Steinberg, E. 1984. To buy or not to buy: Technology acquisition under prospective payment. *New England Journal of Medicine* 312:1349-1353.

Anderson, G., Lave, J., Russe, C., and Neuman, P. 1989. *Providing Hospital Services*. Baltimore, Md.: The Johns Hopkins University Press.

Anderson, H. J. 1990. Survey identifies trends in equipment acquisitions. *Hospitals* 64:30-35.

Darling v. Charleston Community Memorial Hospital, 33 I11. 2d. 326, 211 N.E.2d. 253 (1965).

Davis, K., Anderson, G., Rowland, D., and Steinberg, E. 1990. *Health Care Cost Containment*. Baltimore, Md.: The Johns Hopkins University Press.

Feldstein, P. 1988. *Health Care Economics*. New York: John Wiley & Sons.

Fuchs, V., and Garber, A. 1990. The new technology assessment. *New England Journal of Medicine* 323:673-677.

Griner, P. 1992. New technology adoption in the hospital. In: Institute of Medicine. *Medical Innovation at the Crossroads*. Vol. 3, *Technology and Health Care in an*

Era of Limits. A. C. Gelijns, ed. Washington, D.C.: National Academy Press, pp. 123-132.

Hall, M., and Anderson, G. 1992. Health insurers' assessment of medical necessity. *Pennsylvania Law Review* 140(5):1637-1712.

Johnsson, J., Anderson, H. J., and Burke, M. 1991. Technology acquisition: Trends in imaging. *Hospitals* 65:26-36.

Legorreta, A. P., Silber, J. H., Costantino, G. N., Kobylinski, R. W., and Zatz, S. L. 1993. Increased cholecystectomy rate after the introduction of laparoscopic cholecystectomy. *Journal of the American Medical Association* 270:1429-1432.

Lumsdon, K. 1992. Beyond technology assessment: Balancing needs, strategy. *Hospitals* 66:20-26.

Steinberg, E. P., Stason, W. B., diMonda, R., and Schroeder, S. A. 1988. Determinants of acquisition of MR imaging units in an era of prospective payment. *Radiology* 168(1):265-270.

5

Physicians' Decisions Regarding the Acquisition of Technology

A. MARK FENDRICK AND J. SANFORD SCHWARTZ

The quality and cost of medical care have recently come under intense scrutiny. Identification of the forces that drive the health care system may help policymakers determine ways to allocate those scarce resources devoted to health care more equitably and efficiently. Although payments to physicians account for less than 20 percent of total health care expenditures, physicians generate nearly 80 percent of the total services delivered (Eisenberg, 1986). Further understanding of the physician's decisionmaking process for the adoption of medical innovations may aid in the enormous task of bringing significant health care reform to the United States.

INCENTIVES FOR THE ADOPTION OF MEDICAL INNOVATIONS

> Medical tradition emphasizes giving the best care that is technically possible; the only legitimate and explicitly recognized constraint is the state of the art (Fuchs, 1968).

Substantial evidence indicates that physicians are receptive to technological advances. The "technological imperative," or the desire to do anything and everything possible for a patient, is considered to be a major influence on the adoption of medical innovation (Altman and Blendon, 1979; Kressley, 1981). The pharmaceutical and medical device industries annually supply thousands of new products that offer the potential for improved diagnostic capabilities and new, more sophisticated treatments. Approximately one in three practitioners adopts a new technology in a given year (Freiman, 1985). Although the adoption and use of each of these innovative technologies is guided by the expectation of improved clinical outcomes, these decisions are frequently based on less-than-sufficient data.

Ideally, decisions regarding the adoption of a medical innovation by physicians would be based on results drawn from research performed from a number of different perspectives, addressing endpoints important to patients, providers, payers, and society. In theory, this information would be derived from rigorously designed and conducted controlled experiments that produce unambiguous results. The findings from these investigations would allow physicians to make better-informed and more rational choices, leading to the rapid adoption of relatively beneficial innovations, inhibition of the adoption of interventions that are judged to provide fewer benefits relative to their costs, and prevention of the diffusion of those technologies that are not beneficial (or that are even harmful).

Although the adoption of quality-enhancing, cost-saving, or cost-effective medical innovations is desirable, the early and more widespread adoption of expensive innovations with unknown benefits is not. There is much room for improvement in the ways that we assess the net benefits of medical care interventions (Fineberg and Hiatt, 1979). In addition, there is general agreement that the reimbursement process for medical innovation, which currently requires little in the way of information on clinical and economic outcomes, must be modified to slow the adoption of unproved interventions and to facilitate or even encourage more rigorous evaluation efforts. The implementation of a nonprofit reimbursement system during the evaluative stages of a novel technology would dampen the usual market forces that may encourage the early dissemination of innovations not yet determined effective (James, 1991) while also minimizing economic disincentives that may prevent further technological advances.

Unfortunately, reality diverges from theory in that financial incentives in the form of generous reimbursement of providers for new procedures and diagnostic tests have been identified as a particularly important stimulus to the adoption of medical innovations (Hemenway et al., 1990; Hichson et al., 1987; Hillman et al., 1989; McGivney, 1988). Furthermore, there may be a disincentive for providers to adopt an innovation when reimbursement levels are deemed less than adequate for its use (e.g., cochlear implants). In addition, valid and reliable outcomes data on the safety, efficacy, and cost-effectiveness of many medical interventions do not exist prior to widespread adoption (Chalmers, 1974). Limitations on time, expense, and practicality are primarily responsible for the absence of controlled experiments in many clinical areas. In today's competitive health care environment, decisions regarding the adoption and reimbursement of medical technology must be made quickly and, often, those who make the decisions must rely on imperfect or nonexistent effectiveness data generated by evaluative methodologies of suboptimal rigor. The end result is an inconsistent pattern of adoption and diffusion that has led to the underutilization of some effective technologies (e.g., immunizations), the widespread utilization of some technologies of unproven efficacy (e.g., fetal monitoring), and the use of some later found to be ineffective and even harmful (e.g., gastric bubble).

CONCEPTUAL MODEL

Conceptual models can facilitate understanding of why and how physicians adopt a medical innovation. The model shown in Figure 5-1 is adapted from earlier research in the field of diffusion of innovation (Greer, 1977, 1988; Kaluzny, 1974; Rogers and Shoemaker, 1971; Warner, 1974). The use of schematics such as this can help provide an understanding of physician decisionmaking behavior. However, the evidence available to date indicates that it is difficult to change physician behavior on a significant level (Eisenberg, 1986; Eisenberg and Williams, 1981; Kanouse and Jacoby, 1988).

Innovation Characteristics

Factors inherent to an innovation itself can influence its adoption by physicians and other health care providers (Lee and Waldman, 1986). The advantages of a new technology compared with those of currently available technology are important in establishing the level and speed of its acceptance. When financial

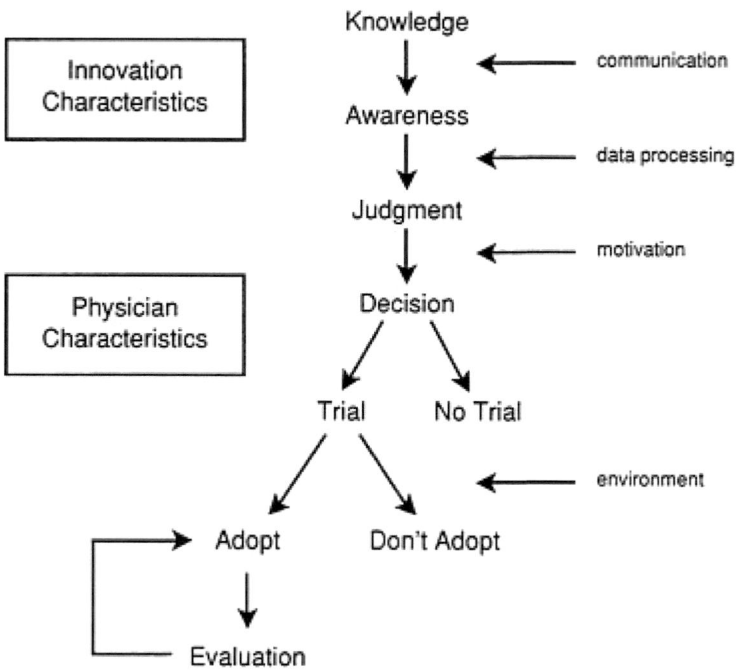

FIGURE 5-1 Conceptual model of the diffusion of innovation to physicians.

incentives are neutral "breakthrough" technologies, such as antibiotics for bacterial infections or chemotherapy for childhood malignancies, are likely to be adopted more rapidly than "me-too" innovations, such as an additional entry into a class of established pharmaceutical drugs that can offer only marginal benefits over the drugs currently in use (Warner, 1975).

The adoption and diffusion of a technology are also a function of the resources and organizational commitment necessary to experiment with the innovation (Baker, 1979; Hillman and Schwartz, 1986). As a rule of thumb, the fewer resources required to implement a change, the greater likelihood that adoption of that innovation will occur. Pharmaceutical agents and many diagnostic tests do not require large capital investments, organizational change, or physical plant alterations, and therefore are easily tried out by physicians. In contrast, interventions that require substantial financial expenditures or training of skilled personnel to acquire proficiency (e.g., magnetic resonance imaging scanners) necessitate a complicated decisionmaking process, which may inhibit the rate of adoption of that intervention. All other factors being equal, less expensive or more profitable innovations will tend to replace existing technologies that produce similar outcomes.

Provider Characteristics

Because the resources that can be devoted to health care are not infinite, physicians are now being charged with a complex and sometimes inherently contradictory set of responsibilities. On the one hand, physicians' primary responsibility is to provide the necessary services to optimize their patients' health. On the other hand, as health care costs continue to increase providers are required to incorporate economic principles into their clinical practices. As a result, the physician's role has expanded beyond that of the doctor-patient relationship (Mulley, 1992; Williams, 1992).

The most important role of the physician is serving the patient. Ideally, physicians successfully act as their patients' agents, providing the care that patients would choose if the patients possessed the scientific knowledge and judgment that the physicians possess. In this role, ideally, the physician's decision to adopt an innovation would focus on an individual patient's outcome and not on those outcomes of more interest to society.

It is known, however, that physicians are not perfect agents. Physician behavior is influenced by a number of factors in addition to patient outcomes. As rational individuals, physicians seek to optimize personal gratification (the second role of the physician), and the benefits realized from being "on the cutting edge" may play a role in an individual's adoptive behavior by contributing to their personal satisfaction. Other personal characteristics may affect their likelihood of adopting new technologies. For example, younger physicians often adopt innovative interventions more quickly than their older counterparts. Independent of physician age, an inverse correlation exists between the time since completion of medical training and the adoption of medical innovation. Speaking broadly, adoption of a new technology is more rapid among subspecialists than generalists, group practitioners than solo practitioners, and urban providers than those practicing in rural settings. Physicians with academic or national affiliations also have a greater proclivity to adopt and use new technology than do those without them (Freiman, 1985). As provider reimbursements are constrained and competition for patients increases, market factors may also stimulate physicians to adopt medical innovations more quickly (Hillman et al., 1989; McCarthy, 1985; Wilensky and Rossiter, 1983). Thus, physicians who are most subject to competitive processes (e.g., those in urban locations) can be expected to adopt innovations earlier. Although postulated, and surely present to some degree, proof of these behaviors has yet to be quantified.

A third and increasingly important role of physicians is that of allocator of scarce resources. However, it is inherently difficult to apply societal concerns on the level of the doctor-patient relationship. Practitioners have limited exposure to the formal training in decisionmaking analysis required to effectively integrate societal perspectives into day-to-day clinical decisions. Increased attention by providers to this underemphasized role would lead to improved efficiency in the delivery of medical care services.

Knowledge

Technologies are evaluated along a number of dimensions: safety, efficacy, effectiveness, and economic impact as well as those related to legal, ethical, and societal concerns. The methodologies used in outcomes research differ in terms of validity, reliability, and rigor; and studies vary in terms of populations examined, sample size, inclusion and exclusion criteria, and study site. The randomized controlled trial, often referred to as the "gold standard" of investigative methods, is performed infrequently, except when mandated by regulatory authorities (e.g., the Food and Drug Administration [FDA]). Regardless of the source of the outcomes data, limitations exist regarding the usefulness of the resultant information. Because of the rapid evolution of medical innovations, changes occur in the real and perceived values of benefit and cost parameters and, moreover, there are difficulties generalizing assessments of efficacy (measured under optimal operating conditions) to effectiveness (measured under average operating conditions).

Much of the effectiveness research in use today reports surrogate outcomes —which are imperfectly associated with the outcomes of true interest—as study endpoints. This reliance on proxy measures is most likely a function of (1) the lack of available research instruments, (2) the complexities of the necessary analyses, and (3) an unwillingness to wait for data on the true outcomes of interest, which often take years and whose generation requires great expense.

The disadvantages of the use of surrogate outcomes are well illustrated by the case of thrombolytic therapy used in the setting of an acute myocardial infarction. The prices of the available thrombolytic agents differed approximately tenfold. At the time of FDA approval, there were no direct comparative studies on reinfarction rates, patient morbidity, or the primary outcome of interest reduction in the rate of mortality rate from acute myocardial infarction. Rather, certain agents were demonstrated to clear the clot in the coronary artery (felt to be the etiology of the infarction) more quickly. Dissemination of the findings reporting these surrogate outcomes led half of the users of one agent to switch to the perceived "better," and more costly drug, and thousands more, who had become convinced of the effectiveness of thrombolytic therapy, began using it almost exclusively. Only recently have randomized trials compared the three most frequently used agents head to head (ISIS-3 Collaborative Group, 1992). Results from the study of over 40,000 cases of acute myocardial infarction suggest that the three agents have equal efficacies in terms of saving lives from acute myocardial infarction. Despite the wide differential in price and the lack of evidence suggesting an added clinical benefit from any particular thrombolytic therapy, in the United States there appeared to be continued widespread use of those agents with lower cost-effectiveness ratios.

In the published literature, there appears to be a positive bias toward studies that promote the adoption of new technologies and a negative bias toward those studies that recommend the "disadoption" of accepted interventions. Rarely will physicians do something that they feel is against a patient's interest. But if an additional intervention that is thought to benefit a patient becomes available, no matter how small a benefit or how great the expenditure, there is a likelihood that a provider will try it (the "technological imperative"). On the other hand, it is difficult to get physicians to stop doing something they are comfortable doing on the basis of a study that is not directly applicable to their day-to-day practice (e.g., delivery by cesarean section) (Goyert et al., 1989). Thus, the adoption of medical innovations may have a long-lasting impact and may be difficult to reverse (Eisenberg et al., 1989).

Awareness

The effectiveness data generated from well-designed and well-conducted outcomes studies is necessary, but not sufficient, for understanding physician adoption decisions. Once effectiveness data are available, physicians must become aware of them. A number of communications channels are now used to convey information regarding health care services and medical innovations. The pertinent issue is not how the message is sent, but how physicians assess the quality of its content.

Inconsistencies exist in the dissemination of knowledge (Winkler et al., 1985). Peer-reviewed medical journals occupy a central role in communicating the risks and benefits of medical innovations to physicians. However, more informal communications techniques (e.g., scientific meetings, continuing medical education courses, the views of opinion leaders, discussions with peers) are also important ways for physicians to learn of technological advances (Fineberg et al., 1978; Manning and Denson, 1979; McLaughlin and Penchansky, 1965; Stross and Harlan, 1978). Physicians demonstrate a pattern of preference in how they receive information pertaining to medical innovation (Coleman et al., 1966; Manning and Denson, 1980; Stross and Harlan, 1979). They appear to place greater value on information acquired from personal interactions, especially those with local opinion leaders (Coleman et al., 1966, Williamson et al., 1989). More recently, scientific advances are also being heralded by the lay press, which directs its messages at both patients and providers.

Speed in reporting medical innovation is a double-edged sword, resulting in a trade-off between the slower, more methodical process geared at ensuring scientific fact that is exemplified by peer-reviewed journals, and the far swifter, less definitive process represented by the mass media whose aim is to provide instant, if not totally reliable, information ("news"). If left solely to the peer review process, the dissemination of innovation would be slowed. However, this controlled method does appear better fit to meet the goals of a health care delivery system devoted to determining the risks and benefits associated with an innovation prior to its widespread diffusion. Without evaluation of this type, the (basically irreversible) implementation of innovation would proceed without a guarantee of the safety and efficacy associated with its use.

However, the effects of bypassing the peer-reviewed reporting process on the adoption of technology, health outcomes, and resource use has yet to be determined. Reporting in the lay press should not be viewed as an exclusively negative influence; use of the mass media can lead to increased awareness of effective underutilized technologies and lead to societal health gains (e.g., immunization information programs) (Herlitz et al., 1989).

The lay press and word of mouth among patients were major forces behind the rapid and widespread adoption of laparoscopic cholecystectomy. These media claimed that the procedural innovation produced excellent surgical results, while providing the following advantages to the patient and the payer over conventional open surgery: less pain, shorter hospital length of stay, and decreased recovery time (Southern Surgeons Club, 1991). Over half of the general surgeons in the United States invested time and resources to learn the technique, even though controlled clinical trials comparing the laparoscopic technique to available treatments had not been performed (White, 1992). It seems clear that the popularity of laparoscopic cholecystectomy did not result from the usual scientific discourse. Factors such as intense patient demand, competition among general surgeons for the cholecystectomy "market," and vigorous marketing efforts by surgical device manufacturers played important roles in the remarkably rapid adoption of this innovation (Gelijns and Fendrick, 1993).

Direct public advertising of products available only with a physician's prescription is a recent phenomenon affecting providers' awareness of innovations. The resultant effects on patient demand for services and physician awareness of advertised products have yet to be quantified. The use of information systems such as television broadcasting (e.g., Lifetime network on cable television), continuing medical education courses, on-line databases (e.g., Medline), or clinical decisionmaking software packages may also improve physicians' access to information about emerging technologies.

Despite these multiple avenues of communication, it is not possible for an individual practitioner to keep abreast of every event that has a clinical consequence of potential interest (Stinson and Mueller, 1980). An example of a failure to appropriately communicate information of an effective medical intervention is the case of the treatment of diabetic retinopathy, the most common cause of severe vision loss among those of working age (Kohner and Barry, 1984). The Diabetic Retinopathy Study was a randomized controlled trial which demonstrated that timely treatment of diabetic retinopathy reduced by one-half severe vision loss in the diabetic population (Diabetic Retinopathy Study Research Group, 1976). But the results from this trial were published in the ophthalmology literature, sources that are not widely read by primary-care practitioners, who provide the majority of medical care to individuals with diabetes (Stross and Harlan, 1979). Thus, a majority of providers went unaware of the research findings and individuals with diabetes suffered unnecessary morbidity simply because of a failure to effectively disseminate the findings of this carefully conducted investigation.

In an effort to improve the dissemination of the results of outcomes research, a special program has been established by the Agency for Health Care Policy and Research to study the different methods of effectively communicating information regarding medical innovations to physicians. More studies are needed on the dissemination of information on medical innovations by both the scientific community and the mass media. Greater emphasis on safety, efficacy, effectiveness, and cost and less focus on unproven benefits may turn out to improve the efficiency, but slow the rate, of adoption of medical innovation by physicians.

Judgment

Technology itself is not the culprit for the high cost of medical care; rather, it is society's current inability to make and enforce decisions about what medical services it needs and can afford (Schroeder and Showstack, 1979).

Political, social, and legal influences have a direct impact on the failure to efficiently allocate spending on our health care resources, estimated to approach $1 trillion in 1993. The generation and dissemination of scientific knowledge are only a few of the necessary pieces to the health care delivery puzzle. Once data on the value of an innovation are available, physicians must synthesize the infor mation and pass judgment on whether the technology is worthy of a trial on their patients. A number of external factors influence this decision. The adoptive behaviors of local peers (and competitors) appear to be the most important predictor of whether an individual physician will try an innovation. Also important are the decisions of regulatory agencies and recommendations of national, professional, and scientific organizations (Lomas et al., 1989).

A hurdle often encountered by physicians in deciding whether or not to try an innovation is the generalizability of results from published clinical trials to individual patients. Research studies have carefully specified inclusion and exclusion criteria. These criteria commonly exclude many patients who are potentially eligible for the innovation once it receives regulatory approval. Thus, physicians must extrapolate the results of clinical trials (efficacy) to routine clinical practice (effectiveness). This problem may account for the enduring acceptance of anecdotal experience (outcomes related to personal experience) by physicians, one of the least rigorous methods of evaluation.

Trial

Once a positive judgment is made, a trial of the innovation must be undertaken. The propensity to try an innovation is directly related to the ease of experimentation. The lower the investment of time, effort, risk and resources involved in trying an innovation, the more likely a physician will experiment with it (see the section Innovation Characteristics). For example, the adoption threshold is likely to be lower for new pharmaceuticals than for new surgical procedures because it is far easier and convenient to write a prescription than to obtain the proficiency (and perhaps the credentials) for performing the surgery. Again, local practices exert a significant amount of influence on an individual physician's decisionmaking, illustrating that what is happening in one's own backyard is often more important than national trends.

In the competitive environment for physicians in the 1990s, delayed adoption of a popular innovation that has been touted through the mass media (with or without evidence of its effectiveness) may lead to the loss of patients. This concern over the loss of market share stimulated the adoption of computed tomography and magnetic resonance imaging scanners by hospitals (Baker, 1979; Creditor and Garrett, 1977; Ramsey et al., 1993). Other environmental factors, such as the fear of malpractice litigation, may affect the rates of adoption of medical innovation. On the one hand, these factors may drive adoption if a new intervention becomes perceived as a "standard of care," even in the absence of rigorous scientific evidence (e.g., as happened with fetal monitoring). On the other hand, they may inhibit diffusion, for example, obstetricians (who have higher-than-average malpractice claims and insurance rates) adopt new procedures at a slower pace than other clinical specialists do (Freiman, 1985).

Adoption

After a positive trial comes the decision regarding adoption. One of the more important factors influencing adoption of medical innovations by physicians is reimbursement policy. History reveals a pattern of "no pay, no play" by physicians. If fair payment for the use of an innovation cannot be guaranteed, this disincentive alone may delay or retard the eventual acceptance of an innovation (e.g., as happened with cochlear implant for severe hearing impairment). Conversely, the ease of establishing reimbursement for the use of a medical innovation can speed its adoption and diffusion. The spectacular diffusions of both laparoscopic cholecystectomy and percutaneous transluminal coronary angioplasty were facilitated by the fact that physicians could be paid for these new procedures under existing, profitable reimbursement codes for open cholecystectomy and coronary artery bypass grafting (Gelijns and Fendrick, 1993).

With rare exceptions, drugs are automatically reimbursed by payers following approval by the FDA. This practice has, however, recently come under scrutiny by insurance companies fearful of the potential overuse of expensive agents shown in efficacy testing to be of marginal benefit for limited clinical indications. In certain instances, reimbursement may not be provided for expensive FDA-approved agents used for indications other than those specifically approved by the FDA. For diagnostic tests and devices, a less straightforward reimbursement pattern exists that is more dependent on the payers' particular decisionmaking processes. For example, it was not until six months after the approval of magnetic resonance imaging by the FDA that the Health Care Financing Administration announced reimbursement of this imaging technique for Medicare recipients. Only then did the diffusion of magnetic resonance units accelerate (Ramsey et al., 1993).

Administrative and bureaucratic factors such as peer review processes, certificate-of-need legislation, and credentialing requirements may have either positive or negative effects on the adoption of a new technology by physicians (Mechanic, 1977, Russell, 1976). Restricting the use of an innovation (e.g., antibiotics) by instituting a formal process may prevent unnecessary usage and slow adoption. Such a process typically draws on the experience of a specialist physician with expertise in the indications for using the innovation. At the same time, providing a streamlined administrative system for patients to receive effective interventions (e.g., thrombolytic therapy) may increase the level of adoption and use of an innovation and have a positive effect on patient outcomes (Topol et al., 1987).

Evaluation

A physician's decision to adopt a medical innovation is usually reversible. With each opportunity for use, a decision based on experience and the tincture of time is made by the physician regarding the appropriateness of an innovation. Many factors, such as ease of patient selection and opportunities for continued use, will directly influence the longevity of a medical intervention (Banta et al., 1981). Concern over the early obsolescence of a technology can retard the initial adoption of an innovation that is perceived to be easily replaced, eventually, by a better alternative. This concern over early obsolescence is partly a function of the resources committed to the technology (Kimberly, 1978). The changing nature of clinical practice allows for tremendous turnover in the equipment needed to appropriately provide care and medical manufacturers seem happy to oblige the evolving practice of modern medicine with a never-ending supply of tools.

SUMMARY

The understanding of physician adoption of medical innovation is incomplete. The use of conceptual models can help illustrate the complex decisionmaking tasks physicians face when they are confronted with the opportunity to adopt an innovative technology. Scientific knowledge on effectiveness and resource use is essential, but it is not a panacea for the resource allocation problem. Numerous barriers prevent the incorporation of quality-enhancing, cost-effective technologies into everyday clinical practice: method and content of communications, regulatory decisionmaking, reimbursement levels, malpractice claims, and external micromanagement of clinical decisions, to name a few. At the same time, the competitiveness of the U.S. medical care system provides incentives to acquire innovations before proof of their relative usefulness in terms of patient outcomes and cost-effectiveness is generated from rigorous evaluations. Thus, an inconsistent pattern of adoption of innovation by physicians has developed.

Research in understanding physician adoption of an innovation should continue to play a significant role as the nation studies ways to reform the health care delivery system. In addition to the development of clinical guidelines based on outcomes research and medical appropriateness (e.g., the Patient Outcomes Research Team initiative funded by the Agency for Health Care Policy and Research), research in other areas that affect physician behavior warrant increased attention as well. Objectives of this additional effort should be to (1) focus on research that is generalizable to everyday clinical practice, (2) ensure that research findings are disseminated quickly and to all applicable parties in understandable language, and (3) provide incentives-financial and other-to reward the effective and penalize the ineffective behaviors of all stakeholders.

REFERENCES

Altman, S. H., and Blendon, R. J., eds. 1979. *Medical Technology: The Culprit Behind Health Care Costs?* Washington, D.C.: U.S. Government Printing Office.

Baker, S. R. 1979. The diffusion of high technology medical innovation: The computed tomography scanner example. *Social Science & Medicine* 13D: 155-162.

Banta, H. D., Behney, C. J., and Willems, J. S. 1981. *Toward Rational Technology in Medicine: Considerations for Health Policy.* New York, N.Y.: Springer.

Chalmers, T. C. 1974. The impact of controlled trials on the practice of medicine. *Mount Sinai Journal of Medicine* 41:753-759.

Coleman, J. S., Katz, E., and Menzel, H. 1966. *Medical Innovation: A Diffusion Study.* New York, N.Y.: Bobbs-Merrill Company.

Creditor, M. C., and Garrett, J. B. 1977. The information base for diffusion of technology: Computed tomography scanning. *New England Journal of Medicine* 297:4952.

Diabetic Retinopathy Study Research Group. 1976. Preliminary report of the effects of photocoagulation therapy. *American Journal of Ophthalmology* 81:383-396.

Eisenberg, J. M. 1986. *Doctor's Decisions and the Cost of Medical Care.* Ann Arbor, Mich.: Health Administration Press.

Eisenberg, J. M., and Williams, S. V. 1981. Cost containment and changing physician's practice behavior: Can the fox learn to guard the chicken coop? *Journal of the American Medical Association* 246:2195-2201.

Eisenberg, J. M., Schwartz, J. S., McCaslin, F. C., et al. 1989. Substituting diagnostic services: New tests only partly replace older ones. *Journal of the American Medical Association* 262:1196-1200.

Fineberg, H. V., and Hiatt, H. H. 1979. Evaluation of medical practices: The case for technology assessment. *New England Journal of Medicine* 301:1086-1091.

Fineberg, H. V., Gabel, R. A., and Sosman, M. B. 1978. Acquisition and application of new medical knowledge by anesthesiologists. *Anesthesiology* 48:430-436.

Freiman, M. P. 1985. The rate of adoption of new procedures among physicians: The impact of specialty and practice characteristics. *Medical Care* 23:939-945.

Fuchs, V. 1968. The growing demand for medical care. *New England Journal of Medicine* 279:190-195.

Gelijns, A. C., and Fendrick, A. M. 1993. The dynamics of innovation in minimally invasive therapy. *Health Policy* 23:153-166.

Goyert, G. L., Bottoms, S. F., Treadwell, M. C., et al. 1989 The physician factor in Cesarean birth rates. *New England Journal of Medicine* 320:706-709.

Greer, A. L. 1977. Advances in the study of diffusion of innovation in health care organizations. *Milbank Memorial Fund Quarterly* 55:505-532.

Greer, A. L. 1988. The state of the art versus the state of the science: The diffusion of new medical technologies into practice. *International Journal of Technology Assessment in Health Care* 4:5-26.

Hemenway, D., Killen, A., Cashman, S. B., et al. 1990. Physicians' responses to financial incentives: Evidence from a for-profit ambulatory care center. *New England Journal of Medicine* 322:1059-1063.

Herlitz, J., Hartford, M., Blohm, M., et al. 1989. Effect of a media campaign on delay times and ambulance use in suspected acute myocardial infarction. *American Journal of Cardiology* 64:90-93.

Hichson, G. B., Altemeier, W. A., and Perrin, J. M. 1987. Physician reimbursement by salary or fee for service: Effect on physician practice behavior in a randomized prospective study. *Pediatrics* 80:344-350.

Hillman, A. L., and Schwartz, J. S. 1986. The diffusion of MRI: Patterns of siting and ownership in an era of changing incentives . *American Journal of Roentgenology* 146:963-969.

Hillman, A. L., Pauly, M. V., and Kerstein, J. J. 1989. How do financial incentives affect physician's clinical decisions and the financial performance of health maintenance organizations? *New England Journal of Medicine* 321:86-92.

ISIS-3 Collaborative Group. 1992. ISIS-3: A randomized comparison of streptokinase vs tissue plasminogen activator vs anistreplase and of aspirin plus heparin vs aspirin alone among 41,299 cases of suspected acute myocardial infarction. *Lancet* 339:753770.

James, A. E. 1991. The diffusion of medical technology: Free enterprise and regulatory models in the U.S.A. *Journal of Medical Ethics 17:150-155.*

Kaluzny, A. D. 1974. Innovation in health services: Theoretical framework and review of research. *Health Services Research* 9:101-120.

Kanouse, E., and Jacoby, I. 1988. When does information change practitioners' behavior. *International Journal of Technology Assessment in Health Care* 4:27-34.

Kimberly, J. R. 1978. Hospital adoption of innovation: The role of integration into external informational environments. *Journal of Health and Social Behavior* 19:361373.

Kohner, E. M., and Barry, P. J. 1984. Prevention of blindness in diabetic retinopathy. *Diabetologia* 26:173-179.

Kressley, K. M. 1981. Diffusion of high technology medical care and cost control-A public policy dilemma. *Technology in Society* 3:305-322.

Lee, R. H., and Waldman, D. M. 1986. The diffusion of innovation in hospitals. *Journal of Health Economics* 4:103-120.

Lomas, J., Anderson, G. M., Domnick-Pierre, K., et al. 1989. Do practice guidelines guide practice? The effect of a consensus statement on the practice of physicians. *New England Journal of Medicine* 321:1306-1311.

Manning, P. R., and Denson, T. A. 1979. How cardiologists learn about echocardiography: A reminder for medical educators and legislators. *Annals of Internal Medicine* 91:469-471.

Manning, P. R., and Denson, T. A. 1980. How internists learned about cimetidine. *Annals of Internal Medicine* 92:690-692.

McCarthy, T. R. 1985. The competitive nature of the primary care physician services market. *Journal of Health Economics* 4:93-117.

McGivney, W. T. 1988. Regulatory, coverage, and reimbursement changes implications for diffusion of technology in radiology. *Investigative Radiology* 23:795-798.

McLaughlin, C. P., and Penchansky, R. 1965. Diffusion of innovation in medicine: A problem of continuing medical education. *Journal of Medical Education* 40:437447.

Mechanic, D. 1977. The growth of medical technology and bureaucracy: Implications for medical care. *Milbank Memorial Fund Quarterly 55:61-78.*

Mulley, A. G., Jr. 1992. The patient's stake in the changing health care economy. In: Institute of Medicine. *Medical Innovation at the Crossroads.* Vol. 3, *Technology and Health Care in an Era of Limits.* A. C. Gelijns, ed. Washington, D.C.: National Academy Press, pp. 153-163.

Ramsey, S. D., Hillman, A. L., Renshaw, L. R., et al. 1993. How important is the scientific literature in guiding clinical decisions?: The case of magnetic resonance imaging. *International Journal of Technology Assessment in Health Care* 9:253262.

Rogers, E. M., and Shoemaker, F. F. 1971. *Communications of Innovations: A CrossCultural Approach,* 2nd ed. New York, N.Y.: Free Press.

Russell, L. B. 1976. The diffusion of new hospital technologies in the United States. *International Journal of Health Services* 6:557-580.

Schroeder, S. A., and Showstack, J. A. 1979. The dynamics of medical technology use: Analysis and policy options. In: S. H. Altman and R. Blendon, eds. *Medical Technology: The Culprit Behind Health Care Costs?* Washington, D.C.: U.S. Government Printing Office, pp. 178-212.

Southern Surgeons Club. 1991. A prospective analysis of 1,518 laparoscopic cholecystectomies. *New England Journal of Medicine* 324:1073-1078.

Stinson, E. R., and Mueller, D. A. 1980. Survey of health professionals' information habits and needs. *Journal of the American Medical Association* 243:140-143.

Stross, J. K., and Harlan, W. R. 1978. The impact of mandatory continuing medical education. *Journal of the American Medical Association* 239:2663-2666.

Stross, J. K., and Harlan, W. R. 1979. The dissemination of new medical information. *Journal of the American Medical Association* 241:2622-2624.

Topol, E. J., Bates, E. R., Walton, J. A., Jr., et al. 1987. Community hospital administration of intravenous tissue plasminogen activator in acute myocardial infarction. *Journal of the American College of Cardiology* 10: 1173-1177.

Warner, K. E. 1974. The need for some innovative concepts of innovation: An examination of research on the diffusion of innovations. *Policy Science 5:433-451.*

Warner, K. E. 1975. A "desperation-reaction" model of medical diffusion. *Health Services Research* 10:369-383.

White, J. V. 1992. Laparoscopic cholecystectomy: The evolution of general surgery. *Annals of Internal Medicine* 115:651-653.

Wilensky, G. R., and Rossiter, L. F. 1983. The relative importance of physician induced demand for medical care. *Milbank Memorial Fund Quarterly* 61:252-277.

Williams, A. 1992. Priority setting in a needs-based system. In: Institute of Medicine. *Medical Innovation at the Crossroads.* Vol. 3, *Technology and Health Care in an Era of Limits.* A. C. Gelijns, ed. Washington, D.C.: National Academy Press, pp. 79-95.

Williamson, J. W., German, P. S., Weiss, R., et al. 1989. Health science information management and continuing education of physicians: A survey of U.S. primary care practitioners and their opinion leaders. *Annals of Internal Medicine* 110:151-160.

Winkler, J. D., Lohr, K. N., and Brook, R. H. 1985. Persuasive communication and medical technology assessment. *Archives of Internal Medicine* 145:314-317.

PART III

Third Party Payer Coverage Decisions

6

Decisionmaking in the Health Care Financing Administration

KATHLEEN A. BUTO

Although the Health Care Financing Administration (HCFA) has been providing coverage and payment for medical services and technologies through the Medicare program for more than 25 years, the basis for coverage remains a mystery to many beneficiaries and health care providers. Because so much discretion is left to Medicare's claims-paying agents, coverage varies widely, depending on local medical practices in a given area of the country. This chapter describes how the current, decentralized system of coverage has developed, discusses how it has created problems of equity, and details some of the changes that will improve the basis for coverage decisionmaking and promote more uniformity in covering Medicare benefits.

BACKGROUND ON MEDICARE COVERAGE

When Medicare was enacted in 1965, the U.S. Congress intended that it protect elderly individuals from the catastrophic costs of expensive hospitalizations and post-acute care. The benefits package reflects that purpose: Medicare provides coverage for a broad range of benefits related to hospital care, physicians' services, home health care, skilled nursing care, medical equipment, and laboratory services. Medicare limits coverage for certain items such as immunosuppressive drugs (for a fixed period of time following a covered transplant). The law specifically *excludes* coverage for certain items, including self-administered drugs, many preventive services, and eyeglasses as well as hearing aids. In general, one can conclude from the following statement that the law is intentionally vague and provides the Medicare program broad authority to cover medical items and services:

> Notwithstanding any other provisions of this title, no payment may be made ... for any items or services which are not reasonable and necessary for the diagnosis or treatment of illness or injury or to improve the functioning of a malformed body member (Section 1862(a) (1)(A) of the Social Security Act).

Medicare has operated for more than 25 years without any regulations that spell out its interpretation of how to implement this statutory language and with little explanation to the public of the process used by HCFA to cover items and services under the program. The program has provided no complete list of the items and services that it covers. For example, most inpatient medical or surgical treatments and procedures are not explicitly listed as covered services. Instead, most decisions on coverage are made by contractors, such as Blue Cross and Blue Shield plans, which pay more than 600 million claims per year on behalf of Medicare. For years, the Medicare program was structured to permit these contractors to be responsive to local medical practice patterns in making their decisions on coverage. Only about 10 to 20 national coverage decisions regarding new treatments and procedures are made each year, ranging from significant medical breakthroughs, such as liver transplants, to more modest changes in diagnostic technology, such as new uses of ultrasonography. Generally, an item is referred for a national coverage decision if it has the potential for rapid diffusion, is significantly expensive, or there is a wide variation in coverage among contractors.

Although the Medicare program has changed dramatically over the years, becoming more centralized in its decisionmaking, the overall approach to covering services has remained the same. Additions to coverage have been incremental, with a focus on the categories of services specified in the law and without regard to broader issues, for example, equity across sites of service. Numerous technologies and services have been added as covered items, whereas few changes or deletions have been made among those items and procedures that are already covered. Although previously decentralized decisionmaking meant, at times, greater speed in coverage and the flexibility to recognize emerging technologies, demands are increasing for more consistency and equity in Medicare coverage policy.

PROBLEMS WITH THIS APPROACH

Medicare coverage has been tied to the specific categories of benefits ("pigeonholes") set up in the law. Because coverage questions are considered narrowly—in the context of these coverage categories—Medicare has extended coverage to items never considered by Congress to be part of the Medicare benefits package. One example is that, despite the narrow coverage for drugs, some years ago Medicare began covering drugs used in infusion pumps because they were categorized as part of the covered durable medical equipment and were essential for making the equipment useful (Section 60-14; Coverages Issues Manual).

Medicare also covers parenteral and enteral food nutrients, not otherwise allowed in the program, as a part of the prosthetic device benefit. This is because the technology is considered a replacement for essential parts of the gastrointestinal system, and the food nutrients are covered because they are critical to the successful use of the technology (Section 65-10; Coverage Issues Manual). This peculiar way of approaching coverage results in apparent inequities; for example, food nutrients are not billable to Medicare—other than for the use indicated above—even if the requirement for them stems from a medical need.

The flexibility and discretion permitted Medicare contractors in paying claims has sometimes resulted in widely varying coverage across the country. This has been especially noticeable as suppliers, manufacturers, and clinical laboratories have expanded from local to national markets. Oncologists have pointed to problems with inconsistent coverage of chemotherapy drugs used for indications other than their approved labeling (unlabeled uses). Patients with cancer who receive treatment at a regional cancer center may learn, when they return home to a different area with a different carrier, that their coverage does not continue. The General Accounting Office has pointed out that inconsistency in covering these drugs for "unindicated" uses has driven some oncologists to admit some cancer patients to hospitals, incurring higher-than-necessary total costs for treatment because different payment rules apply (General Accounting Office, 1992) (Section 13553 of the Omnibus Reconciliation Act of 1993 [P.L. 103-66] will require uniform coverage of unlabeled anticancer drugs, effective January 1, 1994).

The current process for setting national Medicare coverage policy is considered to be a major obstacle in ensuring access for beneficiaries to important technologies and procedures in a timely way. There are no final regulations setting out the rules and criteria for national decisionmaking, although proposed regulations were issued in 1989 (*Federal Register,* 1989). Concerns exist about the length of time that it takes for national Medicare coverage decisions to be made, possible duplication with Food and Drug Administration review of devices or drugs, and general discomfort that decisions are made "in the dark" (National Advisory Council on Health Care Technology Assessment, 1988). The proposal to include cost-effectiveness as a criterion for Medicare coverage raised concerns on the part of providers, physicians, manufacturers, and beneficiaries that Medicare would use this yardstick as a way to unduly restrict coverage of new items and services (McCarthy et al., 1989). Although all groups would agree that improvements in the national coverage approach are needed, reaching a consensus on how that should be done is still a long way from being achieved.

The Medicare program traditionally has used its contractor structure to monitor the utilization of procedures and technologies. A combination of resource constraints on contractors and a lack of clear coverage policies has led many physicians and others to complain about the paperwork burden and "hassle factor" that they believe characterize the Medicare program. One of the worst-case scenarios is when two reviewing authorities send different signals. For example, a peer review organization approved an admission for laparoscopic cholecystectomy as medically necessary, whereas the carrier denied the physician's claim for that admission on the basis that the procedure was still investigational. Although it may be impossible to completely eliminate these problems in clinical areas when there are legitimate differences of medical judgment about the value of certain procedures, the lack of clarity about what Medicare covers contributes to the adversarial and frustrating relationships between contractors and providers.

Unlike private insurers, the Medicare program must often issue national coverage policies through formal rulemaking to give the public an opportunity to comment before coverage policies are finalized. This is especially true where coverage is limited or withdrawn for a particular technology. Although the process ensures broad input and participation in decisions affecting beneficiaries and providers, the regulatory apparatus creates some problems when making coverage decisions. For policies requiring input on the terms of coverage (e.g., heart transplants), many coverage decisions can be implemented quickly, but formal rulemaking has meant delaying coverage of a significant new procedure up to one year, the typical time required to complete the rulemaking process. Technology assessments appear to take too long to complete—in many cases more than one year. This is at least partly because decisionmakers are aware that coverage decisions are virtually irreversible, and formal rulemaking makes it very difficult to modify or withdraw coverage for a technology or procedure. For example, it took three years to withdraw coverage for extracranial-intracranial bypass surgery for the treatment or prevention of stroke, even though only 10 comments on the proposed change were received and there was broad agreement among clinicians that coverage should be withdrawn. In considering any changes in the current coverage process, the Medicare program must find ways to balance the need for public input in decisionmaking with better flexibility to modify or change coverage decisions over time.

PAYMENT CHANGES

Although dissatisfaction with the current coverage process has highlighted the need to modify the current Medicare coverage system, the driving force for greater uniformity and clarity in Medicare coverage of technologies and procedures is from changes in Medicare payment methodologies. Increasingly, the payment approaches historically based on an individual provider's costs or charges are being replaced by national fee schedules or payment methods. The first such major change was to a prospective payment system (PPS) for inpatient hospital services. PPS sets a payment rate on the basis of a patient's diagnosis. Because the payment groupings are set nationally, hospitals, physicians, and manufacturers have demanded centralized decisionmaking on assigning technologies and procedures to specific groupings. They have increased pressure further for quicker response times and clear-cut criteria for coverage.

PPS has also influenced how particular technologies disseminate into clinical practice. For example, prior to 1991, expenses related to capital plant and equipment were still reimbursed on a retrospective cost basis (*Federal Register,* 1991). Thus, even under a method that provided incentives to reduce costs in other areas, hospitals were given incentives to continue to acquire many expensive items of equipment, indeed, to substitute capital for labor when possible. For some technologies, such as magnetic resonance imaging (MRI) scanners, the lack of an *add-on payment* in the inpatient PPS payment helped to encourage the proliferation of freestanding outpatient MRI facilities. In those settings, MRI is eligible for the more generous *charge-based payments.*

The Medicare physician fee schedule, or resource-based relative value scale, is similarly forcing greater uniformity in coverage rules for physicians' services. Now that Medicare pays for physicians' services on a similar basis around the country, there is increased demand for more uniformity and greater clarity and predictability in the services that are covered. In constructing the fee schedule, HCFA had to arrive at a common agreement about the amount and nature of physician work associated with each of the 7,000 procedure codes used by physicians. In many cases, packages of services or "bundles" were established when several services are commonly provided in relation to a procedure. In that way, Medicare explicitly recognized and accepted practice patterns and made coverage and payment for those services more uniform.

Numerous individual examples indicate how payment policy affects the use and diffusion of technologies under the Medicare program. When Medicare began paying for erythropoietin for patients with end-stage renal disease, the payment was based on the optimal dose of 3,600 units of the drug. Facilities had an incentive to keep the dose as low as possible and to retain the difference in payment between the optimal dose and the actual dose administered. When the payment was changed to $11 per 1,000 units, the average dose rose from 2,724 units in December 1990 to an average in September 1992 of 3,899 units (data from the Medicare Decision Support System, Bureau of Data Management and Strategy [BDMS], HCFA, 1991 bills paid). For echocardiography, a combination of non-specific coverage guidelines, the available payment under the Medicare program, and inexpensive equipment has contributed to a rapid growth in spending, from $40.8 million in 1988 to $405.3 million in 1991 (data from the Medicare Decision Support System, BDMS, HCFA, 1991 National Claims History Data System). No evidence suggests that better clinical outcomes are associated with the explosion in use of this particular technology.

TOWARD A MORE REASONABLE COVERAGE APPROACH

HCFA is taking a number of steps to make the Medicare coverage of items and services more understandable, more responsive to changes in technology, and more uniform. One important change is to involve the medical directors of claims-paying contractors such as Blue Cross and Blue Shield and Travelers', as well as the HCFA physicians who provide advice on national coverage decisions, in the identification of coverage questions and in the technology assessments used as a basis for making decisions. To that end HCFA has merged these two previously created advisory groups into a HCFA Technology Advisory Committee (TAC). For example, in the spring of 1993 the TAC conducted an assessment of a new ventricular assist device approved by the Food and Drug Administration for use in patients suffering from postcardiotomy ventricular dysfunction. Rather than requesting an assessment by the Public Health Service, HCFA developed a rational policy to cover the device for its labeled indication based on the TAC assessment. It was issued in October 1993. This process is akin to the one used by Blue Cross and Blue Shield's Technology Evaluation and Coverage Program, which makes recommendations on coverage for selected technologies for local Blue Cross and Blue Shield plans (see chapter 7).

HCFA is also considering contracting out some aspects of technology assessments, including literature reviews or analyses of the quality of medical evidence supporting the use of a medical practice or technology. These efforts should increase both the timeliness and the quantity of assessments produced for the Medicare program.

HCFA has organized special CMD review groups to consider certain issues when there has been a widespread lack of uniformity. These include carrier policies on uses of approved drugs for purposes other than those listed on the label and items of medical equipment (e.g., wheelchairs). In addition, each carrier is setting up a local physician advisory group to help identify problems in coverage and payment and to promote more openness and uniformity in carrier decisionmaking. Beginning in October 1993, HCFA reduced the number of carriers from 34 to 4 regional carriers to process claims for durable medical equipment, prosthetics and orthotics, and supplies. This initiative is designed to reduce fraud and abuse, as well as promote uniform coverage of these items.

In the proposed regulation of January 1989, HCFA discussed some major changes in its approach to covering items and services under Medicare. It proposed that cost-effectiveness be included as a coverage criterion along with the longstanding criteria of safety, effectiveness, and appropriateness. Cost-effectiveness was to be used as an additional consideration in reviewing expensive new technologies that add little or nothing to the efficacy or effectiveness of existing alternatives. If Medicare proceeds to include cost-effectiveness as a coverage criterion in final regulations, the rules will need to clarify that the use of cost-effectiveness as a consideration is intended to encourage development of better outcomes data in support of coverage and to explain how it will not be used to limit access under Medicare to important but expensive new technologies.

In the same regulation, HCFA also suggested the greater use of coverage limited by time or provider, similar to the approach now taken by Medicare in covering heart and liver transplants. As already noted, the regulatory apparatus makes it difficult to change the terms of Medicare coverage once initial decisions have been made, even in the face of better data on outcomes or the usefulness of a technology. Industry groups have urged that Medicare consider interim coverage for important new technologies, with a revision of coverage once the technology has diffused and more is known about its usefulness. For example, HCFA should not withhold coverage of a health care technology when there is evidence of effectiveness in a limited set of circumstances simply because its effectiveness in a broader set of circumstances is still unknown. HCFA is considering greater use of time- or provider-limited coverage similar to the approach now taken by Medicare in covering heart and liver transplants. That is, Medicare would cover a technology but set certain restrictions, such as limiting the site of service or requiring specific data to be submitted to HCFA by the provider of the service. Because data submission would be a condition of coverage, this approach would also ensure that data, uniformly collected and reported, could be evaluated at an early stage.

The Medicare program is working with the Agency for Health Care Policy and Research (AHCPR) to look at the applicability of AHCPR-supported practice guidelines in Medicare coverage. Few coverage questions have arisen in the practice guidelines issued so far on pain management, pressure sores, and urinary incontinence (Acute Pain Management Guideline Panel, 1992; Panel for the Prediction and Prevention of Pressure Ulcers in Adults, 1992; Urinary Incontinence Guideline Panel, 1992). Most of the physicians' services and institutional care described in the guidelines are already covered under the Medicare program. A few items, such as self-administered pain management drugs, are excluded under the statute. HCFA expects the next two practice guidelines—on cataract surgery and benign prostatic hypertrophy—to raise many more coverage questions. Over time, HCFA expects practice guidelines, whether developed through AHCPR or other organizations using similarly rigorous methods, to play an increasingly important role in defining coverage parameters and medical review criteria and in raising questions about the appropriateness of existing coverage.

HCFA is also moving ahead on its own to use Medicare patient data and medical society practice guidelines to assess patterns of care for hospitals. Early in 1993, four peer review organizations (PROs) began a pilot test that focuses on several cardiovascular procedures, such as treatment of myocardial infarction, bypass surgery, and angioplasty (Jencks and Wilensky, 1992). These PROs are developing approaches for profiling hospitals for mortality, complications, readmissions, and other outcomes. They are working with hospitals, physicians, and others to understand and interpret data on practice guidelines and to develop plans for addressing problem areas for hospitals whose performance are below benchmarks. This change in the approach used by PROs moves away from a quality-of-care review that relies on penalties to bring about changes. Instead, PROs expect to use information and feedback on practice patterns to help stimulate more lasting changes in the ways that institutions and practitioners assess their own quality of care. Although the principal purpose of this change is to improve patterns of care for hospitals and physicians, longer-term data on patterns of care and outcomes may lead to improvements in Medicare coverage criteria. For example, Medicare could limit coverage of certain diagnostic tests routinely administered if it appears that they add little or no value to improved diagnosis or treatment of coronary artery disease.

Coverage policy, designed to ensure access for beneficiaries to appropriate medical technologies and services, falls short to the extent that current payment rules dictate the site of service for a given technology or create incentives to use an expensive technology when a more cost-effective alternative exists. As HCFA begins to develop alternatives for a PPS for outpatient hospital services, it will be looking at ways to recognize appropriate differences in costs by site, without having payment levels dictate the site of service. HCFA is considering questions about how to classify services for payment, the extent to which diagnostic tests and other items should be included in a payment bundle, and the impact of such a system on other sites of service. HCFA also plans to consider more systematically, in any future changes in the reimbursement system, the effect of Medicare payment incentives on the use of technologies.

CONCLUSION

The landscape has changed dramatically for the Medicare program since its inception in 1965. The program originated as a highly decentralized operation, with coverage and payment for services determined largely by local patterns and conventions. Now, the Medicare program has moved to national payment approaches, like PPS and the resource-based relative value scale. The rules for covering items and services, however, remain an artifact of the earlier era. Coverage still varies widely from area to area, and the coverage decisionmaking process appears slow and mysterious. In addition, different payment amounts for technologies, depending on the site of service, can inappropriately influence where services are available and how often they are provided.

The Medicare program has begun to make changes that will result in more uniform coverage, the ability to modify coverage on the basis of experience with an item or procedure, and more timely and outcome-based analyses of technologies. Beneficiaries, providers, and physicians deserve to know what is or is not covered under Medicare and to have the same rules apply across the country. Medicare coverage should also be capable of changing as data become available on outcomes related to the use of technologies and services. The rules for coverage should be explicit, and the process should be an open one. Medicare must face these issues squarely. Not only are they significant for Medicare, they are critically important in considering health care reform for the broader population.

REFERENCES

Acute Pain Management Guideline Panel. 1992. *Acute Pain Management: Operative or Medical Procedures and Trauma. Clinical Practice Guideline.* AHCPR Publication No. 92-0032. Rockville, Md.: Agency for Health Care Policy and Research, Public Health Service, Department of Health and Human Services.

Coverage Issues Manual. Section 60-14. HCFA Publication 6, internal document.

Coverage Issues Manual. Section 65-10. HCFA Publication 6, internal document.

Federal Register. 1989. Criteria and procedures for making medical services coverage decisions that relate to health care technology. 54 FR 4302 (January 30, 1989).

Federal Register. 1991. Prospective payment system for inpatient hospital capital-related costs. 56 FR 43358 (August 30, 1991).

General Accounting Office. 1992. *Medicare Reimbursement Policies Can Influence the Setting and Cost of Chemotherapy.* Publication No. GAO/PEMD-92-28. Washington, D.C.: U.S. Government Printing Office.

Jencks, S. F., and Wilensky, G. R. 1992. The health care quality improvement initiative. *Journal of the American Medical Association* 268(7):900-903.

McCarthy, C. M., Samuel, F. E., Sammons, J. H., and Rother, J. March 30, 1989 . Letter to Louis W. Sullivan, Secretary of the U.S. Department of Health and Human Services, Washington, D.C.

National Advisory Council on Health Care Technology Assessment. 1988. *The Medicare Coverage Process.* Internal document.

Panel for the Prediction and Prevention of Pressure Ulcers in Adults. 1992. *Pressure Ulcers in Adults: Prediction and Prevention. Clinical Practice Guideline, Number* 3. AHCPR Publication No. 92-0047. Rockville, Md.: Agency for Health Care Policy and Research, Public Health Service, U.S. Department of Health and Human Services.

Social Security Act, as amended. 1965. Section 1862(a)(1)(A).

Urinary Incontinence Guideline Panel. 1992. *Urinary Incontinence in Adults: Clinical Practice Guideline.* AHCPR Publication No. 92-0038. Rockville, Md.: Agency for Health Care Policy and Research, Public Health Service, U.S. Department of Health and Human Services.

7

Blue Cross and Blue Shield Association Initiatives in Technology Assessment

SUSAN GLEESON

The Blue Cross and Blue Shield Association (BCBSA) is the national coordinating agency for the 73 independent, locally governed Blue Cross and Blue Shield plans. BCBSA serves as the cohesive force that brings these autonomous, nonprofit plans together into a national system. As a system, BCBS is the nation's largest and oldest provider of health care coverage, currently covering 68 million members, or more than one in four Americans. The plans operate 92 health maintenance organizations (HMOs) and 56 preferred provider organizations (PPOs) nationwide. This chapter describes the BCBSA technology assessment program and a recent initiative to support clinical trials for breast cancer treatments.

Each independent Blue Cross and Blue Shield plan provides insurance coverage to its members in accordance with locally drafted contract language and coverage policies. In many cases, the contract terms and services covered are selected by the employer purchasing the coverage on behalf of his or her employees. BCBSA provides many support services to Blue Cross and Blue Shield plans, and one of these services consists of technology assessment and the provision of coverage information. The technology assessment and coverage guidance given to the plans, however, is advisory and informational. Local plans are responsible for formulating their own administrative and coverage policies. Nevertheless, certain large national accounts request that coverage for their employees be administered in accordance with BCBSA coverage recommendations.

TECHNOLOGY ASSESSMENT

Health insurers have an increasingly important mission to be prudent purchasers of health care services for their members. With mounting national con cern over the uninsured and underinsured, we must all find ways to moderate increases in health care costs if the promise of universal access to health insurance is to become a reality. The challenge of health care reform is to provide universal access to effective health care at a cost that is acceptable to government, employers, and the American people in general.

The benefits contracts provided by Blue Cross and Blue Shield plans contain three types of provisions to ensure that premiums are used to purchase services of known efficacy and appropriateness. These provisions typically appear in traditional, HMO, and PPO benefits contracts. The first type of provision requires that services be medically necessary, that is, appropriate and reasonable for the patient's disease or injury. The second type of provision excludes coverage for services that are determined by the local plan to be investigational, that is, of unknown efficacy. The third type of provision requires that services, procedures, medications, and devices have the approval of the appropriate regulatory body before they are covered, for example, Food and Drug Administration (FDA) approval of drugs and certain categories of devices. However, the requirement for consistency with regulatory agencies is broad and extends to the licensure of professionals and the accreditation of institutions.

This chapter focuses on the Technology, Evaluation, and Coverage (TEC) Program of BCBSA that provides technology assessment information and guidance to plans. The TEC Program evaluates the health effects of a given technology, whether it is a service, drug, device, or procedure.

The TEC Program uses five criteria (see below) to determine whether the technology in question improves health outcomes such as length of life, ability to function, or quality of life. The staff of BCBSA evaluate new technologies against the criteria and report to BCBSA's Medical Advisory Panel. The Medical Advisory Panel determines whether or not a specific technology meets the criteria. BCBSA has also instituted semiannual forums at which clinical research experts present directly to the panel the most recent evidence regarding important new technologies. Recent forums have been on high-dose chemotherapy and autologous bone marrow transplantation for breast cancer and multiple myeloma, and on lung transplantation. Another forum addressed high dose chemotherapy and autologous bone marrow transplant for ovarian cancer and ambulatory home uterine monitoring.

Below is presented a brief summary of the five technology assessment criteria used by the BCBSA to determine whether a technology improves health outcomes and can be recommended as eligible for coverage.

1. The technology under consideration must have final approval from the appropriate government regulatory bodies when such approval is applicable. Surgical procedures such as transplants generally involve no regulatory approval (Blue Cross and Blue Shield Association, 1991). A drug, biological product, or certain devices, however, must have final approval from the FDA. Any approval

for use of a drug that is granted as an interim step in the FDA regulatory process is not sufficient. Final approval is not required for all indications for these technologies, however. The use of approved drugs for indications other than those listed on the label will be considered eligible for coverage when they are demonstrated to be effective in improving health outcomes.

2. The scientific evidence must permit conclusions to be made concerning the effect of technologies on health outcomes. The evidence should consist of well-designed and well-conducted investigations published in peer-reviewed journals. The quality of the studies and the consistency of the results are considered in evaluating the evidence.
3. The technology under consideration must improve net health outcomes; that is, the technology's beneficial effects on health outcomes should outweigh any harmful effects on health outcomes.
4. The particular technology must be as beneficial as any established alternatives. The technology should improve the net health outcomes as much or more than established alternatives.
5. The improvement must be attainable outside the investigational setting; the technology should be expected to satisfy the other above-mentioned criteria, when used under the usual conditions of medical practice.

Recent Changes to Program

In September 1993, BCBSA announced three major changes to the TEC Program. First, the Association announced that it would collaborate with Kaiser Permanente on technology assessment activities. Both organizations will contribute resources and expertise. This collaboration will allow the TEC Program to expand its activities. Second, BCBSA appointed a new nineteen-member Medical Advisory Panel, of which the majority of members have no affiliation with Kaiser Permanente or the BCBS plans. Members are noted experts in technology assessment, research, and clinical areas and Dr. David Eddy is the scientific advisor to the Panel. Third, BCBSA made a policy decision that technology assessments were scientific information and should not be proprietary to the BCBS system. The information contained in the assessment would be useful to consumers, physicians, health plans, and other decisionmakers. Starting in 1994, the TEC assessments are available on an annual subscription basis.

THE DEMONSTRATION PROJECT ON BREAST CANCER TREATMENT

Major controversy has arisen in recent years over coverage for promising new treatments for life-threatening conditions that are considered to be investigational. A treatment that has been the source of much controversy is high dose chemotherapy with autologous bone marrow transplantation (HDC-ABMT) for breast cancer.

Clinical studies of HDC-ABMT conducted thus far have not established that the treatment is as safe and effective as conventional chemotherapy in the treatment of advanced breast cancer. Many Blue Cross and Blue Shield plans exclude coverage for the treatment because they consider it to be investigational. HDC-ABMT for breast cancer has been evaluated twice by the Medical Advisory Panel since 1988, most recently in 1991 by David Eddy, M.D., Ph.D. Application of BCBSA's technology evaluation criteria clearly leads to the recommendation that the treatment is investigational. There has been an absence of well-controlled trials, existing clinical series are poorly matched, and small differences in survival demonstrated between HDC-ABMT and conventional chemotherapy for breast cancer to date have not been statistically significant. Furthermore, treatment-related mortality and morbidity from HDC-ABMT exceed those from conventional chemotherapy.

Despite the lack of conclusive evidence that HDC-ABMT is as good as, worse than, or better than conventional chemotherapy, coverage denials have generated unprecedented media concern and litigation. Some researchers advocate the treatment and women have sued to be allowed to receive the treatment, convinced that it is their last hope. Blue Cross and Blue Shield subscribers want access to this service, regardless of the lack of scientific evidence supporting efficacy. Unfortunately, as an editorial in the *Journal of the National Cancer Institute* stated, some members of the oncology community "have raised the public's expectation far above what is supported by the published data. We have no evidence as of yet that any patient will be cured by this therapy who would not have been cured by more conventional treatment" (Henderson, 1991).

The Demonstration Project on Breast Cancer Treatment is an innovative effort of the BCBSA, participating plans, and the Blue Cross and Blue Shield Federal Employee Program to help resolve the clinical controversy surrounding the efficacy of HDC-ABMT for treating breast cancer. The demonstration project is an attempt to return the debate to the appropriate forum of clinical research and away from the courtroom and mass media. Only clinical research can answer the question "does HDC-ABMT work for breast cancer?"

The purpose of the demonstration project is to support randomized controlled clinical trials comparing the efficacy of HDC-ABMT with that of conventional chemotherapy in the treatment of advanced breast cancer with a poor prognosis. The clinical trials are sponsored by the National Cancer Institute, the Clinical Trials Cooperative Groups, and the Philadelphia Bone Marrow Transplant Group. It is hoped that increased financial support for this costly investigational treatment will speed accruals to the trials while providing Blue Cross and Blue Shield subscribers with access to this treatment. The demonstration project is supporting two multicenter randomized trials for women with stage II or III disease and 10 or more positive nodes (CALGB 9082 and INT 0121) and two multicenter randomized trials for women with stage IV metastatic disease (INT 0127 and the Philadelphia Protocol, PBT-1).

The demonstration project provides payments on behalf of Blue Cross and Blue Shield subscribers to the bone marrow transplant centers that are participating in the trials and that have entered into contracts with BCBSA. The all-inclusive payments are separate and distinct from payments made when a new technology is covered. They constitute support for clinical research and defray a significant portion of the patient care costs of HDC-ABMT. Participating institutions, however, are expected to share in the costs of treatment as well.

Currently 17 plans and the Federal Employee Program, accounting for 40 percent of Blue Cross and Blue Shield membership, are participating in the demonstration project. To date, 41 hospitals are participating and contracting is ongoing. Several of the supported trials are accruing patients very well, and Blue Cross and Blue Shield believes its support contributes to the rapid accrual.

FUTURE DIRECTIONS

The Blue Cross and Blue Shield Association, the Blue Cross and Blue Shield plans, and all third-party payers are closely following the progress of the demonstration project. It may serve as a model for how insurers can support clinical research for promising investigational treatments targeted to life-threatening or seriously disabling conditions. Key elements of such a model would be (1) limited support to networks of providers, (2) conducting clinical trials approved or sponsored by peer-reviewed entities, and (3) continued exclusion of technology from full coverage until efficacy has been demonstrated.

The Blue Cross and Blue Shield system wants to work cooperatively with the research community and sponsors to ensure that critical clinical trials are completed and that reimbursements are provided for new technologies when those technologies are known to be effective.

REFERENCES

Blue Cross and Blue Shield Association. 1991. Blue Cross and Blue Shield Association Technology Evaluation Criteria, revised 1991. Chicago, I11.: Blue Cross and Blue Shield Association.

Henderson, I. C. 1991. Window of opportunity. *Journal of the National Cancer Institute* 83(13):895.

8

Kaiser Permanente's New Technology Committee: Coverage Decisionmaking in a Group Model Health Maintenance Organization

PAUL D. LAIRSON

A few years ago Alain Enthoven asked me to give a presentation to one of his classes at Stanford University on how the Kaiser Permanente Program made decisions related to the coverage of emerging new medical technologies. Alain knew that I was chairman of the program's New Technologies Committee, and I believe that he expected a discussion of a sophisticated decisionmaking process that carried a heavy dosage of cost-effectiveness analysis. I am not totally sure that Dr. Enthoven has fully recovered from my presentation related to how decisions are made in the complicated, multifactorial world of medical care delivery, and I believe that the presentation shook his rational view of the world. However, he has been kind enough to invite me back every year since to give a view of the "real" world to his graduate students.

In this chapter, I plan to discuss that process and attempt to describe the complex arena in which group and staff model health maintenance organizations (HMOs) make coverage decisions. Most of the things that I will cover apply to most of us who provide or insure medical services, although there are some differences. To understand the decisionmaking process that Kaiser Permanente uses, I believe that it would be useful to understand the structure of the organization in which these decisions are made.

THE KAISER PERMANENTE PROGRAM

The Kaiser Permanente Program comprises 12 regions that have a large degree of autonomy, held together by a common history and a centralized corporate office in Oakland, California, where many functions that are of mutual bene fit to the overall program are carried out. Much of the autonomy of the 12 regions is driven by the 12 independent Permanente Medical Groups, which have in common their contracts with the Kaiser Foundation Health Plan in their region, the name Permanente, and the fact that they are group practices. The medical groups also have a commonly funded central office, The Permanente Medical Groups Interregional Services, which I direct.

The largest of our regions has about 2.5 million members, and the smallest has about 50,000 members. The degree of independence and the ability to perform functions internal to the region vary with the size of the region. The larger regions greatly support the activities of the Interregional New Technologies Committee, which I will describe. They support the activities of the committee by using committees of physicians and nonphysician personnel in their region; those people track and review in detail technologies related to their areas of expertise. An example would be the Bone Marrow Transplantation Committee in our Northern California region, which tracks and advises the Interregional Committee on bone marrow transplant indications.

THE NEW TECHNOLOGY COMMITTEE

In 1984, because of the explosion in emerging new technologies and because government and large national employers looked upon Kaiser Permanente as one nationwide program and not 12 independent plans, the New Technologies Committee was created to recommend to the 12 regions when and how emerging new medical technologies should be covered. We had begun to find ourselves in the position in which one of our regions covered a particular technology and another region denied coverage of the same technology—sometimes in the same state.

Under the HMO Act of 1973, all "medically necessary services" must be provided by a qualified HMO except in two situations—when the service is experimental or when the service is not medically necessary, such as cosmetic surgery. The HMO Act does not define "experimental."

The New Technologies Committee was established in the offices of the Permanente Medical Groups, but from the beginning it was viewed as a committee for the Kaiser Permanente Program and not solely for the physicians. Although some members of the committee have changed over the past eight years, the representation of the membership has remained stable. Currently, there are 16 members representing physicians (internists, surgeons, oncologists, and pediatricians), health plan administrators, hospital officers, attorneys, and the director of quality assurance. In addition, there are two members of the committee who represent interests outside of the program—a physician and an ethicist.

In our offices one full-time employee staffs the committee, represents the committee directly to the 12 regions and to committees in the individual regions, tracks the technologies brought to that person's attention, and maintains a com puterized database that contains all discussions of technologies, all decisions of the committee, any issue that has been brought to that person's or the committee's attention and, in fact, any inquiry made of any technology from any source. This database is of great value in that it can give a quick status report to any inquiry.

Inquiries relating to a technology come from multiple sources. Often a service involving a new technology will be provided by an outside provider with whom we have a contractual relationship, such as a medical school or an individual physician or group of physicians. The first time that we are aware of these services may be when we are presented with a bill to cover the service and a region—either the benefits office or an individual physician—will ask our office if the program has ever covered or considered covering the particular procedure or treatment. If it is a first-time inquiry, most of the regions are polled to see if they have encountered the procedure and what was done and, in all cases, the inquiry becomes a part of our ongoing data bank.

CATEGORIES OF NEW TECHNOLOGIES

For convenience, we divide the procedures and technologies addressed by the New Technologies Committee into four broad categories. The first category includes new procedures that involve new and often expensive equipment. An example of this would be lithotripsy. In these cases, some guidelines must be followed, such as Food and Drug Administration (FDA) approval of the new equipment. The second category is a new procedure that does not involve new equipment or drugs. An example of this is in vitro fertilization. In these cases, there are few guidelines that must be followed as to when a procedure moves from being experimental to being an acceptable medical practice of proven efficacy and safety. The risks, benefits, and costs are often more difficult to document, and there is no FDA approval process to follow, as there is with new drugs and new equipment that needs FDA approval. In other words, it is often difficult to identify a discrete moment in time when a procedure moves from being experimental to being nonexperimental. Because innovation in clinical practice often occurs in an incremental fashion, the benefits and risks are moving targets, which complicate decisionmaking.

The third category is new drugs. These occupy more and more of our attention as genetically engineered drugs and drugs that are extremely expensive, such as Ceridase, are developed under the Orphan Drug Act. We usually, but not always, follow FDA approval; the exceptions are likely to occur because, although FDA looks at safety and efficacy, it doesn't look at *relative* efficacy. We have, at times, covered medications prior to full FDA approval. As an example, we covered zidovudine (AZT) years before it had full FDA approval. The converse is also true. We have discouraged the use of finasteride, an antineoplastic agent, because of questions related to its efficacy in comparison to alternative technologies. The last category is of those new technologies that have been developed for life-threatening diseases, such as organ transplantation.

These categories are of some benefit to us because of the information base from which we can make decisions and because the ethical considerations are different for life-threatening diseases with no available treatment alternatives.

COSTS OF NEW TECHNOLOGIES

The cost of a technology is not a prominent part of the discussions and deliberations of the New Technologies Committee, although it is clear that many of the agenda items would not be selected if it were not for the costs involved in providing the technology. We use safety, efficacy, and proven benefit of the procedure, device, or drug to guide our decisions. One exception to the use of cost data is when we are looking at a new technology when a well-established, equally effective, alternative therapy or diagnostic test exists. If the old technology costs less and is of equal value, we will not provide the new modality. Rarely, however, do we as an organization have good information on the actual costs of the procedure.

In looking at the costs of a new technology, one must have good information on whether a technology substitutes for other types of technologies, or whether other types of technologies will need to be employed in association with the new technology in question. Sufficient and reliable data does not exist in which to make these types of assessments. It is also not always practical to look at the cost-effectiveness[1] of a technology in making decisions. The cost and benefit to whom are societal questions that are impossible for a single organization to answer.

Research Done by the Committee

Before a decision is made to bring a technology to the New Technologies Committee, research is undertaken. In fact, the research begins at the first inquiry, and the research may determine when an issue will be discussed at the committee level or, better stated, when we think there is enough information on which to make a decision. Committee members are also kept aware of emerging technologies that may be coming to the committee in the future.

In gathering information, a particular technology or drug will often be assigned to one of our regional committees, such as the Bone Marrow Transplantation Committee or the chiefs of a particular department, to be discussed at their regional or interregional meetings. The Kaiser Permanente Program has over 9,000 physicians representing essentially all specialties. We gather information from individuals inside and outside of the program with expertise in the appropriate area. We obviously look at the published literature; however, we often rely more on unpublished information, for example, information presented at scientif ic meetings prior to publication, than on actual publications. By the time information is published, it is often beyond the time we had to make a decision related to a particular patient about whether coverage is indicated. We directly contact research centers involved in the development of a technology to gather their expertise. We also have numerous telephone conversations with researchers to determine the long-range potential of the technology for improving health outcomes.

We rely relatively little on published technology assessments. Again, we usually must make coverage decisions related to a new technology before such studies have been performed and published. These technology assessments, in my opinion, are of much greater value for reviewing established technologies and making decisions as to whether or not they should continue to be covered as benefits to our members. Is the technology more or less outmoded and replaced by newer, safer, and less costly technologies?

We do not do this assessment of "old" or existing technologies at the present time on a program-wide basis at Kaiser Permanente, but rather, these decisions are made by the individual regions and are driven mostly by the practice preferences of individual medical groups and their evaluations of existing technologies. We have had numerous discussions of a centralized review of existing technologies, and we may, like the Blue Cross and Blue Shield Association, move in that direction.

The Interregional New Technologies Committee also does not recommend which type of equipment or device the program should use. This review and decisionmaking is done in a different arena. For example, the New Technologies Committee might recommend that we cover artificial hip joint replacements, but the actual type of artificial joint to be used would be decided by regional committees, often through department chief meetings.

FACTORS AFFECTING DECISIONMAKING

As I indicated earlier, our decisions are guided by our definition of *experimental* which encompasses safety and efficacy. We always try to keep a balance between our responsibilities to individual members and the benefit to our entire enrolled population. It is the enrolled population whose money we have in trust to provide the greatest benefit to the population that we serve. These decisions are not and cannot be made on a cost-effectiveness basis by any single health care provider in the United States. There must be better societal guidelines that we can follow.

Decisions about the use of health care resources and the application of technologies is a social issue. Some guidance must come from the greater society as to what is and is not acceptable and what society is willing to spend on health care. Other forces that are outside of any organization have an impact on deci sionmaking. Our decisions are strongly influenced by three factors not directly related to the technology itself.

The first factor can be found in the current legal environment. In recent years many individuals have resorted to lawsuits when their insurance companies have refused to provide a medical service under the experimental exclusion. In the past these verdicts by the courts meant only that the insurer would have to pay for the medical service or new technology that was in dispute. At times, however, the courts have ordered the coverage of the technology and sometimes awarded punitive damages to the individual, which may amount to millions of dollars. The risk of ending up defending a decision in court—an unpredictable decisionmaking body—and the subsequent costs must be factored into any analysis of whether to cover a new technology. Although these decisions may offer some protection to the individual being insured, they also result in individuals receiving expensive, often painful, and useless treatments.

The second factor is the role of the mass media. If a patient is refused coverage of a procedure or treatment by any insurer, the individual may resort to the press to pressure the organization to provide the intervention. The cost of bad publicity to the organization or insurer cannot be calculated; however, it must also be considered in any decisionmaking process. The mass media generally supports the individual in any dispute between an individual and an organization.

The third factor to be taken into account is the dynamics of employer decisionmaking. Employers, looking for ways to insulate themselves from the costs of their health benefits, have developed multiple ways to attack costs. Emerging technologies have largely been ignored by most employers, despite their significant impact. Although employers have pushed for reduced premiums they often, through employee assistance programs, push insurers to provide technologies of questionable benefit and technologies that are clearly experimental. When an employee is refused a procedure or treatment they often seek help from their employee assistance program, which becomes a strong patient advocate, pressuring insurers to provide services that will ultimately increase the costs of providing insurance for their employees.

The New Technologies Committee makes broad policy decisions for the Kaiser Permanente Program related to whether or not to cover an emerging new technology, or at what point in time the technology is of proven value and safety. Over time, the committee has been asked for assistance in making coverage decisions for individual patients that did not fit within specific guidelines or that could be considered as exceptions to the broad policy that the New Technology Committee had established. Because of the number of requests from within the program to consider individuals and individual decisions, the Kaiser Permanente Program established a separate but interrelated committee, the Situation Management Committee, in each region to make recommendations related to how a coverage policy should be applied to an individual patient. If a region had a question related, for example, to a specific patient and a specific organ transplan tation, the Situation Management Committee would manage the process related to the individual patient. These cases might relate to a patient who did not specifically fit existing criteria or for whom there were extenuating circumstances.

Experimental Exclusions

On the basis of the experiences of both the New Technologies Committee and the Situation Management Committee, we have begun to question the value of the "experimental" exclusion. As indicated earlier, the experimental exclusion is a part of the HMO Act of 1973. We find that if we inform one of our members that we will not provide coverage of a particular technology, an adversarial relationship often develops immediately. These adversarial relationships always seem to involve an inordinate number of attorneys, and true patient-provider communication comes to a grinding halt.

Although we still use the experimental exclusion, and will continue to do so in some form to keep out truly charlatanic practices, we are considering and have used a more participatory format. This means that we approach our member in the following manner: "Coverage of this particular technology may not be the issue. Instead, let us decide together what the best course of treatment for you is in your current condition and explain the risks versus the potential benefits (and the pain, if any) involved in the use of this technology." This allows for much more participation in the decision by the patient and family. In those cases in which we have used this approach it has worked well, for it clearly puts the physician, the organization, and the patient on the same side. We as an organization are moving in that direction as it relates to the experimental exclusion. We also are moving toward having more member representatives on committees such as the New Technologies Committee. Finally, we also use medical ethicists to focus on issues related to coverage and the rights of the individual versus the rights of our collective membership.

CONCLUSION

The issues related to the adoption and use of emerging medical technologies are obviously complex. Who will develop new technologies, who will pay for them, and who will receive them are critical societal issues. Decisions cannot continue to be made by individual insurers trying to manage a process in which the players often have conflicting goals and society, represented by government, will not step forth to give some direction.

A complicating factor related to emerging technologies is who will benefit (or not benefit, as the case may be) from the technical advancement. Many of the costs of the application of technological advances are related to the inappropriate use of the technology. As we make a decision on whether to cover a medical advance, we are also beginning to develop protocols and guidelines for their use.

When, for whom, and under what conditions is the technology appropriate? I believe that this offers great hope, if done properly, for controlling the expenses associated with advances in technology and appropriately applying technology. Appropriate use of technology also requires giving everyone involved-the patient, the physician, the family, and the hospital—the appropriate incentives to use the technology for those who will indeed benefit from the therapy. Improperly applied technologies are costly, are a waste of resources, are often painful, and represent poor quality of care.

Clearly, the increase in the overall expenditures on health care are related to the way in which the U.S. health care system uses technology. Until there are some clearer guidelines of how society wishes to manage the costs of care and the resources it is willing to devote to health care, individual providers and insurers must continue to struggle with the questions that arise from the application of and economic costs of new medical technologies.

9

Autologous Bone Marrow Transplantation: A Microcosm of the U.S. Health Care System

WILLIAM T. McGIVNEY[1]

The controversy over the appropriate utilization of high-dose chemotherapy—autologous bone marrow transplantation (HDC-ABMT) in the treatment of cancer epitomizes the debate in the United States over increasing expenditures for the application of health care technology (drugs, devices, procedures, and techniques). The debate includes all imaginable constituencies-patients, physicians, hospitals, payers, employers, lawyers, economists, and the mass media. The issue is fascinating, because it continually presents new twists and turns. The major question raised is whether or not the utilization and payment for such expensive, potentially high-volume technologies should proceed only after rigorous outcomes data concerning its use for a particular indication are available. In the last decade, the concept of basing clinical and coverage policies on cold, hard data has become an axiom in medicine that is widely quoted yet often ignored. The manner in which the HDC-ABMT issue is resolved (or not resolved) will presage the manner in which similar pressing issues are addressed in the 1990s and the century beyond.

This chapter reviews the controversy surrounding HDC-ABMT, discusses the consensus on the use of outcomes data in health care decisionmaking, describes one payer's process for the difficult coverage decisions associated with HDC-ABMT, and proposes a system for the evaluation and diffusion of significant new technologies.

---

[1] The views expressed in this chapter are those of the author and are not necessarily those of AEtna Health Plans.

THE CONTROVERSY SURROUNDING HDC-ABMT

The high expense of HDC-ABMT is a major reason for the attention that has been given to decisions regarding its clinical application. Charges for the process of bone marrow harvest, high-dose chemotherapy, and bone marrow reinfusion range from $150,000 to $200,000, with most being in the vicinity of the latter value. The use of peripheral blood as the source of stem cell support in combination with the use of colony-stimulating factors has the potential to reduce these charges significantly. Nevertheless, the cost of an individual procedure is magnified by the approximately 1 million new cases of cancer diagnosed each year, including 135,000 to 150,000 new cases of breast cancer. The potential for high-volume use of HDC-ABMT is being realized by an expanding list of indications and by the application of HDC-ABMT earlier and earlier in therapeutic regimens.

HDC-ABMT continues to be used for the established indications of acute leukemia, Hodgkin's disease, non-Hodgkin's lymphoma, and stage III and IV neuroblastoma. It also is being applied for the treatment of stage II, III, and IV (metastatic) breast cancer and multiple myelomas. Finally, a variety of new applications of HDC-ABMT has been observed, including brain tumors in adults and children, ovarian cancer, testicular cancer, Ewing's sarcoma, and metastatic melanoma. The shift toward using HDC-ABMT in earlier stages of the disease process is exemplified by the use of the regimen in stage II and III breast cancer and earlier stages of multiple myelomas. Additional factors influencing utilization include the use of regimens that involve tandem transplants, repeating HDC-ABMT at some predetermined interval after the first treatment and applying HDC-ABMT to treat the recurrence of a cancer anywhere from one to three years after the initial HDC-ABMT treatment. A final issue involves the appropriateness of the harvest and storage of bone marrow for patients who at that time are not candidates for HDC-ABMT but who in the future may be, if a cancer progresses or if the outcomes associated with HDC-ABMT improve.

Thus, the high expense, the size of the potential patient population, rapidly expanding applications, and the scarcity of outcomes data clearly identify HDC-ABMT as a controversial clinical issue with substantial policy implications. These factors and that of critical patient need raised the issue to the national public policy level. The courtroom often has become the forum for this debate in the context of challenges to payer denials of HDC-ABMT. In a clear majority of these cases, the plaintiff has prevailed. In most of these cases, court decisions have turned not so much on the merits (e.g., data) available to support the use of HDC-ABMT as on the coverage decisionmaking process and the accurate translation of the terms (e.g., investigational) and criteria used in this process into specific contractual language (see chapter 10, this volume).

Outside the courtroom, there have been hyperbole and posturing suggesting that payer cooperation with the National Cancer Institute (NCI) in trials on breast cancer represents an attempt on the part of payers to avoid payment for a larger number (e.g., 40,000) of cases for breast cancer. When viewed from a societal perspective, one must ask if the expenditure of $7 billion (40,000 x $175,000 per procedure) for the use of HDC-ABMT in breast cancer is justified by the available outcomes data. Furthermore, such posturing ignores the fact that the trials would not be sponsored by the NCI if outcomes data had convincingly demonstrated a therapeutic advantage for HDC-ABMT over conventional therapy for the treatment of breast cancer. Indeed, if such an advantage had been shown, it would be unethical for such trials to continue. Rather, the NCI trials represent attempts by responsible parties to obtain objective data that can be incorporated into their processes for making these difficult decisions.

OUTCOMES-BASED DECISIONMAKING

The decade of the 1980s will be remembered as a period when the health policy community came to intellectual grips with the fact that the widespread utilization of some health care technologies was based upon no more than the "expert opinion" of a handful of proponents. The sentinel study of Wennberg and colleagues (1988) vividly illustrated the need for the practicing medical community to more firmly ground clinical decisionmaking in outcomes data. Although much homage has been paid to this axiom, there has been sporadic application of the concept.

The heart of the debate over the expanded use of HDC-ABMT proceeds from lingering and justifiable concerns over whether HDC-ABMT improves the final health outcome (e.g., survival) in comparison with that from standard chemotherapeutic regimens. For example, the results for improvement in survival from metastatic breast cancer overlap in large measure for HDC-ABMT and repetitive conventional-dose chemotherapy.

In April, 1992, David Eddy published a review and analysis of all published studies comparing the benefits and harms associated with HDC-ABMT and with conventional doses of chemotherapy in the treatment of metastatic breast cancer. His analysis concluded that:

1. HDC-ABMT had a "higher treatment mortality and morbidity rate than conventional dose chemotherapy";
2. HDC-ABMT had "higher complete response and overall response rates than conventional dose chemotherapy";
3. analysis of available data does not indicate that "median disease-free survival, median overall survival, or actual survival is superior with HDC-ABMT versus conventional dose chemotherapy"; and
4. available evidence did not permit conclusions about the effectiveness of the treatment compared with its alternatives (Eddy, 1992).

Publication of that analysis occurred at a time of rapid diffusion of HDC-ABMT in general oncologic practice, that is, rapid diffusion based upon a modicum of long-term effectiveness data.

PAYER PERSPECTIVE

Requests for coverage for highly expensive, investigational treatments, such as HDC-ABMT in terminally ill cancer patients, are among the most difficult decisions to which payers must respond. The difficulty of the decision to use HDC-ABMT on an investigational basis is compounded by the often desperate situation of the patient and by the aforementioned general lack of data regarding the safety and effectiveness (e.g., survival) of HDC-ABMT compared with those of conventional procedures. Additionally, challenge of payer denials by patients has generally resulted in adverse decisions by the courts and adverse portrayals of payers by the mass media. Thus, payer denials have often lacked clinical, legal, and societal defensibility.

AEtna Health Plans has implemented a process to directly address questions regarding the appropriateness of and coverage for the use of investigational treatments in terminally ill patients with cancer. This process has worked extremely well and has given AEtna Health Plans a thorough, scientific, equitable, and objective process for reviewing these trying cases. Indeed, AEtna's process may serve as a prototype for the involvement of payers and independent expert clinicians in a cooperative decisionmaking process that best serves the needs of desperately ill patients.

HDC in combination with allogeneic or autologous bone marrow transplantation or with peripheral stem cell transplantation most often is the treatment in question. AEtna no longer automatically denies the use of these investigational technologies in terminally ill patients. Rather, AEtna has recognized that both the clinical and the coverage decisionmaking processes really constitute risk-benefit analyses. The sicker the patient is, the less the degree of certitude about the effectiveness of a technology and the greater the risk of harm the patient, physician, and payer may be willing to accept. To address this continuum of care, AEtna has determined that if an investigational treatment for a terminally ill patient is investigational yet "promising," then that treatment is eligible for coverage. A promising treatment is defined as a treatment that "is effective for that disease or shows promise of being effective for that disease as demonstrated by scientific data." citation??

The process for determining whether or not an investigational treatment (e.g., HDC-ABMT) is promising is described below. First, it should be pointed out that AEtna's process affords every opportunity for a decision favorable to the patient if the treatment is appropriate. Basically, AEtna has extended its previous decisionmaking process by adding a clinical review step that relies on two independent and outside sources of expert medical information and advice. These are NCI and the Medical Care Ombudsman Program.

This model process represents a just and equitable solution to a difficult situation. However, it is a short-term solution because it does not address the major problem identified at the outset of this discussion; that is, health care technologies with significant implications for patient well-being and for the substantial expenditure of heath care dollars often diffuse widely into medical practice before there are sufficient outcomes data available to demonstrate the safety and effectiveness of the technology. On the basis of our experience at AEtna, the following proposal describes a system for guiding the introduction and use of health care technologies.[2]

PROPOSAL

A national advisory body should be established to oversee the conduct of evaluative outcomes research on important new technologies. The use and study of these new technologies would be restricted to a network of designated medical centers. Reimbursement for the use of new technologies (e.g., procedures, procedures involving Food and Drug Administration [FDA]-approved devices, and drugs used beyond FDA-approved indications) would be provided but would be restricted to use under the study protocol and within the identified academic centers. In return, outcomes data would be collected and analyzed under the auspices of the independent advisory body. When the outcomes data collected from the study were judged to be sufficient, a comprehensive evaluation would be undertaken, culminating in definitive conclusions about the safety and effectiveness of the technology. Once the national advisory body concluded that a technology was safe and effective for the specified indication, the technology would be allowed to diffuse into practice. At this point, individual payers would decide whether they would pay for the specified use of the technology.

RATIONALE

The rationale for the proposal is that outcomes data should be available to demonstrate the safety and effectiveness of a particular technology (e.g., HDC-ABMT) for its intended use before widespread use of the technology occurs. Assurance of reimbursement would permit earlier access for use as "treatment" for patients in need. The "hassle factor," which is a factor for payers, providers, and sometimes for patients, would be mitigated, if not eliminated. The outcomes data so desperately needed to make the informed risk-benefit determinations integral to the formulation of sound coverage policy and clinical decisionmaking would be generated, collected, and analyzed in a cooperative scientific environment. Inadequate investigator participation in clinical trials would be rectified by

[2] Interestingly, a similar proposal was made in the early 1980s (Bunker et al., 1982). However, the time now seems riper for implementing such a system than perhaps it was then.

the opportunity to use the most advanced technology and the financial incentive of early reimbursement. Inadequacies in patient accrual to trials would be addressed by the concomitant expansion of the size (number of studies) and by restriction of general diffusion. The permissible designs used in the studies also would be expanded. Studies and patient care would be conducted in institutions where rigid quality assurance such as that carried out by NCI helps to ensure consistency, competence, and experience. Payers and society, in general, would achieve answers to important medical issues in a much more efficient and expeditious manner. Finally, as an added bonus, the sagging infrastructure of academic medicine would be buttressed by the restriction of payment for new technology to the setting where its initial diffusion and study belong, that is, in institutions dedicated to the deliberate evaluation of and advancement of patient care.

DISCUSSION

HDC-ABMT crystallized the issues and concerns that have surrounded the debate over ways to deliver high-quality health care while controlling the rate of rise in health care expenditures. With over 1 million new cases of cancer diagnosed every year and with an approximate cost of $175,000 per procedure, HDC-ABMT is a rapidly diffusing technology that has significant implications for the expenditure of health care dollars. One would then expect that with such a large attendant cost, the cancer care community would proceed cautiously with the use of this technology for investigational indications on a limited basis until scientific data convincingly demonstrated the safety and effectiveness of HDC-ABMT for these indications. Actually, just the opposite seems to be occurring; that is, the use of HDC-ABMT seems to be growing almost exponentially, far outpacing the ability of clinical research to generate data to support such use.

How much more rational, responsible, efficient, and valuable to patients, physicians, and payers it would have been if HDC-ABMT were introduced into medical practice through an approach such as the one described above. For example, a hypothesis that extends the use of HDC to an investigational indication would be generated. A network of academic medical centers would be established to evaluate the safety and effectiveness of the procedure. Using the NCI model, after initial dosing and tumor activity studies had been successful, studies would be set up to define the clinical effectiveness of the treatment in comparison with that of the state-of-the-art treatment. The "gold standard" of a randomized controlled clinical trial would be utilized, but alternative designs (e.g., controlled case series) would be available to those patients who did not wish to be randomized. HDC-ABMT, however, would be available only to patients participating in these studies in the defined network of institutions.

During these studies the patient care costs would be covered by the payers, whereas the research costs would be borne by the nonprofit research institution.

Patients would be enrolled in the study only if they fulfilled the criteria established for the study. Payers would abide by the clinical judgments of the participating investigators. Thus, there would be no individual case management regarding the appropriateness of patients as candidates for the procedure.

Outcomes data would be collected and analyzed by an objective panel, with representation given to practicing physicians and also to payer medical directors. When sufficient data were available, the independent panel would reach a definitive conclusion and make a recommendation as to whether the technology should be permitted to diffuse into general practice. Individual payers would then formulate their own coverage policy regarding the use of the technology.

The proposed systematic approach seeks to establish a logical and orderly mechanism for the diffusion and utilization of important new technologies. This mechanism would be based on solid outcomes data and expert consensus. Payers would cover the cost of important new technologies early on within a designated network of academic medical centers in exchange for data collection and analysis and definitive conclusions about the safety and effectiveness of the technology. Implementation of this proposal would contribute to the enhancement of societal good by (1) supporting the use and study of technologies that will lead to either definitive support for widespread use or agreement that the technology should be discarded, (2) enhancing the availability of important new technologies to needy and appropriate patients early on, and (3) shoring up the sagging infrastructure of the academic medical center.

Critics will be quick to pounce on the plan and claim that great harm will be done to innovation in technology and access to needed care by patients. In my opinion, however, the proposal at hand will, in the long run, facilitate the innovation, introduction, and diffusion of new technologies by establishing a broader base of financial and scientific support early on and by financing a rapid general diffusion once the value of a technology has been established. Indeed, this proposal recognizes and affirms the import of a technological imperative in medicine, but seeks to avoid a technological Armageddon.

In the near future, HDC-ABMT may achieve the distinction of becoming the technology that annually expends the greatest amount of health care dollars. What will happen to a new technology like HDC-ABMT in the year 2000? Will it be guided expertly through an orderly scientific process with expanded patient access and, then, into full clinical practice? Will it proceed as HDC-ABMT is doing now, with limited scientific study paralleled by rapid and somewhat chaotic diffusion that results in irretrievable patient outcomes data? Or, will HDC-ABMT be prioritized as, for example, technology no. 798, with national health care funding available only for technologies 1 through 612?

A workable solution to maintaining the delicate balance between sustaining the technological imperative and avoiding technological gluttony must be achieved. All sides will have to give in on something. The present proposal and others underscore the fact that major parties are willing to subordinate individual interests to improve a health care system that has served this country and the world very well.

REFERENCES

Bunker, J. P., Fowles, J., and Schaffarzick, R. 1982. Evaluation of medical-technology strategies: Effects of coverage and reimbursement (first of two parts). *New England Journal of Medicine* 206:620-624.

Eddy, D. M. 1992. High dose chemotherapy with autologous bone marrow transplantation for the treatment of metastatic breast cancer. *Journal of Clinical Oncology* 10:657-670.

Wennberg, J. E., Mulley, A. G., Jr., Hanley, T. D., Fowler, F. J., et al. 1988. An assessment of prostatectomy for benign urinary tract obstruction. *Journal of the American Medical Association* 259:3027-3030.

10

Technology Assessment, Benefit Coverage, and the Courts

LEE N. NEWCOMER

"If you want bad public policy, let a judge write it." The quotation is attributed to Isaac Nisley, an appellate court judge who was presiding as my grandfather in a family debate at dinner. Judge Nisley, who served over 40 years on the bench, is not notable for establishing legal precedent. But it is striking that someone with his experience believed that public policy should be debated, without the constraints of legal rules, by all constituencies of the legislative branch.

That theme dominates this chapter. The legal history of experimental exclusions for new technology is a model study of the judiciary establishing social policy. Despite the altruistic motives for this trend, the judicial actions have left the insurance industry and society with a policy characterized by uncertainty. Understanding these issues requires an overview of the court cases and social changes surrounding exclusions for new technology.

LEGAL HISTORY OF EXPERIMENTAL EXCLUSIONS

Insurers originally needed a mechanism to prevent payment for quackery. Treatments rendered by charlatans were not considered medical therapy as defined by medical insurance contracts. Using the term *medically necessary* to define their parameters of coverage, insurers denied payments for quack treatments.

Physicians were willing allies in these cases. They, too, viewed quackery as potentially harmful to patients and outside mainstream medicine. The definition of *medically necessary* was implicitly understood by physicians, and they agreed with its purpose. Insurers and physicians stood together and attacked these treatments in the courts; quacks and charlatans were mutually threatening.

Judges saw the issue from a different perspective. The term *medically necessary* was vague and contract law required more specific language. In *Fassio v. Montana Physician Services* (1976), the Fassio family petitioned the insurer for coverage of "miracle therapies" to treat their child with Down's syndrome. Both the insurer and the physician reviewers felt the treatments were worthless and therefore medically unnecessary. Benefit coverage was denied. The court ruled in favor of the Fassios, stating that exclusions in insurance contracts must "do so in words that leave no doubt." The same court, however, failed to follow its own advice and did not cite examples of unambiguous wording.

In another case testing medical necessity, *Dronge v. Monarch Insurance of Ohio* (1979), the court again ruled for the plaintiff, citing vague contract terms when using the phrase *medically necessary.* The court further stated, "the test is not what the insurer intends the contract language to mean, but rather what a reasonable person placed in the position of the insured would have understood the words to mean."

Additional cases support this concept. *Victum v. Martin* (1975) defined the term *medically necessary* as "wise in the light of facts known at the time rendered." Judgments occasionally bordered on the absurd. In *Abernathy v. Prudential Insurance Co. of America* (1980), the court stated that Prudential should cover any treatment that is "appropriate," a term as elusive as *medically necessary.* Using its definition, the court approved coverage for depilatory treatment for hairiness.

Judges perceive these cases as an opportunity to provide a social benefit. Individual patients appear as underdogs in a fight against large insurers with extensive legal resources. Judges reason there is no harm in allowing coverage for individual cases. Mary Ader, an attorney for Blue Cross and Blue Shield, summarizes judicial thinking on this matter:

> First, judges view health plans, particularly insurance companies, not as the private companies they are, but rather as quasi-governmental bodies whose purpose is to distribute societal benefits across the community. Second, judges see subscriber complaints as their opportunity, or even obligation, to distribute a benefit to the individual at no cost to the community at large. These assumptions on the redistribution of wealth translate into a general judicial predisposition to find for coverage, regardless of the wording of the relevant policy provisions.... The long-run effect of this is that we now have judge-made insurance. Courts are designing the coverage, not insurers. (Ader, 1992).

EFFECTS OF SOCIAL CHANGES

The judicial propensity to determine coverage threatened the industry. Case law at that time forced insurers to increase their risk by paying for benefits they had not underwritten, but the problems were not limited to the courtroom. At the same time, social changes affected insurers' ability to adapt.

Employers discovered that their future survival depended on their ability to reduce or control medical costs. For most industries, the cost of medical care is the single largest expenditure on the balance sheet. Lacking internal expertise for these problems, the companies turned to insurers for solutions. The mandate was clear—reduce medical cost trends immediately.

Elimination of unproven technology presents a logical way to reduce expenditures without jeopardizing the quality of medical care. In the past, insurers often paid claims unknowingly. They now began to rapidly acquire the medical and claims expertise to identify such unproven technologies. But insurers also expanded the scope of their denials. By definition, academic research treatments were not proven effective; it would be unethical to conduct research comparing treatments if one therapy was already proven to be superior. The costs of clinical care for research treatments were denied under the same exclusions as quackery. From the insurer perspective, these treatments were just as speculative.

Physicians, previously allies with insurers against unnecessary care, were also experiencing new pressures. The demand for accountability forced insurers to begin examining standard medical practices. As a professional group, physicians believed they were accountable only to themselves. Their autonomy was threatened and they saw insurers as the primary threat. Once collegial, the two groups became adversarial.

Insurers then began to ask physicians to support the concept that research treatments in academic medical centers were "unproven" and "medically unnecessary." The two terms were paradoxical to physicians. They could readily agree that many treatments were unproven—that is the nature of research. But they had difficulty accepting the premise that the same treatments were medically unnecessary. Wasn't some treatment necessary for a patient with no other options? How could medical science develop without additional research? Every physician had been trained in an academic medical center; they perceived this function as fundamental to medicine. Denigrating quackery was easy; testifying against academic research was not.

Finally, physicians shifted from *professionalism* to *consumerism.* These terms are best defined with examples. Consider the mother who brings her nine-year-old son to a family practitioner in the 1960s. The child has a fever and a cough with copious sputum and looks sick. He is able to swallow liquids and medicine, so the physician prescribes an oral antibiotic with instructions to return if the fever remains after 48 hours.

The 1960s mother asks the physician, "What if he has pneumonia? Shouldn't he have a chest X-ray?" The doctor probably didn't even turn around as he said no. He knew the X-ray wouldn't change his treatment and he was too busy to waste the time. The waiting room was jammed and he was usually the only physician in the neighborhood; patients had no other choices.

Consider that same scenario today. Acutely aware that the patient's mother will take her child elsewhere, it is easy for the physician to reason that the chest

X-ray won't cause any harm, the insurance company will pay for it, and the mother will be reassured by the findings. He orders the X—ray and the therapy doesn't change.

In the professionalism model, physicians chose technologies based primarily on their determination of medical needs. This model included careful consideration of the value or necessity of technology against the potential harms (including economic damages), and patient preference was secondary or ignored. Consumerism shifts the decisionmaking focus to patient values and desires over medical appropriateness. Physicians become patient advocates who are often unwilling to state that a patient is requesting technology that is probably worthless. The new standard asks, "Does the patient want the technology and is there any harm?"

During these social changes, and after losing several court cases, insurers sought new terms to clarify their exclusions. The phrases *experimental* and *investigational* emerged to exclude unproven care. These terms were often supported with additional language like "as determined by the balance of physician opinion" or the "preponderance of scientific evidence" to clarify their meanings. The new language not only eliminated coverage for quackery but expanded the denials to unproven treatment conducted by legitimate medical research organizations.

Like their predecessors, these terms were also challenged in court. The cases evolved along two lines of logic. In *Sweeney v. Gerber Products Company Medical Benefits Plan* (1989), the patient petitioned the court for coverage of an autologous bone marrow transplantation with high-dose chemotherapy for the treatment of metastatic breast carcinoma. The court examined consent forms signed by the patient and found the word *experimental* in several paragraphs. The medical literature revealed that there was no consistent agreement on the type of medication or the dosage to be used in the procedure. The treatment was used only in phase II trials. Using the common definition of *experimental,* the court concluded that the exclusion was valid for this treatment. The *Sweeney* case, however, was not the norm of judicial reasoning.

Pirozzi v. Blue Cross-Blue Shield (1990) is more typical of cases decided across the country. The *Pirozzi* court also examined autologous bone marrow transplantation and ruled that the treatment was not experimental because it was used in major medical centers and published reports in the literature indicated that tumor shrinkage had occurred with the procedure. The court ignored the fact that the medical centers performing the procedure were the same ones conducting research.

A common feature at each of these trials is the expert witness, who developed the technology, testifying for the plaintiff patient. These experts are characterized by faculty appointments, strong biases in favor of the technology, and persuasive arguments that the technology is "state of the art." Defense attorneys also produce witnesses in the same specialty, but these witnesses do not use the technology because they believe it is not yet proven. These witnesses are less credible to the judiciary; how could they understand the technology if they don't use it? If the defense expert is convincing, the judge then faces conflicting credible experts. In these situations the judge is obligated to rule in favor of the plaintiff patient; reasonable doubt produces losses for the defense.

INSURERS' OPTIONS

The Pirozzi case is typical of most litigation involving experimental technology. Given these precedents, what options do insurers have to exclude coverage for technologies that they believe are unproven?

The first option is to list all specific excluded technologies in the contract. This approach is irrefutable if the language is clear. But there are still pitfalls. Blue Cross and Blue Shield wrote a specific exclusion for "temporomandibular joint syndrome" in their contracts, but was overruled in *Ponder v. Blue Cross of Southern California* (1983) because it "failed the plain and clear test because the undefined technical terminology (temporomandibular joint syndrome) is not calculated to be part of the working vocabulary of average lay persons."

The approach has several disadvantages. What can the insurer do if new information proves that the procedure should be the standard of care? Making an exception to an exclusion jeopardizes the entire contract; the insurer is subject to bad faith contract litigation. Conversely, a new technology invented after the contract list publication must be covered until the next contract renewal, regardless of its efficacy.

Issuing a new contract for each group or individual annually would be a major logistical problem for insurers. And the document would require amendments at least annually for this tactic to be successful.

Finally, the approach invites legislative retaliation. Specifically denying a procedure in a contract without considering the unique circumstances of an individual's request appears arbitrary. If legal appeal is not possible, a rejected policyholder may seek legislative solutions. Infertility treatment is an excellent example of this action; several states now mandate coverage.

Specifying in the contract the decisionmaking process for determination of experimental status is a second alternative approach. The process focuses on objective standards whenever possible. Asking whether an experimental consent form is required to obtain the treatment or requiring Food and Drug Administration approval are examples of objective parameters.

This tactic individualizes the decision and allows people to examine how the decisions are made. They must be carefully reasoned against the facts of each circumstance. Unfortunately, courts can disagree with the reasoning. In *Reilly v. Blue Cross and Blue Shield* (1988), the insurer stated in the contract that a new technology must have a success rate of 50 percent or greater to qualify for cover age. The court rejected the criterion, stating that a per se success ratio was inadequate to determine whether the course of treatment is experimental.

The major disadvantage to this approach is the requirement to follow the process exactly. Insurers cannot change or modify the process to fit a need. Several cases demonstrate the courts' intolerance of deviation from the contract process. In *Dorza v. Crum and Forster Insurance Company* (1989), technology not "commonly and customarily recognized throughout the doctor's profession as appropriate in the treatment of sickness or injury or ... provided primarily for research purposes" is excluded from coverage. The Prudential Insurance Company, acting as the agent for Crum and Forster, did not conduct a poll or survey physicians about the treatments they denied. Prudential chose to rely on the medical literature and expert opinion as a proxy for recognition. The court overruled the exclusion stating that Prudential failed to meet their own standards.

In a similar case, *Adams v. Blue Cross and Blue Shield of Maryland* (1991), the insurer excluded treatment not "accepted by the suitable medical specialty practicing in Maryland." While denying an autologous bone marrow transplantation, the insurer cited multiple articles from the medical literature supporting its own position. The plaintiff produced several physicians from Maryland who performed the procedure. The judge applied the language of the contract and awarded coverage to the plaintiff.

This approach also requires an individual review for each request. For example, use of an internal policy document stating that the insurer does not cover autologous bone marrow transplantation procedures is insufficient when considering an individual case. It is expected that the relevant contract language, the medical records, and the process criteria are reviewed for each case. This approach increases administrative costs for insurers.

CONCLUSIONS

Reviewing the history of experimental exclusions for new technology suggests four conclusions. First, insurers deserved the court intervention. During development of this process too many decisions were arbitrary or were made with insufficient information. This system left no alternative to the patient but persistent appeals or litigation to win a balanced hearing. As stated before, "The meek did not inherit the treatment" (Newcomer, 1990).

Second, insurers failed to tell the public why they denied experimental technology. New developing technologies are not "state of the art" but rather "state of the theory." These treatments or devices are based on promising evidence from studies in the laboratory or in animals, but they have yet to prove their value in the clinic. There is a definite chance for harm. Paul Molino states the issues clearly:

> However, when evaluating the exclusion language of a policy, a court needs to be aware that the purpose of such exclusions is not simply to avoid payment to a

specific insured in any one case. Rather these exclusions, by requiring medical treatment to meet minimal accepted standards, help protect insured from ineffective, unproven and potentially harmful treatments; help eliminate worthless treatments from the marketplace; and help control skyrocketing health care costs (Molino, 1991).

The general public needs to understand that effective technology assessment serves them as a consumer protection agency. Insurers must convey that message.

Third, the judiciary must cease creating social policy and writing benefit coverage. The courts served a useful purpose by raising the standards for technology assessment and coverage decisions. They should now stick to interpretation of the language.

In a recent decision from *Harris v. Mutual of Omaha* (1992), Judge John Daniel Tinder places the entire issue in perspective. He begins his decision with a eulogy for a respected colleague and friend who lost her life to breast cancer during the time the *Harris* case was heard. Now, facing a woman petitioning for coverage of an autologous bond marrow transplantation for the same disease, he writes:

> Despite rumors to the contrary, those who wear judicial robes are human beings and as persons, as inspired and motivated by compassion as anyone would be. Consequently, we often must remind ourselves that in our official capacities, we have authority only to issue ruling within the narrow parameters of the law and the facts before us. The temptation to go about, doing good where we see fit, and to make things less difficult for those who come before us, regardless of the law, is strong. But the law, without which judges are nothing, abjures such unlicensed formulation of unauthorized social policy by the judiciary (*Harris v. Mutual of Omaha,* 1992).

Judge Tinder's courageous statement serves as a guide to all judges.

Finally, all of these judicial strategies are only temporary tactics. Society must debate and answer two questions if it expects any progress on the issue of new technology coverage. First, who should pay the cost of clinical research? Is this a taxpayer, manufacturer, or insurer obligation? Second, can universal criteria be written to define the transition from experimental or investigational status to a technology's being a standard, widely accepted treatment modality?

When these questions are answered—and they are answerable—there will no longer be a need for courtroom decisions about coverage.

REFERENCES

Abernathy v. Prudential Insurance Company of America, 264 S.E.2d 836 (S.C. 1980).
Adams v. Blue Cross and Blue Shield of Maryland, 757 F. Supp. 661 (D. Md. 1991).
Dorza v. Crum and Forster Insurance Company, 716 F. Supp. 131 (D. N.J. 1989).
Dronge v. Monarch Insurance of Ohio, 511 F. Supp. 1, 41 (D. Kan. 1979).

Fassio v. Montana Physician Services, 563 P.2d 998 (Mont. 1976).
Harris v. Mutual of Omaha, No. IP92-1089-C (S.D. Ind., Aug. 26, 1992).
Molino, P. J. 1991. Reimbursement disputes involving experimental medical treatment. *Journal of Health and Hospital Law* 24:329-336.
Newcomer, L. N. 1990. Defining experimental therapy-A third party payer's dilemma. *New England Journal of Medicine* 323:1702-1704.
Pirozzi v. Blue Cross-Blue Shield, 741 F. Supp. 586 (E.D. Va. 1990).
Ponder v. Blue Cross of Southern California, 145 Cal. App. 3d 709, 193 Cal. Rptr. 632 (2d Dist. 1983).
Reilly v. Blue Cross & Blue Shield United, 846 F.2d 416 (7th Cir. 1988).
Sweeney v. Gerber Products Company Medical Benefits Plan, 728 F. Supp. 594 (D. Neb. 1989).
Victum v. Martin, 326 N.E.2d 12, 16 (Mass. 1975).

PART IV

Increasing the Rationality of Coverage Decisionmaking

11

Strengthening the Connection Between Evaluative Research and Coverage Decisionmaking

LUCIAN L. LEAPE

In late 1989, the U.S. Congress upgraded the status and expanded the scope of government activity in the quality of health care research when it created the Agency for Health Care Policy and Research (AHCPR) to replace the National Center for Health Services Research and Health Care Technology Assessment. The charge of the new agency was to "enhance the quality, appropriateness, and effectiveness of health care services." In addition to the expansion of outcomes related research projects, the agency's mandate included the creation of new initiatives in clinical practice guidelines development and dissemination (*Congressional Record,* 1989).

This significant expansion of federal support for medical effectiveness research resulted in part from evidence, accumulated over the previous two decades, of significant variations in the use of a wide variety of medical and surgical technologies (Chassin et al., 1986; Lewis, 1969; Wennberg and Gittlesohn, 1973, 1982) as well as accumulating evidence that a significant fraction of technologies may be ineffective (Chassin et al., 1987; Graboys et al., 1987; Greenspan et al., 1988; Kahn et al., 1988; Leape et al., 1990; Winslow et al., 1988a,b). It was also apparent that many of the tools developed for these research activities could be used to improve the outcomes of care. Payers, policymakers, and physicians saw the potential in these developments for improving both the quality and the value of health care.

The historical significance of concerns about quality of care should not be overlooked. Prior to World War II, the effectiveness of most treatments was dubious. Physicians could do little to alter the natural course of most ailments, and patients expected little more. All of that changed with the incredible flower ing of biomedical science over the past 40 years. It has been medicine's extraordinary successes that have led to rising public expectations and an intolerance of medical failures. Indeed, it seems quite legitimate today to ask why it is that patients receive ineffective treatments.

EVALUATIVE RESEARCH

The term *evaluative research* means different things to different people. The traditional biomedical and industrial perspective was to evaluate safety and efficacy, and these are still the primary focus of Food and Drug Administration concerns. In recent years, researchers have devoted more and more attention to evaluation of a service or product *after* research has demonstrated that it is of some value. Evaluative research asks the question how beneficial is it?—in terms of outcomes, good and bad, and in comparison with alternative treatment or diagnostic options.

Fuchs and Garber (1990) have suggested that technology assessment should now embrace a wide spectrum of consequences—clinical, economic, and social, as well as ethical. Eddy states that equally important is how patients value the procedures that physicians and companies believe are effective and, most importantly, whether they think they should be provided (Eddy, 1990c).

To understand the place of evaluative research, let us first look at how medical practices in the United States incorporate new technologies. For example, consider a surgeon who develops a new operation. He or she first tries the new idea out in the animal laboratory and then on an appropriate patient. It seems to work. The patient and other physicians are impressed. The surgeon tries it on a few more patients. After doing 5 or 10, the results are reported at a national meeting and published in a scientific journal. Other surgeons are also stimulated to try it. They get into fights with insurance companies that refuse to pay for an experimental procedure—unless, that is, they are ingenious enough to classify the new operation under an old name and fool the payers. In any case, they persist, and after a-while the payers cave in, declaring that the procedure is "accepted." How soon they cave in depends on how expensive the procedure is.

The process is a bit different with a new device. it is the manufacturer who must convince the payer, as well as physicians, that the device is worth using—although often the device has been developed in collaboration with a physician, who is equally enthusiastic. The manufacturer also must convince the FDA that the device works and is not grossly hazardous, but that is relatively easy considering that the FDA division that assesses devices is underfunded and understaffed. For drugs, it is-much more difficult, because drug approval requires several stages of clinical trials.

Whether it is a drug, a device, or a procedure, the end result is similar: a new technology is usually disseminated, and paid for, without it having been established that the technology is either (1) substantially better than the existing alter natives or (2) worth the additional cost over the alternatives (they almost never cost less!). Not surprisingly, some are later found to be of no value, even harmful, or at best of marginal benefit.

A medical technology may also be effective for some uses but not for others. It is likely that most inappropriate use falls into this category. After all, relatively few technologies that are worthless are adopted. However, every medical technology can be used inappropriately. For example, there is good evidence that carotid endarterectomy (removal of an obstruction within one of the arteries to the brain) will help prevent stroke if the artery is obstructed by 70 percent or more (Mayberg et al., 1991). But there is no evidence that removal of a 30 percent obstruction is beneficial, and experts do not recommend the operation in that circumstance (Winslow et al., 1988b). Similarly, coronary artery bypass graft (CABG) surgery clearly improves long-term survival in patients with three vessel or left main coronary artery disease (Alderman et al., 1990), but there is little evidence that survival is improved in patients with single-vessel disease. (CABG surgery is usually effective at relieving angina in these patients, however.)

The reasons for adopting a medical technology before there is adequate proof of effectiveness or for extending its use beyond the original purposes are neither pure self-interest nor negligence. The developer or manufacturer of a new treatment or diagnostic tool always has *some* evidence of efficacy; the early experience may be encouraging or the new technology offers at least marginal benefit over current options. In a society such as ours, a number of forces combine to stimulate such use of a technology before there is adequate proof of its effectiveness. As a society, Americans place value on action; doing something is better than doing nothing. It is better to take a chance than to lose from inaction. Then, too, Americans have a love affair with technology: patients, as well as physicians, are attracted to high-technology solutions. It is assumed that they are better than nontechnical alternatives. And, importantly, those who make the decisions to use a new technology, physicians and patients, are insulated from cost considerations; usually, neither pays the entire bill directly.

Unfortunately, once a new procedure, drug, or device has been used and is thought to be of value, it is much more difficult to carry out an unbiased evaluation of its effectiveness. Patients and physicians are reluctant to participate in a randomized trial once they are convinced that the technology works.

How can the process be improved? How can payment be more effectively linked to evidence of effectiveness? To rationalize decisions about the provision of any health care service, three questions must be answered: Does the technology work? If so, for whom is it indicated? Should it be provided (Eddy, 1990a)? Evaluative research attempts to answer these questions. In the following sections I will review the currently used evaluative research methods. Then, I will consider some of the limitations of evaluative research and barriers to its implementation. Finally, I will propose a plan for improving evaluative research and linking it to payment decisions.

DOES IT WORK?

The test of whether a medical technology works is in the outcomes: Is the patient better off? This is what the current emphasis on outcomes research is all about: Do the benefits outweigh the risks? How do health care providers tell whether the patient is better off? What are the important outcomes that should be measured? How should they be measured? What are the sources of information?

Efficacy is used to indicate that a treatment or diagnostic technology accomplishes its alleged objectives under ideal conditions (usually those in which it was developed). Does CABG surgery prevent early death from coronary artery disease? Does it prevent heart attacks? Does carotid endarterectomy prevent stroke?

Effectiveness is a measure of whether the technology works in general clinical practice-—outside of the research environment. For example, CABG surgery has been shown to reduce substantially the death rate in patients with left main coronary artery disease, but not in patients with disease in a single branch vessel. Effectiveness considerations also include examination of the competence of the users.

Types of Outcomes

At least four types of outcomes can be differentiated: clinical, health status, functional capacity, and quality of life.

Clinical Outcomes

Until quite recently, the traditional outcomes that were considered to define the success, or effectiveness, of a medical technology were clinical, that is, they were defined by physicians. These may be positive, that is, the "benefits" of a medical technology, such as diagnosis or cure of disease, relief of symptoms, prevention of complications or disability, and prevention of premature death. Or they may be negative, that is, the risks or "harms" of a treatment or diagnostic tool, such as mortality, pain, anxiety, and complications.

The oldest, simplest, and often still most relevant clinical measure is death. If a treatment reduces mortality from a disease, it is effective, or if the treatment causes a high rate of mortality its risk may be unacceptable. Mortality is easy to measure. There are no quibbles about its definition, its occurrence is almost always accurately recorded, and it is information that is usually readily available from a variety of sources. The purpose of many treatments, however, is not to prevent death but to relieve symptoms. And most treatments are rarely fatal. Thus, mortality may not be the most relevant outcome to measure in many situations.

Health Status, Functional Capacity, and Quality of Life Outcomes

Although few would quibble with the importance of relieving symptoms, curing disease, or reducing mortality, in recent years it has become apparent that classic clinical outcomes alone are sometimes inadequate measures of the value of a technology to the patient. Under certain circumstances, other outcomes may be more important. After all, the ultimate test is whether the patient feels that he or she is better off. What is the patient's perception of his or her health status or ability to carry out normal daily functions? After which treatment is the overall quality of life better? The answers to these questions do not necessarily coincide with "good" outcomes that are defined only in terms of mortality or disease state. Included in health status assessments are measures of functional status, emotional health, social interaction, cognitive function, and disability, as well as simple measures such as the ability to return to work (Epstein, 1990). Evaluations of health status and quality of life almost invariably require interviews or questionnaires, because these kinds of information are not routinely part of the hospital medical record (Cleary, 1988; Greenfield and Nelson, 1992; Lohr, 1992) and because they usually must be measured after the patient is discharged from the hospital.

Sources of Outcomes Data

Outcomes data may be collected prospectively or retrospectively. For prospective data collection, the investigators determine in advance which patients to study and what outcomes to measure. This information is then obtained for every study patient. Data sources include the patient's medical record, laboratory test results, and interviews or questionnaires administered to patients or care givers. Prospective data collection is regarded as superior to retrospective data collection because the necessary data are identified in advance and mechanisms are established to ensure that they are collected. Retrospective data usually consist of information collected for another purpose, such as medical records, discharge abstracts, or health insurance claims, but retrospective data may also include interviews or surveys of patients or care givers.

The most useful outcomes information comes from controlled studies in which treatment effects are determined by comparing outcomes in patients who receive the treatment with those in similar patients who do not. Uncontrolled studies typically collect data only on treated patients or on unselected groups of patients. Evaluation of effectiveness from data from an uncontrolled study requires the investigator to make assumptions or to have knowledge about outcomes in untreated patients. However, outcomes data from an study without a control group can nonetheless often be very useful. For example, if it is known that the mortality from a condition is 100 percent without treatment, then a treatment that reduces mortality to 50 percent is clearly effective.

Measuring Outcomes

The Randomized Clinical Trial

The randomized clinical trial (RCT) is considered the "gold standard" method for assessing clinical outcomes. Patients are identified as candidates by preset criteria and are then randomly assigned to receive the study treatment or an alternative treatment (the control treatment). The outcomes data to be collected (survival, symptom relief, health status, etc.) are agreed upon in advance and are collected concurrently on study and control patients. The outcomes in the two groups are then compared to determine whether the study treatment is advantageous.

If the selection criteria are rigidly adhered to, an RCT provides a valid comparison of two forms of treatment in comparable groups of patients. The random assignment of patients to study or control groups also distributes any unrecognized differences among patients randomly and evenly. Accordingly, differences in outcomes should be attributable solely to the treatment. For these reasons, many regard RCTs as the most valid way to measure efficacy.

The major disadvantage of RCTs is that they are expensive, time-consuming, and difficult to carry out. As a result, relatively few have been performed, so that rigorous comparative information on efficacy is available for only a small fraction of the indications for a small number of treatments. The other major problem with RCTs is that, to the extent that a treatment is perceived as efficacious, it may be difficult to get physicians and patients to agree to accept random assignment to treatment or no treatment groups. Subconsciously or otherwise, physicians may disqualify many of their patients who otherwise appear to be logical candidates. For example, it would now be difficult to conduct a randomized trial of laparoscopic cholecystectomy versus operative cholecystectomy because patients clearly prefer the laparoscopic approach. Finally, RCTs are typically conducted in or by academic medical centers, whose patients and doctors may not represent the population at large. Thus, results may not be fully generalizable to care in community hospitals.

Uncontrolled Clinical Series

Uncontrolled clinical series, usually from a single academic center, may provide data that are collected prospectively or retrospectively from patients receiving a single treatment. Their strength is that they demonstrate what can be accomplished in an optimal environment by skilled physicians. Their disadvantage is that they provide no comparison with alternative treatments. The results also may not be generalizable in that others may be unable to match them.

Data Registries

Data registries collect data prospectively from multiple institutions on patients with certain conditions or treatments such as those who have liver transplants or who have used a thrombolytic therapy. Because participants agree on the data to be collected and send the data to a central source as patients are encountered, registry data are usually reasonably complete. By pooling data from multiple sources, registries make it possible to assess outcomes for conditions or treatment groups that no individual institution treats in large numbers.

Like clinical series, the major deficiency of most registry series is the omission of a control group. Although registry data can be helpful in estimating operative mortality, long-term survival, and complication rates, the absence of similar information for untreated patients limits the ability to determine whether the treatment is better than the alternatives.

Cohort-Controlled Studies

Cohort-controlled studies attempt to measure outcomes by retrospectively comparing outcomes in treated and untreated patients who are selected according to the similarity of their clinical characteristics and risk factors as reflected in the available data. A well-done cohort-controlled study can be an acceptable substitute for an RCT. The principal hazard of cohort-controlled studies is that the investigator may fail to adequately identify or control for all of the important nontreatment variables that determine outcomes.

Hospital Patient Records

Hospital patient records are a rich and readily available source of clinical data that can be collected and analyzed retrospectively. The major disadvantage of abstracting data from hospital charts is that it is expensive. In addition, for most patients there is little or no long-term follow-up information. Getting further information from patient records in clinics and physicians' offices may be difficult and adds further expense.

Statewide Discharge Databases

Statewide discharge databases use data from patients' hospital records which have been abstracted by personnel from the medical records office. These discharge abstracts summarize key clinical and demographic data that can be used for outcomes analysis. In 23 states, all hospitals furnish discharge abstracts to a central health data registry, which provides statewide data for all discharged patients. These databases are virtually the only source of health care data for entire populations, as opposed to data from survey samples or data on subsets of the U.S. population, such as the Medicare population or the beneficiaries of an insurance plan. As such, they permit population-based analyses of regional variations in the use of various services and calculation of overall mortality rates as well as provide some other outcomes data, such as readmission or reoperation rates. Like registry data, this information is uncontrolled. However, because discharge data include all patients receiving a service, they provide an accurate measure of the outcomes that are actually achieved in practice. Not surprisingly, the results are typically inferior to those reported from uncontrolled series from academic centers or RCTs. For example, the average statewide mortality rate from CABG surgery in the early 1980s reported from California (Showstack et al., 1987), New York (Hannan et al., 1990), and Massachusetts (Dalen et al., 1990) was 3.7 percent, whereas that from the Cleveland Clinic series was 0.8 percent (Cosgrove et al., 1984).

A disadvantage of using discharge abstract data is that the amount of data in the abstracts is limited. Many important clinical details are not routinely captured and critical data, such as the results of tests done outside the hospital, may not be available. Errors in abstracting information from hospital records are common. In addition, the absence of universal patient identifiers in many state hospital discharge databases may make it impossible to determine long-term outcomes by tracking a patient and linking one hospital admission to another or to a transfer.

Claims Data Analysis

The availability of a nationwide database, the Medicare claims files, has spawned a large number of studies that attempt to assess the outcomes of various treatments and to demonstrate regional variations in use of various treatments. Mortality and readmission rates are the outcomes measures most commonly studied. The availability of large quantities of data without the need to abstract charts or perform surveys is appealing to researchers. With the Medicare databases, the outcomes of huge numbers of patients may be analyzed for almost any treatment.

Because claims data are obtained for a different purpose, it is not surprising that claims data often fail to include critical information on the patient's condition. Seldom is enough information present to permit adjustments for patient risk. This can lead to unjustified comparisons. For example, using claims data, it is possible to compare mortality in the year following a heart attack between those patients who underwent bypass surgery after the heart attack and those who did not. But the outcome is more related to the patient's condition than to the treatment. For example, if surgery is reserved for those who are in greatest danger of dying, the mortality rate from CABG surgery may be higher than that for patients who did not receive CABG surgery. Conversely, if only those with a good prognosis get operated on, surgical mortality will be less than that for the remainder. Without adjustment for patient risk, the data may lead to inaccurate or unproved conclusions.

Claims data analysis also does not deal with the selection effect, that is, the unmeasured characteristics of the patient that lead some to be selected and others not to be selected for surgery. Even RCTs have trouble dealing with this, despite their rigid and detailed entry criteria. Claims data may also distort or rearrange diagnoses or treatments so as to maximize payments. Finally, the use of multiple provider identification numbers and the separation of hospital and physician claims by Medicare has made attributing the provision of care to specific physicians difficult. This has recently been corrected.

The Uniform Clinical Data Set

The Health Care Financing Administration has investigated the practicality of abstracting much more clinical information directly from medical records. The information is incorporated into a large database, the Uniform Clinical Data Set. Although the validity of this approach is still unknown, the time and expense of record abstraction to obtain the data may limit the application of this method of data collection.

Evaluating Outcomes Data

Even when outcomes information is adequate, it must be evaluated and interpreted. It cannot be used "raw." Risk adjustment or patient selection may not have been optimal. Combining data from multiple sources may be difficult because studies may have been carried out on different populations, at different times, under different conditions, and either before and after a major technical advance. Data may be incomplete; even RCTs do not provide data on the benefits and risks of a treatment for *all* of its uses. Finally, data may be conflicting: two apparently excellent studies may come to opposite conclusions.

Two techniques have been developed to evaluate outcomes data: metaanalysis and appropriateness studies.

Meta-Analysis

Meta-analysis is a technique for combining the results of multiple RCTs to arrive at a conclusion that may not be justified by the results any of the individual studies alone (Lau et al., 1992; Sacks et al., 1987; Thacker, 1988). All of the data in each study are examined, categorized, and grouped according to important subcategories. The major effect of meta-analysis is to establish statistical significance. A difference in outcomes due to the use of a particular technology that is not significant in one study may turn out to be significant when the results from several studies are pooled. Conversely, pooling of data from a number of inconclusive studies may establish that a technology is ineffective.

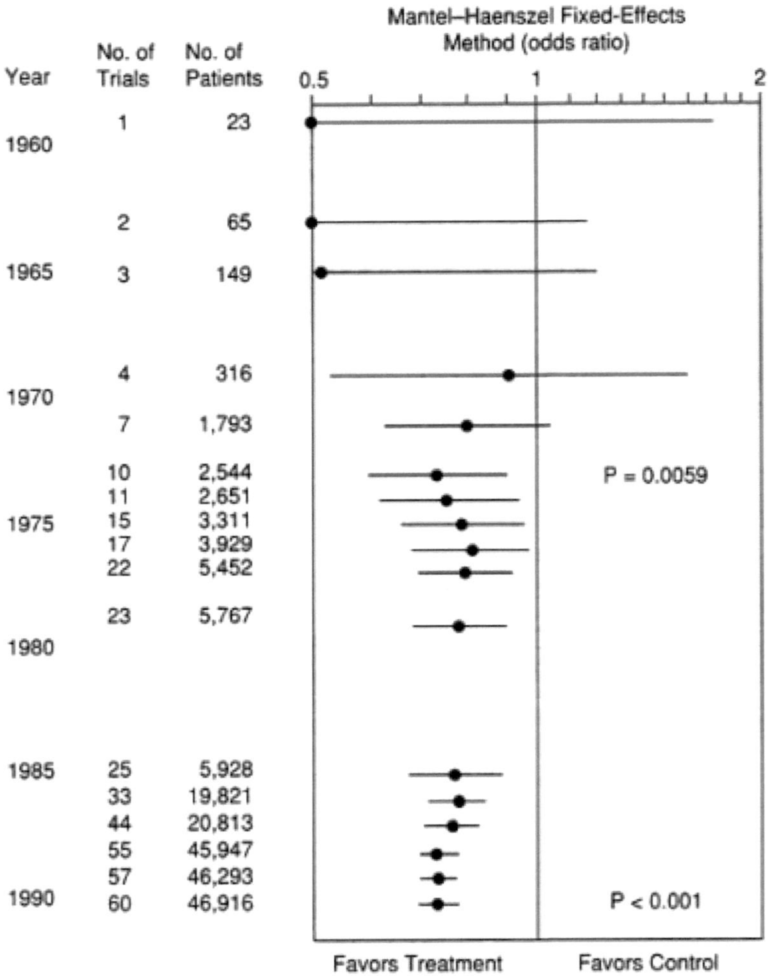

FIGURE 11-1 Cumulative meta-analyses of 60 trials of intravenous thrombolytic agents. "1" indicates that no difference from untreated patients. Less than "1" indicates that fewer numbers of patients died. SOURCE: Lau et al. (1992, p. 248).

Figure 11-1, from Lau et al. (1992), shows the results of cumulative metaanalyses of the efficacy of streptokinase treatment on acute myocardial infarction. The position of the dot indicates whether there were fewer deaths among treated patients. In this example, the very first trials showed that streptokinase was very effective (dot is to the left of the "1" in Figure 11-1). But the studies included low numbers of subjects, only 23 and 65 patients, so the validity of the findings was open to question. The confidence intervals were wide, as indicated by the line that crosses over the "1" in Figure 11-1. By 1974, 10 trials that included 2,544 patients had been carried out. The treatment was found to be effective in most of them, and the confidence limits were reduced so that the result was stable. Because meta-analyses were not being performed in 1974, however, questions about the efficacy of streptokinase treatment remained until several large RCTs were carried out in the late 1980s, more than 10 years later.

Unfortunately, most of the available outcomes data are not from RCTs, and therefore they are not suitable for meta-analysis. Furthermore, outcomes studies vary markedly in the selection of the populations, their nature, and in the quality of the data gathering process. Although all would agree that the assessment of outcomes should be based on science, someone needs to interpret what the science is.

Appropriateness Studies

Appropriateness studies address the issue of interpreting diverse outcomes data by obtaining group judgments from expert clinicians (Chassin et al., 1987; Park et al., 1986). Although the primary purpose of appropriateness studies is to determine for whom the treatment is indicated (see below), the first step in the process is evaluation of the evidence. Outcomes data from all sources—RCTs, meta-analyses, and studies of claims data, discharge data, registries, and clinical series—are evaluated. The expert panels comprise individuals who have vast clinical experience and who often have participated in many of the studies that generated the outcomes data. Thus, they have an intimate knowledge of the strengths and weaknesses of the data as well as of the clinical realities. From these data, their experience, and discussions they make independent subjective judgments of the benefits and harms of a treatment.

PORT Projects

Outcomes research received a major boost in 1990 when AHCPR expanded its Patient Outcomes Assessment Research Programs into the Patient Outcomes Research Teams (PORTs). These PORTs are centered in major medical schools and hospitals to conduct comprehensive outcomes studies of specific conditions, such as prostatic disease, stroke, and myocardial infarction (*Health Services Research,* 1990). These centers employ a variety of techniques, such as metaanalysis, decision analysis, claims data analysis, and surveys, to gather and analyze all available information concerning the effectiveness and appropriateness of use of treatments for the study conditions. Some PORT projects also evaluate health status and functional outcomes in deriving recommendations for preferred care.

FOR WHOM IS THE TREATMENT INDICATED?

As noted above, although a new technology might work in general for patients with a particular problem, it may not—and probably will not—work for all patients with that condition, and it may not be superior to alternative technologies for any patients. The term *appropriate* has been applied to the definition of the specific types of patients for whom a given therapeutic or diagnostic technology is preferred. A treatment is considered appropriate if the benefits sufficiently exceed the risks and negative effects and if it is superior to the alternatives (Park et al., 1986).

Two questions must be asked to translate outcomes information into patient care decisions and to determine for which patient a treatment is indicated: What are the *probabilities* of occurrence of good and bad outcomes from the treatment and its alternatives, and how do patients *value* each of those outcomes? Two methods have been developed to answer these questions: decision analysis and appropriateness methodology.

Both methods compare the effectiveness of alternative treatments in relieving symptoms or preventing death or disability for specific types of patients. Is bypass surgery preferable to angioplasty for patients with pain caused by coronary artery disease (angina)? How do the results of the two treatments compare with regard to early and late mortality, relief of pain, the prevention of heart attacks, and the need for later intervention?

However, the task is even more complex. The extent of disease and the nature and severity of the symptoms vary considerably among patients with the same condition. For example, the RAND evaluation scheme for CABG surgery required appropriateness judgments for nearly 3,000 distinct and different clinical scenarios that incorporate the major risk and severity factors for coronary artery disease (Leape et al., 1991).

Decision Analysis

Decision analysis is an analytic tool for assessing alternative treatments by the use of branched chain logic (Kassirer et al., 1987; Lusted, 1968; McNeil et al., 1975; Weinstein et al., 1980). A decision tree is created to display the choices, and numerical values are assigned to the probabilities of each outcome and to its value or, in the parlance, "utility" to the patient. Figure 11-2 shows an example of a decision analysis for a patient with an infected foot because of a poor blood supply caused by diabetes. The question is whether to amputate the lower leg or wait to see whether rest and antibiotics heal it.

The decision tree in Figure 11-2 outlines the options (the square node), which are to amputate or wait; the possible consequences or outcomes of each option (survival or death for amputation; healing or spread of infection for waiting); the probability of occurrence of each outcome (in parentheses); and the value (utility) of the possible outcomes (far right of diagram). By multiplying the utility by the probability of each outcome and adding the results for each option, one can compare the value (circle nodes) of each option. In the example, "wait" receives a value of 0.92 whereas "amputate" receives a value of 0.89. Therefore, waiting would be recommended.

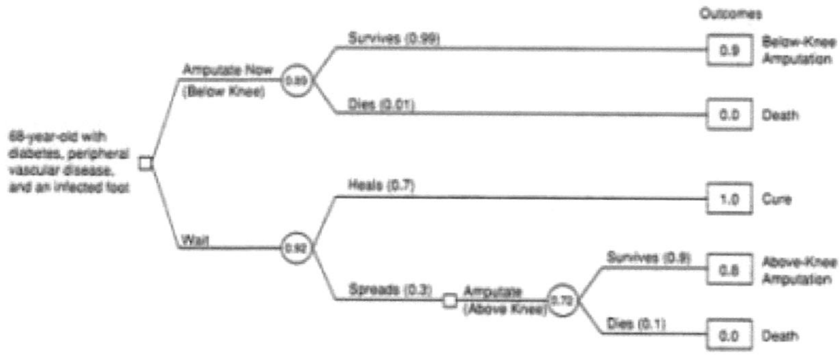

FIGURE 11-2 Example of a decision tree. Management of a 68-year-old man with diabetes, peripheral vascular disease, and an infected foot. SOURCE: Weinstein et al. (1980).

The advantages of decision analysis are that it requires that the clinical problem be formulated explicitly, identifying clearly all of the options and their consequences, and it requires quantitative estimates of both outcome probabilities and patient preferences. If outcomes data are available, probability estimates are sound and reproducible. When outcomes data are absent, probabilities must be estimated; experts may be asked to estimate probabilities. Patient utilities are usually determined by assigning values to reduced life expectancy. In some domains, such as cancer and renal disease, patient interviews have been used to generate utilities (Kassirer et al., 1987).

The validity of decision analysis depends on the validity of the values used for probability and utility. If outcomes data and measures of patient utilities are available, they are used. Otherwise, they must be estimated. The methods for doing this are crude. Furthermore, as Eddy (1984) demonstrated (Figure 11-3), expert estimates of probabilities are incredibly variable. Reproducible methods of eliciting preferences from a diverse or representative population of citizens also have not been developed. In the absence of good estimates of outcome probabilities or utilities, sensitivity analyses can be performed to determine whether variations in the estimates affect the conclusions. Often, they do not.

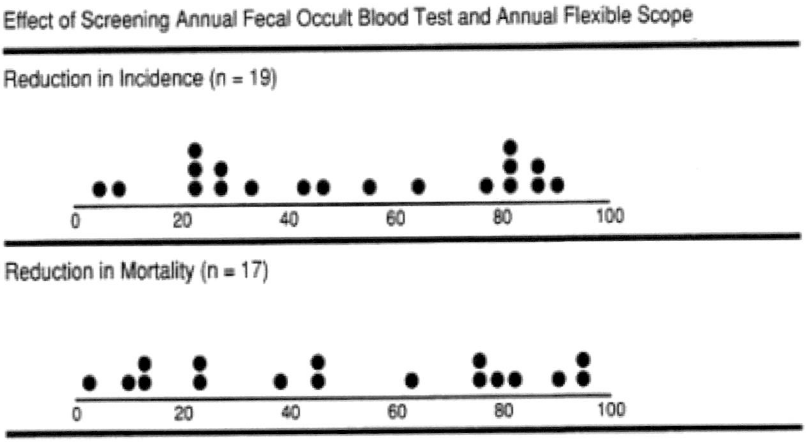

FIGURE 11-3 Probability estimates of experts in colorectal cancer detection. SOURCE: Adapted from Eddy (1984, p. 74).

Appropriateness Methodology

The appropriateness methodology is a group judgment process that asks a multidisciplinary panel of nationally esteemed clinical experts to evaluate the evidence and to make recommendations for use of a particular medical technology (Park et al., 1986). Its rationale is that RCTs and clinical series address only a small subset of patients with a disease. Therefore, data on outcomes are not available for most clinical situations. To determine the appropriateness of using a treatment for a specific clinical scenario, it is necessary to evaluate the outcomes data that do exist and "fill in the holes" when data are lacking.

Appropriateness studies address these issues by obtaining group judgments from expert clinicians who evaluate all the available outcomes data and provide judgments from their own clinical experience for those situations where scientific evidence of effectiveness does not exist. Because the instances of insufficient data far outnumber the instances of sufficient data, this methodology functions as a supplement to the use of outcomes data as well as a necessary bridge between science and clinical practice.

The expert panel rates the appropriateness of providing a treatment for each of its possible indications. A treatment is deemed appropriate if the trade-off between benefit and risk is sufficiently positive, i.e., the benefits outweigh the risks or negative effects by a sufficient margin that the treatment is worth providing. To be meaningful, the appropriateness decision (determining for whom a treatment is indicated) must be made at a highly specific level, which means that hundreds of indications must be rated for a single procedure.

The advantages of the appropriateness method is that it identifies all of the key factors that enter into the clinical decision, is highly specific, is exhaustive of the clinical possibilities, and provides a quantitative representation of the extent of agreement among the panelists.

Its disadvantage is that the ratings are implicit: global judgments of appropriateness by experts who estimate probabilities and impute patient utilities. The validities of the estimates, as well as the global judgments, therefore depend in part on how experts are selected.

Practice Guidelines

Practice guidelines are a means by which the results of outcomes and appropriateness studies are simplified and made accessible to clinicians (Leape, 1990). If sufficiently detailed, they have the potential to identify, and thereby to diminish, inappropriate use. Practice guidelines can also be used as review criteria for evaluating the quality of care or as criteria for payment for services. The development of practice guidelines is an active concern of a number of medical specialty societies, as well as a major mission of AHCPR, which sponsored two Institute of Medicine studies (1990, 1992).

SHOULD IT BE PROVIDED?

Having determined that a treatment is effective for some people, that is, it is superior to the existing alternatives, and having assessed which types of patients will benefit from it, one must then ask whether it should be made available to those patients (i.e., paid for). This requires that three questions be asked, in sequence: How great is the potential benefit? What is the cost-effectiveness of the technology? Is it worth what it costs (Eddy, 1990c, 1991 1a)?

How Great is the Potential Benefit?

The measure of benefit of a treatment is its *value.* A treatment is more valuable if it increases expected survival by five years than if it increases expected survival by only six months. A life-saving treatment (e.g., liver transplantation) is more valuable than one that relieves symptoms (e.g., hernia repair). Value equals the net benefit, that is, relief of symptoms, reduction of pain, or increased survival, minus risks, pain, and psychological effects. Only the patient can do the calculus, because only the patient experiences the symptoms and the risks, fears, anxieties, and pain. And only the patient receives the benefit. Therefore, only the patient can place a value on a treatment (Eddy, 1990c).

A relatively recent innovation that helps patients assess the value of a treatment has been the development of "Patient Shared Decisionmaking," in which patients see videotaped interviews of other patients who have undergone alterna tive treatments (Barry et al., 1988). Using interactive techniques, information on clinical, functional, and satisfaction outcomes is integrated in a highly personal and effective format.

Cost-Effectiveness

Cost-effectiveness calculates the benefits of a treatment in terms of dollars and years of life saved (Weinstein and Stason, 1977). In its simplest form, it asks the question, how much does a treatment cost for each life saved? For example, suppose mammography costs $50 per examination and is carried out every year on 100,000 women over the age of fifty. The annual costs would be $5 million. If this practice resulted in saving the lives of 1,000 women each year, the cost-effectiveness would be $5,000 per life saved ($5,000,000/1,000 lives saved).

Actually, it is more complicated than that, because one must add the costs of treatment for the cases that are discovered and also include the costs of all the negative biopsies that false-positive mammographies generate. One must also subtract the costs of treatment of all of the cases of breast cancer that would have occurred if these women had not gotten mammography. The *net* cost, per life saved, over what is being spent, is the information being sought.

Further refinements are necessary. Saving a life at age 30 is presumably more valuable—and therefore more cost-effective—than saving a life at age 80, so the cost per *year* of life saved is probably a more useful measure than cost per life alone. Furthermore, because a treatment or disease may leave the patient with some disability, the quality of the added life may be less than optimal. To capture these aspects, costs may be measured in terms of quality-adjusted life years (QALYs; LaPuma and Lawlor, 1990). For example, a patient whose life is saved by kidney dialysis may feel that dialysis treatments reduce the quality of life to 80 percent of its value with no disease. If the cost were $20,000 per year, then the cost per QALY is $25,000 ($20,000/0.8).

The major limiting factor in cost-effectiveness analysis, as with all evaluative research, is the lack of accurate outcomes information. Cost information is also not as easy to obtain as one might think. As every hospital administrator and payer knows, costs are not the same as charges. How is charge information adjusted for this? Charges also vary among similar providers in a region and among different regions of the country. How should they be averaged?

Cost-effectiveness analysis, like outcomes assessment, is not useful unless it is *very specific* (Eddy, 1992a,b). Annual screening mammography is not cost-effective for women in their twenties, for example, so specifying the age of the individual for whom a technology is appropriate is critical. For many high-technology therapeutic or diagnostic options, the relevant level of analysis is much more detailed: What is the cost-effectiveness of CABG surgery for a 60-year-old diabetic female with left main artery disease, a normal stress test, and good ventricular function? What is the cost effectiveness of CABG surgery for a hypertensive 75-year-old male with two-vessel disease, a positive stress test, and 60 percent reduction in ventricular function? Probably very different.

Is It Worth It?

This is the trade-off question. It asks: For the population that is paying for health care (whether members of a health maintenance organization, employees of a company, enrollees in a Blue Cross plan, or, in an ideal system, the nation as a whole) do the value and the cost-effectiveness of a technology *compared with those of other health services,* justify the provision of the treatment for all who need it (Eddy, 1990b)? If resources were not limited, then most would choose to provide all treatments that are appropriate, that is, that are "worth doing," even, perhaps, some treatments that provide only a small benefit. Resources are limited, however. Funding one service makes less money available for others. So how does one choose? Consider a simple example. Nationwide, approximately 3,000 liver transplants are performed each year, at a cost of about $300,000 each. Thus, the country spends about $900 million (3,000 x $300,000) for liver transplants annually. Is this preferable to using the same funds to provide prenatal care for 2 million pregnant women who do not now receive it? Or to using the funds to provide $5,000,000 to each of 180 emergency rooms in major cities to enable them to stay open and adequately handle an increasing load of trauma cases?

The methods for making these decisions are underdeveloped, largely because, as a society, the United States has until now refused to recognize the need to address the resource allocation issue. However, the basic steps of the process are clear. First, *community* judgments about the value and the cost-effectiveness of each service—the cost per QALY—must be made. Second, services should be compared and ranked according to these judgments. Third, we must decide what we will and will not pay for as part of a basic benefits package that is provided for all citizens. We must make the trade-offs explicit. The problem is not our lack of techniques for doing this, but our lack of political leadership that recognizes the need and has the will to set in motion the process to make these decisions.

MAJOR PROBLEMS IN THE APPLICATION OF EVALUATIVE RESEARCH

The foregoing summary, while brief, portrays an impressive armamentarium for evaluating technologies, most of which has been developed in the past 25 years. Although methodological questions remain unsolved, evaluative research already has the capacity to provide the guidance that the U.S. health care system so desperately needs. Yet, by any objective assessment, one is forced to conclude that evaluative research has so far had very little influence on the use of medical treatments. Why is this so?

There are at least three reasons. Until they are addressed, rational decisionmaking is unlikely to become much more than a fringe activity of academics. These reasons are:

- Inadequate resources have been committed to the task.
- We fail to deal with costs and trade-offs.
- We have not developed a public process for decisionmaking.

Inadequate Resources

Current expectations for the fruits of outcomes research are unrealistic. Although the recent expansion of the outcomes research effort with PORT projects and guideline development is encouraging, these are really only pilot projects—feasibility studies. I think they will be successful, but the number of treatments being evaluated is a tiny fraction of what is needed for even the high-cost technologies. They must be expanded a hundredfold. In addition, it is seldom possible to use "outcomes" alone to determine whether a treatment is worth doing. Outcomes must be evaluated in the context of a host of clinical variables and costs must be compared with alternatives. It is a complicated and expensive task.

The job to be done is immense. The resources applied to it so far have not been sufficient. Is it too much to ask that one cent of each U.S. health care dollar be spent to determine whether the other 99 cents is well spent? Any successful industry spends at least that much on quality assessment. One percent of current health care expenditures would be $8 billion! Even 1/10 of that, 0.1 percent, would be $800 million, more than six times the amount allocated to AHCPR for evaluative research in fiscal year 1992. Although industry, particularly pharmaceutical manufacturers, spends an additional several hundred million dollars on preapproval drug and device testing, the total of public and private funding for evaluative research is small in comparison with the need. Until we make a much greater commitment, the impact of evaluative research will be limited.

We Fail to Deal with Costs and Trade-offs

The focus of evaluative research has traditionally been on the primary outcome question of effectiveness—does the technology work in practice? In recent years, with decision analysis and appropriateness research, the inquiry has been broadened to ask under which specific circumstances a treatment is better than the alternatives. We have asked whether a treatment is worth doing. And we have finally asked patients to value the care they might receive. But we have shied away from the really important question: Is the additional benefit worth the cost (Eddy, 1990b)?

In fact, some people believe that it is unethical to ask that question. They think that physicians should offer, and payers should cover, anything that might possibly help a patient. Indeed, it is politically dangerous to raise the cost question, especially if the conclusion is that a treatment may *not* be worthwhile for someone who has severe disease with limited life expectancy (such as AIDS), or for somebody for whom the benefit is relatively small (such as CABG surgery is for some), or for a technology for which the cost is very high (such as bone marrow transplantation).

But this is the question that must be asked. It is, in fact, unethical *not* to ask it. Of course, cost counts. Would any payer approve *any* technology that cost $1 billion per patient? No. Would any payer bother to discuss coverage of a technology that cost $1? No. We must ask the trade-off questions. We make the trade-offs now, providing liver transplants for some and no prenatal care for others, but we make them by default and by ability to pay, not by deliberation and choice.

At some point in the not too distant future, we will get serious about reducing health care costs. When that happens, basic and necessary care (care that every payment plan must provide) and care that will not be provided as a basic benefit will need to be identified. Those decisions will turn on comparative value.

The experiment with Medicaid coverage revision in Oregon has pilot tested one way to do this. A comprehensive process was developed to elicit community preferences; this involved local and statewide meetings, a telephone poll of selected citizens, and interviews with special groups. Cost-benefit analysis was then used to prioritize treatments. The initial results were unsatisfactory because life-saving therapies were undervalued. This led to a reconsideration and revision of the list, which was finally approved by the state legislature. The necessary waiver to implement the plan for Medicaid patients was then initially rejected, but subsequently approved, by the federal Department of Health and Human Services.

Although some have objected to the Oregon plan because it rations health care only for the poor, others have lauded the fact that at least it does so explicitly and according to the specific health care service, rather than implicitly by limiting access of individuals, as in the current Medicaid system. Leaving aside the merits of either of these arguments, it is apparent that some valuable lessons about how to begin to make allocation decisions have been learned from the Oregon experience (Eddy, 1991b). First, it demonstrates how difficult it is to place a proper value on services. Researchers found that people valued lifesaving treatments more highly than others, regardless of "years of life saved" or other metrics. Second, the need for a high degree of specificity in describing condition-treatment pairs was reconfirmed. This immensely complicates the allocation process, but it cannot be avoided. Third, it reemphasized the tremendous need for good data regarding outcomes and costs.

The Oregon experiment asked the right question: Should a particular treatment or diagnostic technology be provided? It has moved this issue onto center stage. Although the process has many imperfections, it is, as Eddy (1991b) has noted, at least an open process with the capacity for self-correction. The research agenda for improvement has been established.

There is another lesson from Oregon: health care probably cannot be rationed in the United States unless it is rationed for all citizens. This means that the trade-off decisions must apply to everyone to be accepted. It must appear to be fair. If there is to be a basic benefits package, it must apply to all.

We Have Not Made Decisionmaking a Public Process

We have it all backwards. Adoption decisions are made by hospitals, payers, and plan administrators, and physicians decide which services to provide for their patients. It should be the other way around: society should decide which services it wants for its citizens. Physicians should then provide them and payers should pay for them. The *value* of a new treatment is determined by what it does for the recipient, that is, the patient (Eddy, 1990b,c). Only patients can decide whether that value is worth the cost. It is the patient who gets the benefits and suffers the harms, not the physician or the payer. The patient is far better qualified to decide if a treatment is worth it. It is also all of us—as patients, potential or actual—who, in the aggregate, pay for health care for everyone, either directly or indirectly. The public has the right to make the decisions on how resources are to be allocated.

Not only has the public not been asked to make these decisions, but as patients we are also denied access to knowledge of the crucial ingredient needed to make even individual decisions rationally: monetary costs. Patients almost never pay directly the financial costs of a treatment they receive. In fact, in most cases, the patient does not even *know* the costs of a specific treatment. Similarly, the public has been shielded from any responsibility for allocating resources. By divorcing costs from decisionmaking, we have made it impossible for ordinary citizens to assess the value of health care. By default, the task has fallen to the payers and providers. To rationalize adoption decisions, this process needs to be reversed and coverage decisions need to be made by those who will receive the benefit.

It is necessary to investigate whom to ask and how to frame the questions. What are the relative roles of those who have a disease and would benefit from an expensive treatment, versus the roles of all others who have, say, only a 1:100,000 chance that they might someday need it? What is the treatment worth to each of those groups? What metric should be used to measure worth? Clearly, if you must pay for something directly, "worth" depends in large measure on what you can afford. A treatment cannot be "worth" $100,000 to someone who could never raise that amount of money; it might be worth more than that to someone who could raise a lot of money. How can these points of view be harmonized?

As the Oregon experiment has demonstrated, assessing public values and making public decisions is not easy, but it has begun. We must now proceed to develop an effective and feasible process, one that is balanced, fair, and acceptable to all.

RECOMMENDATIONS

The Federal Government's Role

To relate adoption decisions to evaluative research, we need much more evaluative research. We must vastly expand and strengthen all aspects of technology assessment: effectiveness and outcomes research, appropriateness research, the methodology of determining patient preferences, and methods for performing the trade-off decisions among competing technologies. It seems inescapable that the federal government must play a much larger role.

There are several reasons for this. First, the multifaceted nature of the new technology assessment and, in particular, the need to develop and implement methods for incorporating patient preferences require that technology assessment be a public process. The entire process is driven by the end result, the adoption decision. These decisions about which services will be provided must be public decisions made on the basis of public information of effectiveness, costs, and appropriateness, not private decisions made on the basis of private data, feasibility, and profits. They must express community values.

Second, most of the tasks are those for which industry has neither expertise nor interest in performing. It is reasonable to require the manufacturer of a new drug or device to demonstrate that it performs its stated function and that it does so safely. It is not reasonable to expect the manufacturer to objectively assess whether the new drug or device is superior to competitive products or, if it is, whether it is worth the extra cost. Similarly, the surgeon is not the person best qualified to evaluate the benefit or value of an operation compared with the benefit of another treatment (a drug, for example) for the same condition.

Third, the magnitude of the task requires resources that far exceed the capacity of health-related foundations in the private sector to support, even if they were to devote all of their funds to these activities.

Fourth, the process must be coordinated. Some authority (such as the Food and Drug Administration) must ensure that a new treatment is systematically moved along the assessment pathway from demonstration of efficacy to the final decision as to whether it should be provided as part of basic health services. No private organization can do that.

Finally, centralizing responsibility for coordinating and ensuring that technology assessment is carried out at all levels is the only way to reduce the duplication and inefficiency now incurred because payers and hospitals perform their own evaluations to make needed coverage and adoption decisions. This process, however, should be insulated from the political process. Just as the U.S. Congress does not tell the Food and Drug Administration which drugs to approve, it should not certify effective services.

There are several options. Either the Office of Health Technology Assessment of the Department of Health and Human Services could be given an expanded role or a new Health Technology Board could be established with the responsibility of carrying the products of AHCPR-funded research through the process to final assessment of effectiveness, appropriateness, and cost-effectiveness.

Although these first stages of evaluation of a service could legitimately be centralized, ascertaining public preferences and performing the trade-off decisions that determine what is and what is not paid for is a political decision. It is probably best done at a regional level by those who will have to live by the consequences.

An Optimal Evaluation and Approval Process

The ideal evaluation and approval process ensures an orderly progression of a treatment through the stages of evaluation. The problems presented by new technologies and treatments are very different from those of treatments currently in use.

New Technologies

In the optimal system, the use of a new treatment prior to approval would be prohibited. After a treatment has been shown to be efficacious by the innovator, clinical trials would be carried out. This would be an extension of the current process for new drugs. These trials would be RCTs conducted by a limited number of centers and funded by the federal government under the peer review approval process. The first step, therefore, is to generate outcomes and cost information. Second, the specific indications for which use of a technology is appropriate should be defined. Uses for which a treatment is found to be ineffective would not be evaluated further. Third, the value of effective treatments will need to be assessed by patient panels. Finally, a community-based process would be used to determine whether appropriate and valued services are worth their costs and to rank each new service in comparison with other services being provided. The end result would be a basic benefits package that all payers would be required to provide. Inappropriate services would be prohibited, but other services that were not included in the basic benefits package could be available under a self-pay or optional insurance program.

Established Technologies

For medical technologies now in use, the same judgments described above for new technologies would need to be made. Clearly, this is an immense task, because there are thousands of diagnostic and therapeutic treatments currently in use, each with many indications. Additional outcomes data will need to be obtained for many by means of RCTs or prospective data collection. For debatable technologies, evaluation of effectiveness could be facilitated by making physician and patient participation in data collection a condition of payment. Each service currently being provided will eventually need to be valued and either approved or rejected as part of a basic benefits package.

Payers' Roles

Payers would have several new roles in this coordinated system of evaluation and adoption decisionmaking. First, they would provide the detailed cost information needed for cost-effectiveness analysis and allocation decisions. Second, all payers would be required to cover all services that are defined as part of a basic benefits package. Coverage of optional services could form the basis of a variety of optional insurance packages. Finally, payers would continue to pay for established technologies while they were being evaluated for appropriateness and cost-effectiveness.

A Public Process

It is evident that no one—payers, providers, or patients—is happy with the current methods used to determine which services should be provided. A key reason is that we continue to duck the central issue: What should and what should not be paid for? Although a public process for rendering these judgments will always be a little messy and never entirely satisfactory to all concerned, I believe that it will be far more acceptable, and certainly more equitable, than our current method.

REFERENCES

Alderman, E., Bourassa, M., Cohen, L., et al. 1990. Ten-year follow-up of survival and myocardial infarction in the randomized Coronary Artery Surgery Study. *Circulation* 82:1-18.

Barry, M. J., Mulley, A. G., Jr., Fowler, F. J., and Wennberg, J. E. 1988. Watchful waiting vs immediate transurethral resection for symptomatic prostatism. *Journal of the American Medical Association* 259:3010-3017.

Chassin, M. R., Brook, R. H., Park, R. E., et al. 1986. Variations in the use of medical and surgical services by the Medicare population. *New England Journal of Medicine* 314:285-290.

Chassin, M. R., Kosecoff, J., Park, R. E., et al. 1987. Does inappropriate use explain geographic variations in the use of health care services? A study of three procedures. *Journal of the American Medical Association* 258:2533-2537.

Cleary, P. D. 1988. Patient satisfaction as an indicator of quality care. *Inquiry* 25:25-36. *Congressional Record,* November 21, 1989, pp. H9360-H9363.

Cosgrove, D., Loop, F., Lytle, B., et al. 1984. Primary myocardial revascularization. *Circulation* 88:673-684.

Dalen, J. E., Goldberg, R. J., D'Arpa, D., et al. 1990. Coronary heart disease in Massachusetts: The years of change (1980-1984). *American Heart Journal* 119:502-512.

Eddy, D. M. 1984. Variations in physician practice: The role of uncertainty. *Health Affairs* 3:74-89.

Eddy, D. M. 1990a. Anatomy of a decision. *Journal of the American Medical Association* 263:441-443.

Eddy, D. M. 1990b. What do we do about costs? *Journal of the American Medical Association* 264:1161-1170.

Eddy, D. M. 1990c. Connecting value and costs. *Journal of the American Medical Association* 264:1737-1739.

Eddy, D. M. 1991a. Rationing by patient choice. Journal of the American Medical Association 265:105-108.

Eddy, D. M. 1991b. What's going on in Oregon? *Journal of the American Medical Association* 266:417-420.

Eddy, D. M. 1992a. Cost-effectiveness analysis: A conversation with my father. *Journal of the American Medical Association* 267:1669-1675.

Eddy, D. M. 1992b. Cost-effectiveness analysis: Is it up to the task? *Journal of the American Medical Association* 267:3342-3348.

Epstein, A. M. 1990. The outcome movement—Will it get us where we want to go? *New England Journal of Medicine* 323:266-269.

Fuchs, V. R., and Garber, A. M. 1990. The new technology assessment. *New England Journal of Medicine* 323:673-677.

Graboys, T. B., Headley, A., Lown, B., Lampert, S., and Blatt, C. M. 1987. Results of a second-opinion program for coronary artery bypass graft surgery. *Journal of the American Medical Association* 258:1611-1614.

Greenfield, S., and Nelson, E. C. 1992. Recent developments and future issues in the use of health status assessment measures in clinical settings. *Medical Care* 30:23-41.

Greenspan, A. M., Kay, H. R., Berger, B. C., et al. 1988. Incidence of unwarranted implantation of permanent cardiac pacemakers in a large medical population. *New England Journal of Medicine* 318:158-163.

Hannan, E., Kilburn, H., O'Donnell, J., et al. 1990. Adult open heart surgery in New York State: An analysis of risk factors and hospital mortality rates. *Journal of the American Medical Association* 264:2768-2774.

Health Services Research. 1990. Patient Outcomes Research Teams: A new strategy for health services research on medical care quality. Editorial. *Health Services Research* 25:691-737.

Institute of Medicine. 1990. *Clinical Practice Guidelines: Directions for a New Program.* M. J. Field and K. N. Lohr, eds. Washington, D.C.: National Academy Press.

Institute of Medicine. 1992. *Guidelines for Clinical Practice: From Development to Use.* M. J. Field and K. N. Lohr, eds. Washington, D.C.: National Academy Press.

Kahn, K. L., Kosecoff, J., Chassin, M. R., Solomon, D. H., and Brook, R. H. 1988. The use and misuse of upper gastrointestinal endoscopy. *Annals of Internal Medicine* 109:664-670.

Kassirer, J. P., Moskowitz, A. J., Lau, J., and Pauker, S. G. 1987. Decision analysis: A progress report. *Annals of Internal Medicine* 106:275-291.

LaPuma, J., and Lawlor, E. F. 1990. Quality adjusted life-years. *Journal of the American Medical Association* 263:2917-2921.

Lau, J., Antman, E. M., Jimenez-Silva, J., et al. 1992. Cumulative meta-analysis of therapeutic trials for myocardial infarction. *New England Journal of Medicine* 327:248-254.

Leape, L. L. 1990. Practice guidelines—An overview. *Quality Review Bulletin* 16:42-49.

Leape, L. L., Park, R. E., Solomon, D. H., et al. 1990. Does inappropriate use explain small area variations in the use of health care services? *Journal of the American Medical Association* 263:669-672.

Leape, L. L., Hilbome, L. H., Kahan, J. P., et al. 1991. Coronary Artery Bypass Graft: A Literature Review and Ratings of Appropriateness and Necessity. Publication JRA02. Santa Monica, Calif.: The RAND Corporation.

Lewis, C. E. 1969. Variations in the incidence of surgery. *New England Journal of Medicine* 281:880-884.

Lohr, K. N. 1992. Applications of health status assessment measures in clinical practice. *Medical Care* 30:1-14.

Lusted, L. B. 1968. *Introduction to Medical DecisionMaking.* Springfield, I11.: Charles C Thomas.

Mayberg, M. R., Wilson, E. W., Yatsu, F., et al. 1991. Carotid endarterectomy and prevention of cerebral ischemia in symptomatic carotid stenosis. *Journal of the American Medical Association* 266:3289-3294.

McNeil, B. J., Keeler, E., and Adelstein, S. J. 1975. Primer on certain elements of medical decisionmaking. *New England Journal of Medicine* 293:211-215.

Park, R. E., Fink, A., Brook, R. H., et al. 1986. Physician ratings of appropriate indications for six medical and surgical procedures. *American Journal of Public Health* 76:766-772.

Sacks, H. S., Berrier, J., Reitman, D., Ancona-Berk, V. A., and Chalmers, T. C. 1987. Meta-analyses of randomized controlled trials. *New England Journal of Medicine* 316:450-455.

Showstack, J., Rosenfeld, K., Gamick, D., et al. 1987. Association of volume with outcome of coronary artery bypass graft surgery. Scheduled vs nonscheduled operations. *Journal of the American Medical Association* 257:785-789.

Thacker, S. B. 1988. Meta-analysis: A quantitative approach to research integration. *Journal of the American Medical Association* 259:1685-1689.

Weinstein, M. C., and Stason, W. B. 1977. Foundations of cost-effectiveness analysis for health and medical practices. *New England Journal of Medicine* 296:716-721.

Weinstein, M. C., Fineberg, H. V., Elstein, A. S., et al. 1980. *Clinical Decision Analysis.* New York, N.Y.: W. B. Saunders.

Wennberg, J. E., and Gittlesohn, A. 1973. Small area variations in health care delivery. *Science* 142:1102-1108.

Wennberg, J. E., and Gittelsohn, A. 1982. Variations in medical care among small areas. *Scientific America* 246:120-134.

Winslow, C. M., Kosecoff, J. B., Chassin, M. R., Kanouse, D. E., and Brook, R. H. 1988a. The appropriateness of performing coronary artery bypass surgery. *Journal of the American Medical Association 260:505-509.*

Winslow, C. M., Solomon, D. H., Chassin, M. R., et al. 1988b. The appropriateness of carotid endarterectomy. *New England Journal of Medicine* 318:721-727.

12

Manufacturers' Responses to the Increased Demand for Outcomes Research

ANN K. M. MARSHALL

The title of this chapter would imply that health care manufacturers face a well-defined demand for outcomes research. This is not so. Rather, they confront an evolving and heterogeneous set of market dynamics that may collectively be referred to as the *technology assessment trend.* Simply stated, the technology assessment trend emphasizes the importance of considering comparative effectiveness and relative value in evaluating medical technologies. But the application of this concept varies considerably among providers, payers, and regulators and over time-creating uncertainty on the part of manufacturers as to precisely what sorts of information will be required as the technology assessment trend matures. Manufacturers' activities in the area of outcomes research reflect the nascent stage of this trend.

To gain perspective into manufacturers' outcomes research activities, it is important to highlight the factors that have driven the emphasis on technology assessment and their connection with outcomes research. First, however, it is useful to provide working definitions of *medical technology assessment and outcomes research.*

TECHNOLOGY ASSESSMENT AND OUTCOMES RESEARCH

Medical technology assessment can be defined as the careful evaluation of a medical technology for evidence of the health, economic, social, and ethical consequences of its technical applications, both in absolute terms and in comparison with other competing technologies (Office of Technology Assessment, U.S. Congress, 1982; Perry, 1988). As discussed elsewhere in this volume, real-life technology assessments are less comprehensive than the ideal suggested by the above definition. Moreover, the focus of a technology assessment depends on the technology assessed (e.g., drug, device, or procedure) and the type of organization conducting the assessment (e.g., hospital, managed care organization, third-party payer, government agency, academe, or a manufacturer). The spectrum of technology assessment ranges from more or less informed technology appraisals to controlled clinical studies, as depicted in Figure 12-1.

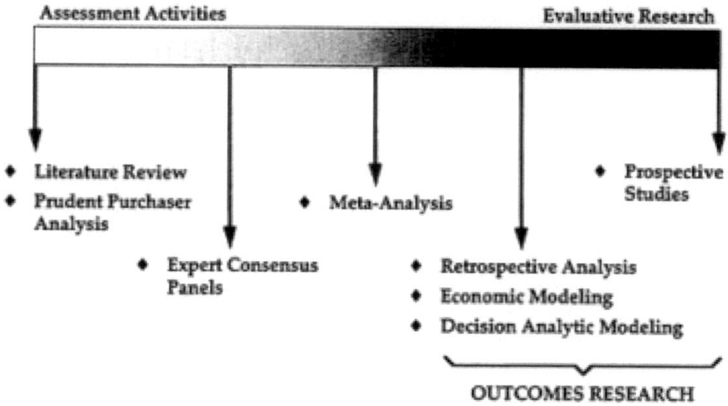

FIGURE 12-1 The spectrum of technology assessment.

Outcomes research can be viewed as a subset of technology assessment activities. It encompasses prospective clinical studies, retrospective analyses of large health databases, and economic and decision-analytic modeling. In addition to relevant areas of clinical expertise, outcomes research draws upon the fields of epidemiology, economics, and health services research. Outcomes research can be roughly divided into two categories: economic outcomes research (cost-benefit, cost-effectiveness, and cost-utility analyses) and patient outcomes research (measurement of treatment outcomes such as functional status, quality of life, and long-term survival). Patient outcomes research extends beyond the safety and efficacy studies traditionally conducted by pharmaceutical companies. First, whereas traditional efficacy research often studies intermediate or surrogate endpoints, patient outcomes research focuses on "outcomes of real interest to patients," such as death and disability (Eddy, 1990). Second, patient outcomes studies generally incorporate comparisons of competing treatments and may even compare different treatment modalities (e.g., drug versus procedure).[1]

[1] Strictly speaking, the traditional safety and efficacy studies conducted by pharmaceutical companies to support New Drug Applications filed with the Food and Drug Administration are also outcomes research. However, the term *outcomes research* is often used to refer to the study of outcomes *other than* classical safety and efficacy outcomes—and will be so used in this chapter.

Although health care providers and third-party payers use outcomes research findings in their technology assessments, they rarely conduct outcomes research themselves. The Agency for Health Care Policy and Research (AHCPR) develops rigorously systematic syntheses of the literature and expert opinion, but it produces little in the way of outcomes research, per se. In the future, more AHCPR and third-party payer activities in meta-analysis, decision-analytic modeling, and retrospective health database analysis can be expected. For the most part, however, experimental research on patient and economic outcomes will continue to be conducted by manufacturers and academic or private-sector researchers, the latter frequently being at least partly funded by manufacturers.

THE TECHNOLOGY ASSESSMENT TREND: WHY NOW?

Although "technology assessment" and "outcomes research" have only recently become household phrases, the origins of the technology assessment trend may be traced back almost 20 years. In the early 1970s, John Wennberg and others documented significant geographic differences in the rates at which certain medical procedures were being performed that could not be explained by differences in the incidence or severity of disease among the populations being compared (Wennberg and Gittelsohn, 1973; Wennberg et al., 1987, 1989). These differences naturally raised questions about appropriateness of care and optimal treatment patterns, questions that triggered a surge of interest in studying patient outcomes.

The challenges of patient outcomes research lead clinical researchers to expand their scope of clinical methodologies and techniques. For example, the limitations of randomized, controlled clinical trials (RCTs) in assessing the relative effectiveness of treatment options in clinical practice encouraged researchers to turn to epidemiology—a field in which researchers have expertise in such areas as observational study design, analysis of large databases, and knowledge of the natural history of diseases. Within the field of health status measurement, new instruments were developed to measure disease-specific parameters. In addition, more responsive instruments were developed to measure more discrete, but clinically relevant, changes in health status and quality of life.[2] These methodological advances helped fuel what Wennberg has called the "outcomes agenda," namely, the "systematic evaluation of all of the outcomes that are relevant to patients-mortality, morbidity, complications, symptom reduction, and functional status improvement" (Wennberg, 1990, p. 45).

[2] See *Medical Innovation at the Crossroads.* Vol. 1, *Modern Methods of Clinical Investigation* (Institute of Medicine, 1990) for an overview of the techniques and methods that have been employed in outcomes research, including observational methodologies, meta-analysis, decision analysis, and health status measurement. See Freund and Dittus (1992) for a concise summary of the techniques and methods specific to economic outcomes research.

Despite its potential to significantly advance the practice of medicine, patient outcomes research probably would have remained in the domain of academic researchers were it not for the intractable escalation of health care costs. As the 1980s progressed and the oft-recited waves of belt-tightening and cost-shifting rippled through the U.S. health care system, policymakers noted the potential of outcomes research concepts and methodologies to help rationalize health care expenditures. Patient outcomes research held out the hope that, by eliminating inappropriate and suboptimal health care, costs could be controlled without diminishing quality of or access to care. Faith in the promise of health care rationalization was the impetus behind the U.S. Congress' creation and aggressive funding of AHCPR in 1989-1990.

The emphasis on *economic* outcomes research has been fueled by public sector "prudent purchaser" initiatives and the growth of managed care. Third-party payers, health maintenance organizations (HMOs), and formulary committees are now important decisionmakers in the process of technology adoption and diffusion. Unlike physicians, these new decisionmakers have a direct interest in cost containment, and they have the consolidated market clout to demand evidence of the comparative effectiveness and relative value of new drugs, devices, and procedures. Hospital, HMO, and Medicaid formulary committees are increasingly considering outcomes research—particularly economic outcomes research—in their drug formulary decisions. Third-party payers, both public and private, now often require evidence of the comparative effectiveness of new therapeutic or diagnostic procedures before granting coverage or adjusting reimbursement levels for those procedures. These market trends are creating new informational requirements for pharmaceutical companies and high-tech, procedure-related device companies.

MANUFACTURERS' RESPONSE TO THE TECHNOLOGY ASSESSMENT TREND[3]

Device Companies

The U.S. medical device industry comprises roughly 7,000 manufacturers whose varied outputs include mundane commodity products such as tongue depressors and surgical masks, expensive capital equipment such as gammaradiation sterilizers and magnetic resonance imaging scanners, high-technology singleuse products such as percutaneous transluminal coronary angioplasty catheters

[3] This chapter utilizes information obtained through 23 interviews with representatives of 15 manufacturers and 4 consulting or research organizations. To ensure the anonymity of interviewees and their companies, only publicly disclosed examples of manufacturer outcomes research activities are cited specifically. The comments and opinions expressed in this chapter are the author's and do not represent the views or policies of Abbott Laboratories.

and biodegradable sutures, and equipment ranging from ventilators to endoscopic staplers. It should be acknowledged from the start that only a small percentage of these companies view outcomes research as critical to the commercial success of their products. For the most part, only manufacturers of high-cost and innovative technologies that have a direct impact on patient therapeutic or diagnostic outcomes are likely to consider conducting outcomes research.

Historically, device companies' introduction to outcomes research arose out of their struggles with coverage and reimbursement in the early to mid-1980s. At that time, a number of essentially new, medically complex devices and technologies had been approved by the Food and Drug Administration (FDA) but were not immediately granted coverage by the Health Care Financing Administration (HCFA), the Blue Cross and Blue Shield carriers (the Blues), or private insurers. Instead, third-party payers conducted their own technology assessments of such FDA-approved devices before making coverage decisions, often consuming two or three years in the process. (Examples of devices subjected to additional third-party payer scrutiny include the implantable infusion pump, cardiac defibrillator, magnetic resonance imaging scanners, extracorporeal shock wave lithotripter, and cochlear implant.) The delay of third-party payer coverage created an extremely costly post-FDA hurdle that had to be crossed before a manufacturer could accomplish full commercialization.[4]

As mentioned above, payers' newly activist stance in questioning costly new technologies was prompted by the cost-containment imperative. When a new medical technology threatened to significantly increase expenditures, payers wanted to know whether and to what extent it improved the quality of patient care in comparison with existing treatment options. Payers were obliged, however, to pose their questions in terms of the regulatory and contractual language that governed their coverage obligations: Was the new device or procedure "reasonable and necessary" (Medicare) or "medically standard and acceptable"/"not investigational" (private payers and the Blues). The underlying question, however, was one of value: Will the additional cost of this new technology yield improved outcomes (or outcomes at least equivalent to those from existing technologies) for the beneficiary?

The fact that payers answered these questions by conducting their own technology assessments sent two clear messages to the involved device manufacturers. First, FDA's process of approval for devices did not leave payers sufficiently comfortable about the effectiveness of novel devices. Second, even granting the effectiveness issue, the fact that FDA approval could be obtained without presenting comparative data left open the question of whether a new technology

[4] See Bucci et al. (1985), Kane and Manoukian (1989), McGivney (1991), and VanAntwerp (1985) for background on the impact of technology assessment activities of third-party payers on the adoption and diffusion of new device and procedure technologies. Bucci et al., Kane and Manoukian, and McGivney also discuss the related but additional impact of inadequate reimbursement.

was worth the (usually) higher cost. These concerns were evident in the negative recommendations of the technology assessments conducted by the Office of Health Technology Assessment (OHTA), as commissioned by the HCFA, during this pivotal period of the mid-1980s. OHTA cited the lack of well-controlled clinical trials demonstrating safety and effectiveness as the basis for its negative recommendations—although it is worth noting that few of the devices receiving *positive* OHTA recommendations had been supported by well-controlled clinical trials showing safety and effectiveness (Bucci et al., 1985). Nonetheless, by the mid-1980s manufacturers began to realize that they could significantly reduce the risk of coverage delay or denial if they produced well-controlled clinical trials that showed the comparative effectiveness of their devices.

It should be mentioned that, since the late 1980s, trends in the FDA device approval process have been consistent with the technology assessment trend. Whereas previously the FDA tended to focus on whether a device was safe and performed as intended, by the late 1980s reviewers also emphasized that "the 'clinical utility' of all devices undergoing review in a ... [pre-marketing approval application] must be established prior to approval" (Office of Drug Evaluation, Food and Drug Administration, 1991). For example, the issue of clinical utility was central to the FDA's unwillingness to approve Healthdyne's home uterine monitor for use in preterm labor. Although the FDA was satisfied that the device accurately monitored the intensity and timing of contractions, it required evidence that such monitoring made a difference in the outcomes of deliveries. More broadly, device manufacturers noted that the FDA had come to require more rigorous biostatistical analyses to support effectiveness claims in premarketing approval applications, and by the end of the 1980s often required control arms and even comparative analysis in cases in which it would not have done so in the past. This new rigor is at the root of the protracted difficulties experienced by the companies Domier and Medstone in trying to show the clinical effectiveness of their biliary lithotripter devices (Stern, 1990).

In this environment, device companies have become much more sensitized to the need to conduct patient outcomes research. However, the decision to conduct such research is very much product specific and depends on affirmative answers to such questions as: Is this an essentially new product (as opposed to a "follow on") that will increase expenditures by the health care system? Is the reimbursement structure for procedures in which this product is used likely to pose difficulties for users of the product? Are payers likely to try to restrict the use of this product to a limited set of indications?

Because a limited number of new medical devices face these issues, the pool of device manufacturers who conduct outcomes research is rather small and quite sophisticated compared with the broader population of device manufacturers. These "high-tech" device manufacturers have tended to sponsor prospective controlled clinical trials, typically focusing on patient outcomes. The types of endpoints that have been studied vary by technology, but include survival, disease, functional status, and quality-of-life measures. Some medical devices are particularly well suited to quality-of-life studies (e.g., artificial hips and incontinence devices), and a fair amount of work has been done in that area. In a number of cases, device manufacturers have undertaken considerable work in support of their outcomes research capabilities. For example, they have developed databases (e.g., using coding and cost data), they have contracted with outside consultants to do meta-analyses of device-relevant therapeutic areas, and they have developed or validated instruments to measure quality of life in patient outcomes research.

Most high-tech device manufacturers employ a professional dedicated to outcomes research activities, usually housed in the "medical" area. Device companies almost always commission outside researchers to run the clinical trials associated with their outcomes research, largely because they do not have the extensive clinical research infrastructures found in pharmaceutical companies. But device companies also emphasize research credibility as an important reason for commissioning independent researchers. On the whole, device companies supporting prospective outcomes research seem to be extremely concerned that the research be conducted to the highest standards, indicating, for example, "We want our clinicals to be run like the highest caliber pharmaceutical trials" or "We follow National Institute of Health standards for clinical trials in contracting with outside researchers." This strong emphasis on credibility makes sense when one recalls that, historically, the need to do outcomes research arose out of payers' skepticism about the effectiveness of devices and procedures.

Most device manufacturers engaged in outcomes research are very clear about why they are doing the research and who their audience is: They do outcomes research to secure coverage and reimbursement for the procedures in which their devices are used. Their primary audience is the HCFA, the Blues, and the large commercial payers. Because third party payers have historically questioned comparative effectiveness, device manufacturers have tended to focus on patient outcomes. However, this is beginning to change. Many now include an economic component in their studies, although patient outcomes still dominate the focus of study designs. Retrospective analyses do not play a large role, because studies are typically conducted prior to widespread coverage.

It is worth reemphasizing that the above remarks refer to a rather small subset of device manufacturers that have developed a fairly sophisticated approach to outcomes research. Most device manufacturers do not conduct multiarm clinical trials, develop economic models, or employ rigorous syntheses of observational and experimental data. This is not to deny the increasing efforts of many device companies to develop cost data pertaining to the use of their products. But these data are typically used to develop accounting-oriented cost analyses, as opposed to cost-benefit or cost-effectiveness analyses based on patient outcomes. It is important to note that accounting-oriented cost analyses can be quite useful, particularly for direct purchasers of devices such as hospitals. As a matter of fact, such cost analyses are better suited to the ways that most hospitals actually make their financial decisions than are true economic outcomes analyses—which is one very good reason why a broad array of device manufacturers produce them.

Pharmaceutical Companies

Pharmaceutical firms did not suffer from the sorts of coverage difficulties experienced by device manufacturers and described above. Throughout the early 1980s, the HCFA and virtually all other third-party payers automatically covered FDA-approved drugs (to the extent that they covered drugs at all). Nevertheless, a few pharmaceutical firms recognized the importance of the burgeoning technology assessment trend. Those firms supported the development of in-house expertise in the evolving methods of clinical investigation. Equally important, they perceived the receptivity of the market toward outcomes information and understood the marketing opportunity inherent in that receptivity (Jack, 1991).

These early efforts in outcomes research began to bear fruit in the mid-1980s. The two classic studies of that period, on auranofin and captopril, were both published in 1986 (Bombardier et al., 1986; Croog et al., 1986). The study of auranofin (for adult rheumatoid arthritis) used well-developed, multidimensional health status measures that provided a consolidated health status score for each patient. The study of captopril (for essential hypertension) employed nine unrelated functional status and quality of life instruments, some of which were newly developed for the study. Despite their methodological differences, both studies used nontraditional methods of clinical investigation to measure clinical endpoints that were too subjective to be measured by traditional approaches. In addition, both companies undertook these studies with the physician audience in mind, to show the impact of their drugs on dimensions of life that are meaningful and important to patients. This contrasts sharply to the payer orientation of device companies.

However, most pharmaceutical firms did not begin to think seriously about outcomes research until the 1987-1989 time frame. By then the increasingly restrictive practices of hospital, HMO, and Medicaid formulary committees had forced pharmaceutical companies to address directly the issue of value with their customers. In the U.S. Congress, the pharmaceutical industry faced escalating criticism of its prices. In addition, the HCFA and some managed care organizations were beginning to voice an interest in new concepts like therapeutic substitution and drug utilization review. It became increasingly evident that key constituencies were narrowly focusing on drug *prices.* To show the *value* of their products, pharmaceutical companies had to move the discussion to the topic of cost-effectiveness—and then provide credible evidence of that cost-effectiveness. Outcomes research, particularly economic outcomes research, was well suited to this task.

In most pharmaceutical firms these market dynamics were initially observed in public policy or managed care marketing functions, and those functional areas often took the lead in espousing the importance of outcomes research. Typically, such early efforts met with widespread skepticism. The business side expressed doubts. After all, outcomes research is costly and one can legitimately question its cost-effectiveness. The clinical research and development (R&D) areas also registered resistance. This resistance was partly due to a lack of confidence in (or familiarity with) the clinical methodologies used in outcomes research, but it also arose from the perception that outcomes research draws resources away from conducting the studies required to support New Drug Application filings. Thus, most pharmaceutical firms went through a period of "conversion" before committing to the importance of outcomes research. Relatively few pharmaceutical firms established departments, or even individual positions, fully dedicated to outcomes research until the 1990s. The companies that did have early involvement of their R&D and marketing divisions in outcomes research have more advanced outcomes research capabilities today.

With few exceptions, pharmaceutical companies are still grappling with the central questions of how to structure their outcomes research activities. Expertise is situated in such widely disparate organizational locations as marketing, public policy, corporate planning, R&D, and medical affairs. In broad terms, there appears to be a general trend to locate the primary outcomes research function in clinical R&D, with communication linkages to the marketing and new product development divisions. That said, however, few companies have satisfactorily integrated outcomes research into their clinical development processes. In most companies, the outcomes research function is still quite protean and will continue to evolve over the coming years (Freeman, 1991; Steward, 1991a,b, 1992; The Zitter Group and Technology Assessment Group, 1992).

Although the very early outcomes research efforts of pharmaceutical companies focused on patient outcomes, recent emphasis has shifted to economic outcomes. In fact, *cost-effectiveness* seems to be the dominant buzzword in pharmaceutical industry conversations about outcomes research and technology assessment. A number of companies report that patient outcomes (e.g., functional status and quality of life) are studied in the course of conducting economic studies, but are rarely the sole subject of a study. Even those companies that follow a more balanced approach to outcomes research acknowledge a bias toward economic outcomes. This is not surprising when one recalls that aggressive cost consciousness has driven most of the market dynamics that lead the majority of pharmaceutical firms to do outcomes research in the first place. Nonetheless, the more balanced approach will likely prevail over time, as indicated in a personal communication from the director of the outcomes research function at a large pharmaceutical firm:

> Given the current market trends, there is increasing emphasis on economic studies. You don't make the market; the market makes you. But, ultimately, good

> medicine is good economics. In the end, if you can show patient benefit, the economics will follow. On the other hand, no amount of pharmacoeconomics studies will support a product that doesn't offer a meaningful clinical advantage —unless you were to price it at a fraction of the price of competitive therapies.

Pharmaceutical firms employ a wide variety of outcomes research methodologies. This variety is as indicative of the infant stage of the discipline as it is of differences among companies. There is a significant degree of disagreement among knowledgeable parties regarding the usefulness, validity, and limits of the investigational methodologies and instruments that are being employed in the service of outcomes research.

Most pharmaceutical firms produce a mix of prospective studies, retrospective analyses, and economic and decision-analytic modeling. Not all of these studies are used as "end products." A significant amount of outcomes research and related work is conducted to support and guide study design for prospective studies. The following are examples of the types of support work conducted by pharmaceutical companies.

- *Historical cohort studies* may be conducted to develop information on the cost and medical resource use associated with a disease and its treatment in populations. Such analyses can also provide limited information on the natural history of a treated disease.
- *Baseline data on the direct and indirect costs* of a specific type of illness may be developed by prospectively or retrospectively collecting cost data. In some cases, companies have invested significant resources to develop cost-of-illness information to provide valid and consistent inputs into cost-effectiveness studies.
- *Economic and decision-analytic models* are often used to identify the most important parameters that should be examined in a prospective study. It is useful to do this sort of preliminary work, because only a limited number of parameters can be studied in any given prospective trial. The researcher wants to study those parameters that are most sensitive to the disease state in question (and to its standard treatment options) to ensure that the results of the study will provide relevant and meaningful data on the compound studied. Similarly, it is not feasible to collect data on every disease- and treatment-related cost when conducting a prospective study. Economic modeling is used to identify which factors account for the bulk of the costs associated with a disease and its treatment; a prospective study can then focus on the major contributors to cost.
- In some cases there is no valid and reliable instrument available for measuring the set of quality-of-life or functional parameters appropriate to the disease state being studied. Researchers may do extensive work to *develop and validate new instruments* or to *validate existing instruments.* These efforts can, on occasion, consume years.

Most firms also use economic modeling and, less frequently, retrospective studies as end products. On the whole, there appears to be a growing reluctance to use retrospective analysis in stand-alone studies. This is because most of the available databases are claims databases—designed to track financial transactions, not clinical data. This raises validity issues with respect to the results, severely limiting a company's ability to communicate those results to customers. Even when it is possible to use existing databases, the adjustments and supplemental work required are usually quite costly.

Economic modeling is much better accepted as a stand-alone study approach. Most companies noted that, as long as a model's assumptions are reasonable and clearly stated, the results can be useful and informative. Companies often follow a three-step process in developing modeling studies: (1) develop the model structure and preliminary assumptions; (2) present the study concept, model, and preliminary assumptions to an expert panel for consensus review; and (3) revise the model and assumptions as appropriate. Modeling is particularly useful when the endpoints being studied are rare events or take a long time to become manifest (e.g., progression of degenerative disease or death from a chronic condition). In such cases, prospective studies could take 10 to 15 years and require tens of thousands of patients. Modeling allows the researcher to project economic or patient outcomes using available data on the disease and its relevant treatment options within a time frame that is practical for real-life decisionmaking.

In addition, modeling has been used as a decisionmaking tool in the early stages of product development. For example, one company reported using decision-analytic modeling to determine the efficacy rate that its investigational compound would have to achieve to be cost-effective. This information was then used in developing the target profile of the product.

In some pharmaceutical firms, those who are involved in the outcomes research function operate primarily as consultants to those who are involved in the clinical R&D functions, who then run the studies (particularly when studies are of investigational compounds and are incorporated into the clinical development program). In other companies, those involved in the outcomes research function operate primarily in a project manager role, and most studies are contracted to outside researchers, including both academe and independent firms. In the majority of companies, however, a mix of internal and external personnel conduct outcomes research.

Virtually all pharmaceutical companies use the consulting services of outside experts in their outcomes research activities, even those companies committed to developing substantial internal capabilities. In the case of quality-of-life studies, companies sometimes access the expertise of consultants on the technical aspects of instrument development or selection, but they typically conduct the studies in-house. Companies' clinical development groups generally feel fairly comfortable in their ability to develop and run a quality-of-life study and tend to view such studies as relatively uncomplicated. In some cases, this betrays an oversimplified view of the methodological issues involved in these studies, as evidenced by the growing practice of fairly routinely inserting "short-form" or abbreviated quality-of-life measures into clinical trials.

By contrast, pharmaceutical firms are more likely to commission outside researchers to conduct economic outcomes studies, whether they be prospective, retrospective, modeled, or a combination thereof. Companies are less comfortable with the methodological issues involved in cost-benefit and cost-effectiveness studies because of the lack of standardized approaches to doing those studies.[5] This uneasiness is accentuated by the fact that many companies have not yet developed sufficient in-house expertise to grapple with the methodological issues involved in designing pharmacoeconomic studies—although several companies stand out as notable exceptions to this general rule.

It is interesting to note that there is considerable difference of opinion regarding whether or not it is optimal to commission outside researchers to perform outcomes research. Some pharmaceutical firms believe that outside researchers enhance the perceived credibility of outcomes research by mitigating the appearance of conflict of interest. These companies tend to view their internal outcomes research function primarily as a knowledgeable and proactive sponsor of externally conducted studies. Other pharmaceutical firms are of the opinion that outcomes research is simply too important for a company to allow itself to be heavily dependent on outside expertise. These companies are committed to expanding their internal expertise in health economics, pharmacoepidemiology, and health services research to increase the proportion of outcomes research conducted in-house. Moreover, they are confident that by producing high-quality studies they will be able to defuse any lingering skepticism about the objectivity of manufacturer-conducted outcomes research. All companies interviewed stated that their studies, whether conducted internally or externally, are designed to be published in peer-reviewed journals. Most companies reported that when they sponsor the work of outside researchers, those researchers are free to publish the results of those studies. In such cases, the sponsoring company generally does not have the right to edit or censor the researcher's publication, although it usually has the right to read the manuscript prior to submission for publication.

Despite some differences in how pharmaceutical firms approach outcomes research, a number of clear trends can be identified. Pharmaceutical companies are initiating outcomes research earlier in the product development cycle, conducting it for more compounds, and using prospective study designs more often. Increasingly, quality-of-life and economic outcomes studies are conducted simultaneously. Although the trend in economic outcomes studies is to collect cost

[5] Most companies reported that they had not done any cost-utility studies, primarily because of methodological concerns. There are very real difficulties with the generalizability of the "health state preferences" used in such studies, because there is little basis for claiming that the health state preferences of the study population represent those of the broader population.

data prospectively, economic modeling studies are still used—but often as a preliminary tool for identifying appropriate prospective study parameters.

Pharmaceutical companies are developing a keener sense of the importance of producing timely outcomes information about new products. It is becoming routine for companies to ask, by phase I or II of the clinical development program for an investigational compound, what sort(s) of outcomes research should be conducted. Prospective studies are now frequently initiated in phase II of a clinical development and evaluation program. At the same time, companies are developing a longer-term approach to outcomes research. A significant number of companies have initiated long-term patient functionality studies. This highlights companies' recognition that the market will require outcomes data, not only when a pharmaceutical product is launched but also as it achieves broader use.

Biotechnology Pharmaceutical Companies

Given the high costs associated with genetically engineered drugs, the market forces driving outcomes research should apply even more convincingly to biotechnology pharmaceutical (biotech) companies. In an increasingly price sensitive market, biotech companies need to show that their products are cost-effective, even though they are expensive in absolute terms.

In comparison with traditional pharmaceutical firms, however, biotech companies have not been very active in outcomes research. This may be because biotech firms are typically more technology driven and less market oriented than traditional pharmaceutical firms. As a group, biotech companies have few marketed pharmaceutical products. Their efforts have largely been focused on developing promising compounds and raising the capital to fuel those development efforts. As a consequence, many biotech companies have been better attuned to the capital markets than to the pharmaceutical marketplace. To date, only a few biotech firms have invested in outcomes research. These are firms that have developed a stronger market orientation either through the experience of marketing a pharmaceutical product or in anticipation of a product launch.

Among biotechnology companies, Amgen was a pioneer in outcomes research, sponsoring both economic and quality-of-life studies of its first marketed product, recombinant human erythropoietin (indicated for anemia associated with chronic renal disease), in 1989.[6] Those studies were undertaken because the low level of Medicare reimbursement for erythropoietin therapy from the HCFA was

[6] Although a number of early economic modeling studies comparing various thrombolytic therapy options, including Genentech's recombinant tissue plasminogen activator, were conducted, those studies were not sponsored by Genentech (Jones-Grizzle and Bootman, 1992). Genentech did provide partial support for the ISIS-3 study of thrombolysis patient outcomes, sponsored by the Department of Veterans Affairs and reported in 1992 (ISIS-3 Collaborative Group, 1992).

prompting providers to underdose patients with chronic renal disease (CRD). By showing that proper dosages of erythropoietin significantly improved the well-being of patients with CRD, Amgen persuaded the HCFA to alter its reimbursement structure for erythropoietin. Building on the success of its erythropoietin studies, Amgen initiated outcomes studies for its next product, filgrastim (recombinant methionyl human granulocyte colony-stimulating factor) during phase III clinical trials. These studies showed that filgrastim substantially reduced the need for postchemotherapy hospitalization and provided a basis for the positive differentiation of filgrastim from other granulocyte colony-stimulating factor products.

Despite the evident success of Amgen's outcomes research efforts, other biotech companies remained inactive for some time. In 1991 Centocor conducted a retrospective cost-effectiveness study of its first therapeutic product, Centoxin[7] (then awaiting FDA approval for the treatment of septic shock). But the study was initiated late in the product development process—well into FDA's review period and, even more important, well after the hospital community had reached a widely publicized consensus about the "devastating" financial impact of a $3,700-per-dose septic shock drug. It is unclear whether the FDA's failure to approve Centoxin without further clinical trials was at all influenced by the tumult surrounding its price. What is clear is that Centocor's response to the hospitals' sticker shock was too little and too late.

In the wake of the Centoxin experience, biotech companies will likely develop a keener appreciation of the importance of timely outcomes research. At least one biotech company, Synergen, has already begun to integrate outcomes research into its clinical development process (Longman, 1992). Indeed, Synergen's efforts rival those of the large, traditional pharmaceutical firms and will probably serve as a model for other biotech companies.

Summary Observations

It is evident from the foregoing discussion that manufacturers' outcomes research is market driven. Manufacturers produce outcomes data for more or less defined audiences in response to the perceived informational requirements of those audiences and to address specific marketing concerns. The audience can include any or all of those decisionmakers who influence the approval, diffusion, pricing, or utilization of medical products. The marketing concerns include the various pricing, reimbursement, coverage, registration, and formulary access issues faced by manufacturers.

Most device companies engaged in outcomes research have identified a primary audience and are pursuing fairly straightforward reimbursement or regula

[7] Centoxin is the registered trademark.

tory goals. Biotech companies also have a well-defined rationale for conducting outcomes research. In a cost-constrained environment, therapies that add substantially to the cost of health care must provide evidence of sufficient value to warrant that cost—even when the therapies are "breakthrough" technologies. The fact that many biotech companies are only now beginning to recognize this rationale for outcomes research does not make it any less clear. By contrast, traditional pharmaceutical firms, whose products rarely embody the biotech extremes of high cost and radical innovation, face more subtle and diffuse market forces.[8]

It is interesting to note, therefore, that traditional pharmaceutical firms have taken the lead in outcomes research. Most pharmaceutical firms are committed to the importance of outcomes research, even though many are uncertain about how the outcomes research movement will evolve. This uncertainty is largely due to the early stage of outcomes research. Most of the studies undertaken to date are still in progress and, until the results become available, one can only guess how diverse decisionmakers will respond to the range of information being generated. Granted, isolated studies have been completed, but the market response to those studies provides little guidance on the long-term role of outcomes research in decisions about the availability, utilization, and pricing of medical technologies.

Simply stated, it is not clear what sort of market dynamic will emerge as outcomes research becomes more widespread. Because the technology assessment trend is young, open questions abound: How extensively will physicians incorporate information from outcomes research in their therapeutic choices? Will patients become a significant audience for information on outcomes? Will formulary committees fall back on simple cost-minimization strategies in the face of tight budgets? Will regulatory bodies become involved in monitoring outcomes research? These issues are of vital importance not only to manufacturers but also to future medical innovation.

IMPLICATIONS FOR THE HEALTH CARE INDUSTRY AND MEDICAL INNOVATION

Outcomes research provides answers to questions about what therapies work best, under what conditions, to promote the outcomes that patients care about. As mentioned above, the answers to these questions should provide a basis for rationalizing health care expenditures and improving patient care—and it is for

[8] The audience for outcomes research is far more diverse in the United States than elsewhere, particularly with respect to pharmaceuticals. Outside of the United States, pharmaceutical prices and reimbursement levels are often controlled by government bodies that, in recent years, have placed increasing importance on outcomes data, particularly economic outcomes data. In some countries, the pricing determination process is closely linked to the approval process. At the extreme, Australia and Canada are moving toward requiring cost-effectiveness data as part of the registration package for pharmaceuticals.

these reasons that outcomes research has deservedly attracted significant attention in recent years. However, at least two major issues must be addressed if the promise of outcomes research is to be realized.

First, although manufacturer-sponsored outcomes research generates important and useful information, that information alone will not support the broader, systemic promise of outcomes research. Manufacturers appropriately focus their outcomes research activities on their own products and on the procedures in which their products are used. Manufacturers do not sponsor outcomes research on medical procedures or therapies that are independent of their products unless a procedure or therapy serves as the established comparator to an alternate procedure or therapy for which a manufacturer's product is used. Moreover, although manufacturer-sponsored outcomes research is almost always comparative, such research rarely addresses every therapeutic option relevant to the disease state in question—nor is it realistic to expect manufacturers to support such broad-based research.

Yet, many of the most striking opportunities for improving patient care and rationalizing health care expenditures depend on conducting outcomes research on (1) procedures that are not product driven (e.g., prostatectomies, hysterectomies, and cesarean deliveries) or (2) clinical conditions whose therapeutic options are only partially product driven (e.g., coronary artery disease, cataracts, lower back pain, and peripheral vascular disease). In the former cases, manufacturers have no rationale to conduct outcomes research. In the latter cases, manufacturers may have a rationale to conduct outcomes research, but most likely it would not be inclusive of all clinically relevant therapeutic modalities. It is important to note that third-party payers have begun to sponsor outcomes research on investigational procedures that are not essentially product driven, such as autologous bone marrow transplantation for breast cancer. However, with the exception of studies conducted by AHCPR-sponsored Patient Outcomes Research Teams, there has been little comprehensive outcomes research conducted on clinical conditions or on noninvestigational, non-product-driven medical procedures. Much more work of this sort is needed if the emerging body of outcomes research is to provide an adequate basis for improving patient care and rationalizing expenditures.

The second issue is more fundamental. Even supposing that an adequate body of outcomes research information is being generated, there remains the critical challenge of appropriately integrating that information into actual medical practice. As indicated in other chapters of this volume, current incentive structures do little to encourage physicians to modify their practice patterns in response to outcomes research, particularly when such modification requires giving up an established and familiar therapeutic approach or a lucrative procedure. Even today, few medical schools incorporate courses on outcomes research or epidemiology in their core curricula, and correspondingly few physicians are inclined to seriously consider outcomes research findings in their day-to-day practice decisions. Recognizing the importance of this issue, AHCPR has undertaken research on the relative effectiveness of various means of disseminating its technology assessment and outcomes research findings to relevant audiences. Dissemination strategies are only part of the picture, however. If outcomes research is to have a meaningfully positive impact on the U.S. health care system, then the systemic factors that affect the ability and willingness of health care professionals to act on outcomes research information must be confronted.

It is important to recognize and address those factors that limit the potential benefits of outcomes research, because substantial resources are being devoted to it. The cost of a single prospective study can easily exceed $1 million. Metaanalyses and retrospective studies are less expensive, but these approaches are usually feasible only after a drug or a device has achieved relatively broad use, which typically happens only after it has been marketed. Since key decisionmakers are increasingly demanding that manufacturers provide outcomes research when a product is launched, manufacturers are increasingly conducting prospective studies, the costliest type of outcomes research.

Thus, an important consequence of heightened market demand for outcomes research is that the investment required to bring a new drug or high-tech device to market has increased. Because the outcomes research trend is still so new, one can only speculate about the ultimate implications of this shift. However, the classic theory of competitive dynamics is suggestive. Generally, as an industry moves toward requiring larger investments to bring new products to market, the number of players in that industry will decrease and the size of each player will increase. This is because larger up-front product development costs require that firms have a larger revenue base (critical mass) to sustain the increased cash outflow during the development stage of product life cycles. This would imply that the increased demand for outcomes research constitutes a competitive advantage for larger firms and will tend to reduce the number of smaller firms through acquisitions, mergers, or failures.

This dynamic is likely to affect high-tech device companies more profoundly than pharmaceutical companies, because (1) the increased expense of outcomes research, viewed as a percentage of total product development costs, is considerably higher for high-tech device companies than for pharmaceutical companies, and (2) unlike the pharmaceutical industry, the high-tech device industry includes a significant number of relatively small companies, which makes the device industry more sensitive to competitive shifts in the requisite critical mass. Indeed, looking at the change in the average size of companies receiving FDA approval for class III devices between 1981 and 1988—a period during which class III device approval times lengthened and the FDA placed increasing emphasis, for devices for which premarketing approval was being sought, on evidence of clinical utility and rigor in biostatistical analysis,—it appears that the high-tech device industry responded predictably to the escalating cost of bringing new products to market. In 1981, the average size of companies who received approval for class III devices was $300 million, whereas by 1988 the average size had increased fourfold to $1.2 billion (in constant 1980 dollars; Bucci et al., 1990).

The competitive dynamics of the pharmaceutical industry are also likely to be affected by the increased demand for outcomes research, but differently. Investment in outcomes research can be used to create barriers to entry in specific markets, particularly in markets for pharmaceutical therapies that treat chronic conditions. This is because key decisionmakers show keen interest in outcomes research on the comparative impact of pharmaceutical therapies on endpoints such as survival and disease progression in patients with chronic diseases; but such studies can take 5 to 15 years, require thousands of patients, and cost millions of dollars. When firms that are established in a chronic therapy market (e.g., for hypertension) invest in such research, they create a twofold barrier to entry. First, they raise the ante for any newcomer wishing to enter the market. Second, they create a "time-buffered" competitive advantage, because the new entrant will have to wait years before the results of outcomes research on its new compound are available. Predictably, this sort of competitive positioning is already under way in some of the markets for therapies that treat chronic conditions such as asthma and hypertension. The strength of such barriers to entry will be directly proportional to the market's insistence on long-term outcomes research information.

The potential impact of these competitive dynamics on innovation is sobering. Clearly, if the above speculations about demand for outcomes research and barriers to entry in the pharmaceutical industry were to prove correct, the effect would be to dampen pharmaceutical innovation in certain markets. Of greater concern is the predicted impact on the high-tech device industry. As Alan Kahn has described, innovation in the medical device industry is characterized by "smaller companies taking the lead, [with] a more fluid innovation process" that can respond to an ill-defined and rapidly changing market (Kahn, 1991, p. 89). Smaller companies are better able to stay close to their customers, approach unmet needs in an entrepreneurial fashion, and respond quickly to market input about product performance and features—qualities that have driven much of the innovation in high-tech devices for the past 20 years. If the high-tech device industry evolves toward fewer and larger companies, the United States can expect a decline in radical medical product innovations.

CONCLUSION

Rarely in life does one encounter an unequivocally positive trend, and the trend toward increasing demand for outcomes research is no exception to this cheerless observation. The growing market demand for outcomes research, particularly as a condition for registration, reimbursement, or formulary acceptance, will likely slow the pace of innovation in drugs and devices to some degree. It would be a mistake, however, to conclude that the outcomes research trend is therefore ill advised. The information generated by outcomes research has real potential to improve patient care and help rationalize health care expenditures. Of course, as discussed above, realizing this potential requires that (1) sufficient outcomes research be conducted on procedures and clinical conditions that are not product driven and (2) outcomes information be appropriately incorporated into actual medical practice. Given the cooperative efforts by the various stakeholders in the U.S. health care system to address these issues, the promise of outcomes research may warrant a limited trade-off with the pace of medical product innovation.

REFERENCES

Bombardier, C., Russell, I. J., Ware, J., et al. 1986. Auranofin therapy and quality of life in patients with rheumatoid arthritis: Results of a multicenter trial. *American Journal of Medicine* 81:565-578.

Bucci, V. A., Hall, N. C., and Reiss, J. B. 1985. New obstacles in the path of marketing new medical devices: The stream of regulation. *Journal of Health Care Technology* 2:81-96.

Bucci, V. A., Hall, N. C. and Norcia, L. A. 1990. FDA DecisionMaking on Class III PMA Products: An Analysis of 124 PMA Approvals. Unpublished manuscript.

Croog, S. H., Levine, S., Testa, M.A., et al. 1986. The effects of antihypertensive therapy on the quality of life. *New England Journal of Medicine* 314:1657-1664.

Eddy, D. M. 1990. Should we change the rules for evaluating medical technologies? In: Institute of Medicine. *Medical Innovation at the Crossroads. Vol. 1, Modern Methods of Clinical Investigation.* A. C. Gelijns, ed. Washington, D.C.: National Academy Press, pp. 117-134.

Freeman, R. A. 1991. Organizational issues in outcomes management research. *Journal of Pharmacoepidemiology* 2(2):59-67.

Freund, D. A., and Dittus, R. S. 1992. Principles of pharmacoeconomic analysis of drug therapy. *PharmacoEconomics* 1(1):20-29.

Institute of Medicine. 1990. *Medical Innovation at the Crossroads. Vol. 1, Modern Methods of Clinical Investigation.* A. C. Gelijns, ed. Washington, D.C.: National Academy Press.

ISIS-3 Collaborative Group. 1992. ISIS-3: A randomized comparison of streptokinase vs tissue plasminogen activator vs anistreplase and of aspirin plus heparin vs aspirin alone among 41,299 cases of suspected acute myocardial infarction. *Lancet* 339:753770.

Jack, W. 1991. Pharmaceutical differentiation through quality of life measurement: A case study. *Journal of Pharmaceutical Marketing and Management* 6(1):65-85.

Jones-Grizzle, A. J., and Bootman, J. L. 1992. Pharmacoeconomics of genetically engineered drugs. *PharmacoEconomics* 1(1):45-53.

Kahn, A. 1991. The dynamics of medical device innovation: An innovator's perspective. In: Institute of Medicine. *Medical Innovation at the Crossroads.* Vol. 2, *The Chang ing Economics of Medical Technology.* A. C. Gelijns and E. A. Halm, eds. Washington, D.C.: National Academy Press, pp. 89-95.

Kane, N. M., and Manoukian, P. D. 1989. The effect of the Medicare prospective payment system on the adoption of new technology. *New England Journal of Medicine* 321:1378-1383.

Longman, R. 1992. Synergen rewrites the pricing debate. *In Vivo* 10(7):20-24.

McGivney, W. T. 1991. Hurdles to technology diffusion: What are expectations for PET? *Journal of Nuclear Medicine* 32:660-664.

Office of Device Evaluation, Food and Drug Administration. May 3, 1991. Clinical utility and premarket approval. Internal memorandum from the director, Office of Drug Evaluation, to the Office of Drug Evaluation review staff.

Office of Technology Assessment, U.S. Congress. 1982. *Strategies for Medical Technology Assessment.* Washington, D.C.: U.S. Government Printing Office.

Perry, S. 1988. Technology assessment in health care: The U.S. perspective. *Health Policy* 9:317-324.

Stern, W. R. 1990. Meeting of the Food and Drug Administration gastroenterology urology device section advisory panel on extracorporeal shock-wave lithotripsy for gallbladder stones, October 19, 1989. *American Journal of Gastroenterology* 85: 238-240.

Steward, S. 1991a. Part 1: Building bridges with cost-effectiveness. *Pharmaceutical Executive* 11 (9):58-70.

Steward, S. 1991b. Part 2: Taking the lead with cost-effectiveness. *Pharmaceutical Executive* 11 (11):46-61.

Steward, S. 1992. Part 3: Developing strategies with cost-effectiveness. *Pharmaceutical Executive* 12(2):74-84, 109.

VanAntwerp, M. 1985. Diffusion of new technologies: Can Medicare payment decisions be made faster and more efficiently? *Journal of Health Care Technology* 2:97-103.

Wennberg, J. E. 1990. What is outcomes research? In: Institute of Medicine. *Medical Innovation at the Crossroads. Vol. 1, Modern Methods of Clinical Investigation.* A. C. Gelijns, ed. Washington, D.C.: National Academy Press, pp. 33-46.

Wennberg, J. E., and Gittelsohn, A. 1973. Small area variations in health care delivery. *Science* 182:1102-1108.

Wennberg, J. E., Freeman, J. L., and Culp, W. J. 1987. Are hospital services rationed in New Haven or over-utilised in Boston? *Lancet* 1:1185-1189.

Wennberg, J. E., Freeman, J. L., Shelton, R. M., and Bubolz, T. A. 1989. Hospital use and mortality among Medicare beneficiaries in Boston and New Haven. *New England Journal of Medicine* 321:1168-1173.

The Zitter Group and Technology Assessment Group. 1992. *Pharmaceutical Outcomes Activities.* The Zitter Group and Technology Assessment Group.

13

Paying for Evaluative Research

ALAN M. GARBER AND DOUGLAS K. OWENS

The sponsors of medical technology assessment, the principal form of evaluative research concerning medical interventions, are as diverse as the goals and methods of the research itself. In this chapter we describe the sponsors of such research in the United States and discuss why sponsorship matters and why some sponsors may be more suitable than others. The identity of the sponsors of technology assessment is important insofar as most of them have an interest in the results of the assessment, so their ability to produce evaluative research of use to parties whose interests do not coincide with their own may be limited.

We first define medical technology assessment and describe the institutions in the United States that sponsor or perform medical technology assessment. Often, the responsibility for evaluating technologies is divided among several institutions, particularly the federal government and private institutions. Each institution may in turn play multiple roles, giving it a set of incentives to perform research that varies with the particular technology and context.

We then discuss mechanisms for sponsoring technology assessment. Specifically, when is it most appropriate for the government to fund such activities and when do such activities properly belong in the private sector? To what extent should sponsorship of technology assessment come from payers and to what extent should it come from consumer groups or the producers of the technologies? We close by drawing some general guidelines about how and by whom technology assessment should be performed.

WHAT IS TECHNOLOGY ASSESSMENT?

One of the most widely used definitions of *technology assessment* comes from an Institute of Medicine publication. According to that definition, technology assessment is

> any process of examining and reporting properties of a medical technology used in health care, such as safety, efficacy, feasibility, and indications for use, cost, and cost-effectiveness, as well as social, economic, and ethical consequences, whether intended or unintended (Institute of Medicine, 1985, p.2).

Medical technology itself can be construed in broad terms; according to the congressional Office of Technology Assessment, medical technology consists of the

> techniques, drugs, equipment, and procedures used by health-care professionals in delivering medical care to individuals, and the systems within which such care is delivered (cited in Institute of Medicine, 1985, pp. 1-2).

These broad and seemingly all-encompassing definitions of medical technologies and formal evaluations of those technologies can be given greater specificity by distinguishing the *stages*[1] of technology assessment. Fuchs and Garber (1990) defined three stages of technology assessment (stages I to III), in which each stage encompasses progressively broader dimensions of evaluation. Stage I, according to this classification, focuses on technical characteristics. This might include measures of the ability of an antibiotic to inhibit the growth of bacteria in a test tube or measures of the resolution, speed, and electromagnetic hazards of a new computed tomography scanner.

Stage II investigates clinical efficacy, in which the clinical outcomes may be surrogate endpoints. For example, a stage II clinical trial of an antihypertensive medication might measure its efficacy at lowering blood pressure, but not its effects on mortality or on the incidence of stroke. Stage II includes most traditional randomized clinical trials as well as nonrandomized evaluations of the efficacy of treatment.

The purview of stage III trials encompasses comprehensive clinical, economic, and social endpoints. Cost-effectiveness analyses of medical technologies are stage III studies, at least when they attempt to incorporate comprehensive measures of health outcomes in addition to costs. Although stage III studies are the most comprehensive, to the extent that they can build upon the results of stage II studies they need not be expensive. A traditional randomized clinical trial, a stage II assessment, is likely to be very expensive; a stage III assessment that combines information from such a trial with data from other sources may be far less costly. Many technologies never receive a stage III assessment.[2]

---

[1] These stages should not be confused with the phases in pharmaceutical evaluation used by the Food and Drug Administration, which have a precise regulatory interpretation.

[2] Recently, clinical trials that assess a broad range of endpoints, including the impact of the intervention on economic endpoints and quality of life, have been initiated. Such trials are likely become the most convincing stage III assessments; by designing trials that encompass these comprehensive endpoints at the outset, the investigators obviate the need to link data from disparate sources and to model phenomena that were not measured as part of the trial.

The distinctions between stages of technology assessment are useful because the purpose of early-stage assessments (stages I and II) differs from that of later stage assessments (stage III). Stage III assessments deal most directly with the policy, reimbursement, and clinical issues that determine when a technology should be used, how it should be implemented, and whether the benefits the technology offers can be obtained at an acceptable cost. These issues are not addressed in stage I or II assessments, which are valuable for different reasons. Stage I and II assessments answer precise technical and clinical questions using well-established methods.

The sponsors of technology assessment also have different incentives for doing studies at different stages. That is why they often concentrate their efforts on a particular stage. The incentives facing the sponsors influence the way they select technologies for study and the endpoints that they use for the evaluation. Seldom will an insurer devote substantial resources toward evaluating an aspect of technical performance—the resolution of a scanner, for example—just as the manufacturer of the scanner may be unwilling to devote resources to determining the impact of its scanner's use on the functional recovery of individuals whose metastatic cancer is found through use of the device.

WHO PERFORMS TECHNOLOGY ASSESSMENTS IN THE UNITED STATES?

The United States has long been a leader in performing medical technology assessment, even though countries with national health insurance would seem to have stronger reasons to support evaluative research. In the United States, assessment activities have not been tightly linked to reimbursement; much of the funding has come from organizations that have a loose connection, if any at all, to major insurers. In this section, we give an overview of medical technology assessment in the United States and describe the groups that perform it. We also briefly describe the amounts that they spend and their methods for choosing which technologies to assess. The available expenditure information does not allow us to distinguish between the stages of technology assessment. However, it seems clear that if stage I assessments were included, the largest sponsors of technology assessment would be drug and device manufacturers, much of whose research and development expenditures can be considered forms of technology assessment. Our discussion below focuses on stage II and III evaluations.

Identifying the Sponsors

The sponsors of evaluative research in the United States are remarkably diverse and numerous. Although no comprehensive inventory of sponsors has been published, two reports prepared by the Institute of Medicine provide helpful overviews (Institute of Medicine, 1985, 1988). In particular, the *Medical Technology Assessment Directory* (Institute of Medicine, 1988) catalogues many of the organizations that sponsor technology assessment.

Most sponsors of evaluative research can be classified broadly into three categories. They are *producers* of technology, *consumers,* and *payers.* The reasons for sponsoring evaluative research differ markedly among the categories (discussed later in the section "Sponsoring Evaluations of Medical Technology"). Because their goals differ, to the extent that the studies are subject to biases and that there is selectivity about the outcomes to be investigated and the technologies to be studied, the sponsor of the research can have a major impact on the nature of the findings. As we discuss below, many of the sponsors of technology assessment play different roles in different contexts, so they do not face the same incentives or bring the same focus to each one of their activities.

Producers

Producers of medical technology include the pharmaceutical industry, device and equipment manufacturers, professional societies and associations, and some government agencies. Professional societies often evaluate the services and products that their members supply. For example, the Diagnostic and Therapeutic Technology Assessment Program of the American Medical Association produces reports that aim to disseminate state-of-the-art information about the effectiveness of medical treatments to the practicing medical community and to the public at large.

Some government agencies, such as the National Institutes of Health (NIH), act in part as producers of technology. NIH is responsible for conducting or sponsoring the research that leads to many important medical innovations. Its function as the major government sponsor of biomedical research in the United States, combined with its large and impressive intramural research program, means that it has contributed in some capacity to most of the major biomedical advances of the years after World War II. In some cases, NIH holds patents or otherwise controls the production of biomedical technology. For example, alglucerase injection, a treatment for the inherited disorder known as Gaucher's disease, is produced in the private sector under a licensing agreement with NIH. NIH, which discovered the drug, holds one patent and has applied for another patent concerning its production (Garber et al., 1992). NIH also has a very large budget for evaluative research, including small clinical studies, small and large randomized clinical trials and, to a limited extent, some stage III evaluations, including cost-effectiveness analyses.

Consumers

Consumers of medical technology are those people who use medical care directly (that is, patients) or those organizations that represent patients' interests. Several agencies of the federal government have the responsibility of safeguarding the interests of patients, such as the Food and Drug Administration in its role as the regulatory agency for medical devices and drugs. The Agency for Health Care Policy and Research (AHCPR) is perhaps the largest federal sponsor of stage III technology assessments. For all three stages of medical technology assessment, however, NIH spends substantially more than AHCPR because it sponsors many clinical trials, which are often large and expensive. A major focus of the research sponsored by AHCPR is determination of the effectiveness and the cost-effectiveness of medical technologies. Medical professional societies also often sponsor evaluations of technologies that they do not produce. For example, the American College of Physicians (ACP), an organization of internists, has studied and issued guidelines regarding the use of mammography; the ACP and its members neither sell the equipment used for mammography nor, typically, do they collect the professional fees for performing mammography (a task that usually falls to radiologists). Rather, internists act as agents for their patients. Other private, nonprofit groups, such as research organizations (for example, the Battelle Memorial Institute, the Hastings Center, and other university-based programs) and foundations (for example, Project HOPE, the Center for Health Affairs, the Hartford Foundation), may sponsor or perform evaluative research that serves to protect the interests of consumers.

Payers

Payers, both public and private, also sponsor technology assessment. Federal payers that participate in evaluative research include the Health Care Financing Administration (HCFA), which is responsible for administering the Medicare program and the federal participation in Medicaid, and the Department of Veterans Affairs (VA). The VA Health Services Research and Development Service, in particular, sponsors a broad range of evaluative research activities. Private-sector payers that sponsor technology assessments include insurance companies (for example, the Blue Cross and Blue Shield Association Technology Evaluation and Coverage Program), health maintenance organizations (McGuire, 1990), and self-insured employers.

Expenditures for Evaluative Research

The diversity of organizations and the varied natures of their activities make precise estimations of total expenditures for evaluative research exceedingly difficult. Nevertheless, the following figures are included to give a broad sense of expenditures for evaluative research. According to the Institute of Medicine, U.S. expenditures for technology assessment in 1984 were almost $1.3 billion, or 0.3 percent of total health care expenditures. This figure includes roughly $750 million spent by the pharmaceutical industry on clinical trials, $235 million spent by NIH on various evaluative activities, and approximately $35 million spent by the medical device industry. The VA Cooperative Studies Program also sponsors clinical trials. Expenditures for these trials may reach $18 million to $20 million when the cost of associated clinical care is included (Janet Gold, Department of Veterans Affairs, personal communication, September 10, 1992). In addition to clinical trials, NIH funds the Consensus Development Program, which sponsors six to eight consensus conferences per year at a cost of $130,000 to $140,000 each (William Hall, Office of Medical Applications Research, NIH, personal communication, September 8, 1992). HCFA sponsors approximately 10 technology assessments per year via contracts from the Bureau of Eligibility, Reimbursement and Coverage to the Office of Health Technology Assessment at AHCPR. These activities cost approximately one million dollars each year (Samuel Dellavecchia, Health Care Financing Administration, personal communication, September 11, 1992).

Table 13-1 indicates the technology assessment expenditures by a number of other organizations. These expenditures are approximate and, because definitions may vary or programs that are responsible for technology assessment often include other activities, they may overstate the magnitude of assessment activities. The sources of funding for technology assessment vary among the types of organizations. Professional societies and trade associations fund technology assessment primarily from the dues of members. The primary funding sources for technology assessment by private, nonprofit organizations are grants and contracts from federal government agencies, industry, and private sources, including foundations. Academic organizations similarly fund technology assessments primarily from grants and contracts from federal and private sources.

Selection of Technologies for Evaluative Research

Although the process of selecting which technologies to assess varies substantially, some common themes emerge. In general, the selection process is influenced strongly by whether an organization is acting primarily as a producer, as a representative of consumers, or as a payer. As discussed below in detail, producers naturally focus on the technologies that they have developed. In contrast, organizations that act on the behalf of consumers have various selection processes. AHCPR has focused many of its large-scale technology assessments on conditions and treatments for which there is significant geographic variation in their use (a potential indicator of inappropriate utilization or uncertainty about efficacy) and that are expected to account for substantial Medicare expenditures.

TABLE 13-1 Sponsors of Technology Assessment

Producers	Budget	Consumers/Representatives	Budget	Payers	Budget
American Academy of Neurology[a]	NA	OTA	$1,600,000	HCFA Bureau Eligibility	$1,000,000
American Academy of Ophthalmology[a]	$7,500	FDA Center for Devices	NA	HCFA Office of Research and Demonstration[a]	NA
American Academy of Pediatrics[a]	NA	FDA Center for Drugs	$250,000	Prospective Payment Assessment Commission[a]	$1,500,000
American College of Cardiology Task Force[a]	$25,000	FDA Center for Food Safety	NA	VA Cooperative Studies Programs[a]	$14,000,000
American College of Obstetrics[a]	$110,000	NHLBI	$29,000,000	BC/BS Medical Necessity Program[a]	$350,000
American College of Physicians[a]	$150,000	NICHD Technology Transfer Program	$200,000	BC/BS Technology Evaluation Program[a]	$600,000
American College of Radiology[a]	$26,000	NIH Consensus Development Program	$900,000		
American Dental Association[a]	NA	National Library of Medicine	$500,000		
American Diabetes Association[a]	$100,000	VA HSRD Special Projects Office	$100,000		
American Gastroenterological Association[a]	NA	AHCPR[b]	$120,000,000		
American Hospital Association[a]	$368,000	OHTA	$1,000,000		
AMA Council on Scientific Affairs[a]	$613,782				
AMA Diagnostic/Therapeutic TA[a]	$380,000				
AMA Drug Evaluation[a]	$500,000				
California Medical Association[a]	$15,000				
College American of Pathologists[a]	$15,000,000				

NOTE: NA, not available; AMA, American Medical Association; TA, Technology Assessment; OTA, Office of Technology Assessment, U.S. Congress; FDA, Food and Drug Administration; NHLBI, National Heart, Lung, and Blood Institute; NICHD, National Institute of Child Health and Human Development; NIH, National Institutes of Health; VA HSRD, Department of Veterans Affairs, Health Services Research and Development Service; AHCPR, Agency for Health Care Policy and Research; OHTA, Office of Health Technology Assessment; HCFA, Health Care Financing Administration; BC/BS, Blue Cross and Blue Shield.

[a] May also act as agents for consumers.

[b] Total expenditures in fiscal year 1991; not all activities are technology assessment.

SOURCE: Updated from Institute of Medicine (1988).

In addition, AHCPR sometimes performs or sponsors evaluations requested by HCFA, as mentioned above.

Professional associations generally select technologies on the basis of requests from members, standing committees, third-party payers, and government organizations. The most notable assessment efforts by a professional society are those of the Clinical Efficacy Assessment Project (CEAP) of ACP. CEAP identifies potential projects on the basis of a review of the current literature, academic opinion, policy needs, as well as requests from other ACP committees and outside organizations including payers. CEAP has had a long and successful collaboration with the Blue Cross and Blue Shield Medical Necessity Project, which commissioned a series of papers from the project. A large number of CEAP assessments of diagnostic procedures and screening tests have been published in the *Annals of Internal Medicine*. These papers were written by ACP members who had particular expertise in evaluative research and are reprinted in two books (Eddy, 1991; Sox, 1987). On the part of ACP, the final selection of topics to be assessed by CEAP depends on, among other factors, the anticipated level of interest to practitioners of internal medicine, the potential for wide application and benefit of the technology, and the risks associated with wide application of the technology. As is true in this example, in general, professional associations assess technologies that are relevant to their members, either because of questions about efficacy or because of controversy about coverage policy.

Payers usually focus on technologies that are likely to result in significant claims. They emphasize technologies that are new, expensive, or of uncertain efficacy. For its collaboration with the ACP, the Blue Cross and Blue Shield Association Medical Necessity Program prioritizes projects on the basis of requests from member plans. HCFA sponsors technology assessments to determine if medical technologies are or continue to be eligible for Medicare coverage. More specifically, for a technology to be assessed it must (1) represent a significant advance in medical science or be potentially outmoded, (2) have the potential for a significant financial impact on the Medicare program, (3) have the potential for rapid diffusion, and (4) have generated controversy regarding its efficacy or appropriateness of coverage (Samuel Dellavecchia, Health Care Financing Administration, personal communication, September 11, 1992).

In summary, a diverse group of people and organizations sponsors medical technology assessments. Although it is difficult to identify all of the participants, it is helpful to categorize the sponsors by the roles they play. Those sponsors that have formulated explicit policies for choosing technologies that should be assessed usually adopt criteria that reflect the interests of the people and the institutions they represent.

WHO SHOULD SPONSOR TECHNOLOGY ASSESSMENT?

As long as the process of technology assessment is open, the quality of the research underlying it is high, and the selection of technologies for study is appropriate, the value of the studies will depend little on the sponsor of the funding. Because these conditions are not always met, the identities of the sponsors can matter a great deal. Another reason for concern about the sponsors of the research is that current funding of technology assessment may well fall short of what is needed. Who might bear the cost of any incremental funding dedicated to this activity?

Of the three main groups of sponsors that we have discussed—producers, consumers, and payers—each has something different to gain from an assessment. Insofar as their goals differ, they will not always agree in their rankings of the importance of specific technologies for study or in the outcomes that matter. The producers of a health care technology have an interest in showing that the technology is valuable; the consumers of the technology have a direct interest in learning about its efficacy, but perhaps not its cost; payers have a direct interest in its cost and a less direct interest in its efficacy.

Producers of Medical Technology

Ordinarily, the producers of a technology sponsor or perform an evaluation of the technology in the early stages of its development. One of the costs of developing a product or technology is establishing its technical characteristics. For some technologies, like medical devices, early evaluations may lead to changes in the design of or manufacturing process for the product. Early assessments may be conducted before the product is publicly announced or when many of its characteristics are known only to the producer. Thus, the producer will be uniquely aware of the limitations and advantages of the technology and might justifiably refuse to cooperate in an external evaluation. The producer also has the incentives to perform the evaluation, insofar as the return to expenditures for evaluation will accrue to the producer. In the United States, a great deal of producer-sponsored evaluation is mandated by regulation, particularly for drug approval.

Producers might not perform certain kinds of evaluative research that would be useful to consumers. The most important impediment arises if the producer cannot expect to gain from performing the research. Consider a manufacturer of acetaminophen, a drug that has been available in generic form for many years. No company has a monopoly on the sale or distribution of acetaminophen, and any research showing its superiority to alternative analgesics would benefit all current and potential producers, not only the sponsor of the research. If the research instead concerned a newly approved nonsteroidal anti-inflammatory drug, the company that had exclusive marketing rights would have strong incentives to fund a study likely to demonstrate its superiority to other nonsteroidal anti-inflammatory drugs. Only when a producer can capture returns that exceed the costs can it be expected to sponsor evaluative research; this situation is unlikely to arise when there are multiple current or potential competitors in the production and sale of the drug or device.

Similarly, a producer cannot be expected to sponsor a study that is unlikely to show that its product is superior to an alternative therapy. If the study is devoid of marketing value and is not required for approval, there is little reason to proceed. Nor will a producer sponsor a study whose results will not be available during the lifetime of a drug or device patent. The financial benefit to the manufacturer of a study that will not produce results until the expiration of the patent or period of monopoly might not exceed its costs. That is one of many reasons why long-term trials of the effects of preventive care on survival are seldom sponsored by producers; how can a manufacturer of an antihypertensive drug conduct a trial that is expected to show a mortality benefit in 15 years if the patent will expire by then?

Even in circumstances in which producers are willing to sponsor technology assessments, however, the studies that result may not have the credibility of studies sponsored independently. For example, if a company can suppress studies with negative findings and selectively release studies favorable to its product(s), published studies will give a misleadingly positive impression of the therapies.[3]

The design of a study may similarly reflect the interests of the producer rather than those of the consumer. Because the producer of a technology will be motivated to perform a study to meet regulatory requirements or to increase revenues, it may select endpoints and study designs that show the technology to its greatest advantage. The resulting endpoints may not be the most relevant to clinical or policy decisions. For example, a producer-sponsored study might emphasize the advantages of a drug in terms of its side effect profile. The producer may be less willing to study the long-term efficacy of the drug, particularly if there are significant doubts that it would be better than older and less expensive alternatives. Therefore, it is critical that standards for the conduct and review of producer-sponsored technology assessments be developed and implemented.

In summary, when a producer is not a monopolist, when an evaluative study is unlikely to demonstrate the superiority of the product, or if the producer will no longer be a monopolist by the time the research is completed, the producer will have little incentive to sponsor a technology assessment. Even when the proper incentives are in place for the producer, however, there are additional reasons why the public, as consumers or payers, might not place much credence in producer-sponsored technology assessments, unless there is clear evidence that the study adheres to rigorous methodologic standards.

---

[3] This bias is similar to, but distinct from, "publication bias." Publication bias refers to the tendency of peer-reviewed medical journals to favor publication of positive findings over negative ones. Although one might presume that readers could adjust for such a bias, it is hard to do so without any information about rejected studies. The same would hold true for company-sponsored negative studies that are never submitted for publication. As a practical matter, a producer of technology would find it difficult to suppress a multi-institutional randomized trial, but it is probably feasible to repress dissemination of the results of a small study.

Consumers of Medical Technology

When producers of a technology are unsuitable as sponsors of an assessment, the consumers of the technology are potential alternative sponsors. No party has a greater direct stake in the efficacy of a health care technology than the patients (consumers) who hope to benefit from it. Unlike the producers of the technology, its consumers do not have an incentive to overstate its benefits, unless it is an issue for negotiation with payers.

There is ample precedent in other contexts for consumers sponsoring assessments. For example, car manufacturers are consumers of steel and other inputs into automobile production; they expend significant time, effort, and money on evaluations of these components. Consumers Union, a nonprofit consumer testing and advocacy group, provides extensive testing of consumer products. Yet, as the preceding section suggests, despite the exceptions of federal agencies and occasional provider groups that may represent consumers, consumers and consumer groups infrequently sponsor formal evaluations of medical technology. The reasons are not hard to appreciate.

Consumers or patients may not have the expertise to evaluate technologies. Although their lack of expertise would make it difficult for them to perform evaluative research, it should not compromise their ability to *sponsor* it. Of greater importance is the set of obstacles that economists label "transaction costs." Consumers of health care are many and decentralized; producers are fewer and in some cases unique. For any one consumer, the cost of sponsoring an evaluation is high and the information acquired is of relatively little value to that individual, although for consumers collectively, the information may be quite valuable. If consumers could easily cooperate and pool their resources to sponsor such studies, they would often be an appropriate source of funding. Thus, consumer interests are most likely to be represented by agencies of the federal government, such as AHCPR, acting on their behalf.

Consumers may also be ill-suited to sponsor such studies, at least as individuals, because insurance coverage may narrow their interests. For consumers whose health care costs are completely covered by insurance, there is little interest in knowing the price of the technology; their sole concern is its safety and effectiveness. If they bear a copayment, they will have a direct stake in the costs of the technology, but to the extent that they are insured, their sensitivity to cost will be blunted. Hence, consumers often have little incentive to sponsor research that evaluates the costs as well as the benefits of medical technologies. Consumers or their representatives can play a role in sponsoring evaluations of medical technologies, but they are unlikely to take the lead in such efforts.

Payers for Use of Medical Technology

Unlike consumers, payers have a direct interest in the costs of the technology, and at least some payers have a large enough share of the insurance market to justify making the expenditures to evaluate medical technologies. Unlike producers, payers may perform evaluations of drugs and devices that are not patented (or that compete with several similar products). The large representation of payers among the entities sponsoring technology assessment attests to the importance of this activity to payers and to their suitability as sponsors of evaluative research.

Although payers are often large organizations with thousands of enrollees, none can be considered a monopsonist (sole buyer) in the market for health services or a monopolist in the sale of insurance. This is one of the reasons that payers have limited incentives to perform evaluative research. Even a large organization may not have sufficient economic interest to sponsor a costly evaluation of a medical technology, particularly if the information will be available to other payers (some of them competitors). Although payers collectively might find it worthwhile to learn who should receive coronary angioplasty, no single payer may be responsible for a large enough share of the market to justify spending the money required for a full evaluation of that procedure. Thus, payers tend to underinvest in such activities, although in many respects they are appropriate sponsors of evaluative research.

Payer-sponsored studies are subject to concerns about payer motivation. Payers are criticized from time to time for inappropriately concentrating on the bottom line of expenditures rather than on the well-being of their enrollees. Undoubtedly, some insurers focus inappropriately on the short-term payouts, but such an attitude cannot be a viable long-term strategy for a payer. Payers, whether they are insurers selling policies to enrollees or companies financing health care for their employees, cannot long retain subscribers or employees if the coverage package they offer does not seem worth the cost. If current insurers are systematically attempting to deny valuable health technologies to enrollees, they are not very successful; it is probably easier for privately insured Americans than for the citizens of any other country to gain access to expensive medical technologies.

Other Sponsors

The federal government (and to a lesser extent, state governments) is perhaps the most important sponsor of evaluative research. It plays multiple roles; hence, it does not fit completely into one of the categories of sponsors of technology assessment discussed above. Some agencies, such as AHCPR, reflect the interests of many parties and take seriously their role as a protector of consumer interests. The FDA similarly protects consumers in its efforts to keep unsafe or ineffective drugs and devices off the market.

In summary, even though many of the entities that sponsor evaluative research do not fit neatly into a single category, the classification is useful because it helps to provide an understanding of the influences and biases of each sponsor (see Table 13-2). Furthermore, a sponsor's willingness and ability to undertake evaluative research depend directly on its role. Payers might be willing to sponsor a study of bypass surgery, but producers—the surgeons who perform the procedure, and the hospitals where the surgery is performed—would not. The producers would be reluctant because they are too dispersed and would benefit too little from the results of such an evaluation to devote resources to it. Consumer groups and government agencies might sponsor a study of the use of aspirin for the prevention of heart attacks, but producers would not, because it is a generic product. Payers would not sponsor such a study, because their expenditures for aspirin are insignificant, and unless the use of aspirin was likely to markedly reduce the expenditures associated with heart disease, the treatment would not have a large financial impact. Any one sponsor—payers, producers, or consumers—would bear significant costs, but the information would be available to all. Hence, no one sponsor is likely to be able to fund studies of all technologies with which it is concerned. Other methods for sponsoring evaluative research may overcome this problem.

TABLE 13-2 Role of Health Care Organizations

Organization	Producer	Consumers/ Representatives	Payers
Health maintenance organizations		X	X
Providers	X	X	
Government agencies	X	X	X
Hospitals	X		X
Research organizations, foundations, IOM		X	
Pharmaceutical industry	X		
Device manufacturers	X		
Health Care Financing Administration			X

SPONSORING EVALUATIONS OF MEDICAL TECHNOLOGY

Previous Proposals for Sponsoring Technology Assessment

Each of the parties identified above can benefit from evaluations of technology. Their interests and capabilities differ, and they may not benefit equally from evaluative research, so they may not be equally suitable as sponsors of evaluative research. Although it is not clear that any one party should bear the responsibility for sponsoring all such research, the responsibility is now shared in a haphazard fashion. Too little is probably spent on such research because the benefits that all groups share undoubtedly exceed the total amount that producers, consumers, and payers spend on evaluative research as individual entities. Furthermore, the small percentage of health care expenditures devoted to formal technology assessments seems reasonable only for technologies that are stable, unchanging, and of well-established effectiveness; it is hard to imagine a less apt description of modern medical technologies. The recognition that too little technology assessment is done has periodically motivated individuals to propose new mechanisms for sponsoring such activities.

Most of the published proposals for changing the funding of technology assessment suggest that payers take a prominent role (Bunker et al., 1982; McGivney, 1992; Relman, 1980; Yarbro and Mortenson, 1985). Of the many individuals and organizations that have an interest in the evaluation of medical technology, payers have the most to gain from accurate assessments. The simple reason is that payers can directly use the results from evaluative research to assist in coverage decisions. A fair process for studying technologies and for using the results of evaluative studies to determine coverage can enable payers to facilitate the delivery of cost-effective care; to the extent that they are successful, and their success is known to employers and potential subscribers, they will attract additional subscribers.

One of the most comprehensive plans was offered by Bunker and colleagues (1982), who proposed the formation of an Institute of Health Care Evaluation. The institute would include representation from the public (employers, employees, and consumers), the medical profession (researchers, academicians, clinical practitioners, and professional societies), payers, and the federal government. Funding would come from a per capita levy on public and private payers, grants and contracts from the federal government, and a fee from all other members. The major goal of the institute would be to perform outcomes-based evaluative research, including cost-effectiveness analysis, on technologies chosen by the members. The institute's role would not include policy decisions; rather, responsibility for policy and coverage decision would rest with the members. Although agencies of the federal government and professional societies would contribute to the institute, much if not most of the funding would come from payers. The proposal does not mention the producers of medical technology explicitly.

A proposal formulated by the Jackson Hole Group, an organization propounding a specific model of managed competition, addresses the issue of sponsoring technology assessment within the framework of a comprehensive plan to reform the health care system (Ellwood, 1992). The plan of the Jackson Hole Group calls for the establishment of several new oversight agencies that together create a public-private health partnership. An independent government agency, the National Health Board, would oversee the transition to a health care system characterized by universal health insurance coverage, private-sector competition, and ongoing technology assessment. The National Health Board would recommend which health benefits should be covered on the basis of an evaluation of their effectiveness. Evaluations of effectiveness depend on the activity of two of three proposed private-sector agencies. A Health Standards Board would assess medical technologies and medical practice variations. This activity would be facilitated by the creation of an Outcomes Management Standards Board, which would set standards for data collection and health outcomes reporting and would oversee the collection of outcomes data on all delivered health care. Both boards would be sponsored by payers, employers, consumers, and health provider groups.

The aspects of the Jackson Hole Group's plan that are relevant to evaluative research are as follows. First, evaluative activities would be made an integral part of health care by requiring that outcomes data be systematically collected, reported, and analyzed. Second, technology assessment would be sponsored primarily by payers (insurance companies and employers), with contributions from consumer and health provider groups. The plan of the Jackson Hole Group is similar to the proposal of Bunker and colleagues (1982) in several important respects. Both plans highlight the need for systematic, increased funding of technology assessment, with participation of public and private entities, and both emphasize the role of payers as sponsors. The Jackson Hole Group model extends to many other aspects of health care, however, and goes considerably further in integrating collection of the data needed for technology assessment into routine health care delivery.

Several other proposals recommend that payers serve as the primary sponsors of technology assessments, perhaps in combination with government payers (Friedman and McCabe, 1992; McGivney and Hendee, 1988; Yarbro and Mortenson, 1985). For example, the payers might cover the medical care costs of patients enrolled in clinical trials but not the incremental research costs attributable to the trial itself.

Sponsorship of Stage III Assessments: The Leading Role of Payers

The chief reason for focusing on payers is that they have both the ability and the need to sponsor evaluative research, particularly stage III studies. Assuming that the research itself is valuable, an assumption that we do not explore here, too little is done for the sole reason that it is a public good. Use of the information by one person does not make it less available to others; in economist's terminology, the information is "nonrival." In contrast, the bread that one person consumes is bread that is not available to another. It is also difficult to charge for access to some kinds of information; economists describe such information as "nonexcludable." Because the information is valuable to many payers, consumers, and other interested parties, its total value may be great, but if access to the information cannot be controlled, no single entity that produces it will be able to recover its costs by selling the information to others.

These conditions characterize a form of market failure, which means that the standard argument that competitive markets produce optimal outcomes does not apply here. For an imperfect market such as this, Ronald Coase (a recent winner of the Nobel prize in economics) provided a useful framework for thinking about regulatory solutions. If there were a costless way to negotiate detailed contracts, to monitor them, and to enforce compliance with them so that everyone with access to the information had to share in the cost, this source of market failure could be overcome. These ideal conditions, called *zero transaction costs,* cannot be met, so the next best solution is to determine who would have the responsibility for producing the information if the ideal conditions were met. Coase's arguments had to do with property rights; he claimed that the legal system should (and did) assign rights to the party that would have purchased them if there were zero transaction costs. The best sponsor of evaluative research can be discovered by analogous means; it is the party or parties that would have the responsibility for sponsoring or producing the research if efficient markets for information could be established.

We believe that payers would have the primary responsibility for sponsoring evaluative research if such market conditions existed, because payers have the most to gain and have natural advantages in sponsoring the relevant research. Insurers can serve their enrollees better if they base their coverage decisions on good information about what medical technologies work best for a given expenditure. Furthermore, payers have unique access to the claims databases that can be used as part of the assessment of the costs and cost-effectiveness of medical technologies. These arguments have far less force for stage I assessments than for stage III assessments because, as we have noted, producers usually have the best access to the information relevant to stage I assessments and also have greater incentives to sponsor them.

Alternatives to Payer Sponsorship

Assigning the sponsorship responsibility to insurers is only one solution to raising the overall financial commitment to evaluative research. An obvious alternative is an increased level of direct government involvement. Why not increase the already substantial federal activity in technology assessment? Inasmuch as the federal government represents all interested parties and has an extensive and successful record of sponsoring such research, it too would seem to have strong reasons to support such work and the competence to do so. For many purposes, involvement of the federal government is desirable. But the means of financing the evaluative research is the most important reason for preferring sponsorship by payers (which includes some federal agencies and programs) to sponsorship by the federal government generally.

Government funding may lack one of the desirable features of sponsorship by payers. Namely, if payers are the sponsors—perhaps contributing to a fund in proportion to their premiums—the "tax" that funds the research falls most heavily on those who benefit most. The people with the most comprehensive insurance coverage would pay the most for the research, whereas those with minimal insurance would pay less. Government-sponsored research could be funded by a variety of mechanisms, but if it were funded by general tax revenues rather than a premium tax, the people who benefit the most from the research would not necessarily pay the most. Funding on the basis of premiums does not eliminate "free rider" problems, however, because people who lack insurance would not contribute to the fund. Nonetheless, the expenditure for technology assessment would be very small in relation to the value of the uncompensated health care the uninsured receive.

Tax Incidence for Evaluative Research

Tax incidence refers to the parties who ultimately bear the burden of a tax. If a tax is levied on groceries and the price of groceries increases by the same amount as the tax, the incidence of the tax is on the consumers. We suspect that the incidence of a tax on health insurance premiums will be on the people who pay the premiums, not the insurers. Similarly, it may matter little whether the money used to sponsor an evaluation comes in the form of a tax on health insurance premiums or as a tax on health care expenditures. In both cases, the cost is likely to be passed on to those consumers who either buy health insurance or use health care heavily. Suppose that the tax is imposed on health care expenditures rather than on the insurance premium. Then the insured person's health care expenditures might be, say, one percent higher than they would be otherwise. If insurance covered the tax as well as the health care expenditures, the added cost would be passed through as an increase in the insurance premium, so it would be nearly equivalent to an insurance premium tax. An important difference between the insurance premium tax and the health care expenditure tax is the liability of the uninsured; the uninsured would have to pay the latter but not the former tax. However, if many of the uninsured are unable to pay their health care expenses, they might also be unable to pay the tax. Furthermore, because many (but not all) of the uninsured and underinsured have less wealth and income than the insured, sparing them the tax might help redistribute income toward the less well off.

If insurers did not cover the health care expenditure tax, the tax would look to the insured individual like an increase in the copayment rate. Since most insured patients prefer insurance coverage for essentially all health expenses (about 80 percent of Medicare enrollees have "Medigap" plans that pay a substantial fraction of Medicare copayments and deductibles), they are likely to prefer to have insurance coverage for the technology assessment tax along with their other health care expenditures. Thus, they would prefer to contribute to the fund in the form of increased premiums rather than to pay an additional charge that would be added to copayments.

We believe that the contribution to stage III evaluative research should equal approximately the level Relman recommended over a decade ago for evaluative research, that is, 0.2 percent of health expenditures (Relman, 1980); at a very minimum, the level of expenditure should be 0.1 percent of health insurance premiums, which would amount to about $200 million (Fuchs and Garber, 1990). A fixed percentage contribution would enable the funding for technology assessments to increase if the adoption of a new technology led to increases in health care expenditures. If the pace of innovation or of the development of new applications of existing technologies increased, a higher level of funding might be needed, whereas if innovation slowed, a smaller contribution might be appropriate. These funds would be used primarily for stage III and, to a lesser extent, stage II assessments and would complement rather than replace the evaluative research sponsored by producers, as we discuss below.

Sponsorship for Early-Stage Technology Assessment

The published recommendations for financing and sponsoring technology assessment typically do not distinguish the stages of research, but most of the recommendations seem to focus on what we call stage II or stage III assessments. Payers have much less to contribute to stage I assessments. Because stage I evaluation is often a key component of the development (or approval process) of a new technology, the producers would usually be best situated to sponsor such evaluations. They also have incentives to perform stage II assessments when they are required for approval. Furthermore, stage II assessments may be necessary for discovering how a technology might best be used; for a drug, a stage II assessment may be required to determine the best dose and dosing interval. The producer will usually have a strong interest in performing such assessments and, to the extent that the assessments are designed to refine the technology, the producer has the incentives to perform a study that consumers, payers, and health care providers will find useful.

Producers would have a diminished role in stage III assessments, however. Drug and device manufacturers are increasingly interested in sponsoring cost-effectiveness evaluations, but they are unlikely to do so if the results of the evaluation might be unfavorable to their product.

Standards for Evaluative Research

Successful expansion of technology assessment activities requires not only adequate funding from appropriate sponsors but also the development of standards for the research. At least as important as the issue of who should sponsor technology assessment is the question of how it can be made as impartial and as useful as possible. Evaluative research can be complex, the data can be overwhelming, and the analytic methods can be difficult; it will not always be amenable to replication without great effort. Consequently, the process itself must be open and credible. One way to ensure this is to concentrate decisionmaking in a group that is insulated from short-term political and economic exigencies but that is responsive to the need to contain health care spending.

Centralization of the sponsorship of technology assessment activities can improve the quality and usefulness by such assessments by helping to aid in the implementation of uniform standards. The cost-effectiveness techniques that are prominent in stage III assessments are fairly well developed, despite a number of areas of disagreement. One of the most imposing obstacles to using cost-effectiveness results to guide resource allocation in health care is the lack of uniformity in the assumptions used by different groups of investigators. Although any two studies might adhere to the same set of principles in computing cost-effectiveness estimates, one might use a rate-of-time discount of five percent, whereas the other might use two percent; one might adopt a societal perspective, whereas the other might adopt the perspective of payers. Although we do not advocate strict adherence to a uniform standard for all cost-effectiveness studies, the establishment of a set of minimum standards can improve comparability of assessments. Thus, for example, the institutions that sponsor or coordinate technology assessments can define a set of basic assumptions that all studies should include, although they might also explore the consequences of following an alternative set of assumptions. This simple step would make the studies much more useful and would not limit the ability of researchers to explore alternative approaches.

The drawbacks of current approaches to technology assessment are not limited to the varied and often contradictory assumptions used by different researchers. A second problem is the selection of technologies to be studied. As we discussed above, sponsors now select the technologies to study on the basis of their own interests. Although they can hardly be faulted for doing so, the process would be more useful to the public if the method for selecting the topics for study were explicit. The major factors that need to be considered in studying technologies are well known: the expense of the technology, the degree of uncertainty about its effectiveness, and the importance of the health condition that is being prevented or treated.

The voices of consumers, providers, producers, and payers need to be heard to help ensure that the assessments address their concerns fairly and as completely as possible. Most proposals for funding technology assessments and most international approaches to sponsoring technology assessments, whether they are part of coverage decisions or not, incorporate representation from the many interested parties.

CONCLUSIONS

Evaluative research has a critical role to play in determination of the efficacy and effectiveness of medical technologies. If we can ensure that evaluative research is of high quality and accessible, it also should have a central role in decisionmaking regarding the coverage of medical technologies and reimbursement policies. Because the U.S. health care system is pluralistic and decentralized, no single entity is suitable as a sponsor of the broad range of medical technology assessment that is needed. Producers have an important role to play in stage I and II technology assessments. Payers have the most direct incentives to sponsor stage III assessments, because they need to anticipate the economic, health, and to a lesser extent, social consequences of covering a technology. We believe that they should be the primary sponsors of stage III technology assessments. Other proposals have contained similar recommendations, and all urge that the assessors possess some independence from short-term economic incentives and direct political control.

This area of research is likely to remain underfunded until cooperative arrangements result in more centralized activities than are currently possible. The continuing and unsustainable growth in health care expenditures will inevitably lead to further attempts to reform health care financing mechanisms. If these reforms are to result in the rational use of U.S. health care dollars, they must be guided by research that determines what works, and at what cost. Powerful economic disincentives currently deter the growth in technology assessment activities that is needed. A system that generates adequate funding for evaluative research will need to be designed to overcome these disincentives. Only then will this country have the opportunity to control expenditures while identifying those technologies that are of the greatest value to consumers of health care.

REFERENCES

Bunker, J. P., Fowles, J., and Schaffarzick, R. 1982. Evaluation of medical-technology strategies: Effects of coverage and reimbursements. *New England Journal of Medicine* 306:687-692.

Eddy, D. M., ed. 1991. *Common Screening Tests.* Philadelphia: American College of Physicians.

Ellwood, P. M., Enthoven, A. C., and Etheredge, L. 1992. The Jackson Hole initiatives for a twenty-first century American health care system. *Health Economics* 1:149168.

Friedman, M. A., and McCabe, M. S. 1992. Assigning care costs associated with therapeutic oncology research: A modest proposal. *Journal of the National Cancer Institute* 84:760-763.

Fuchs, V. R., and Garber, A. M. 1990. The new technology assessment. *New England Journal of Medicine* 323:673-677.

Garber, A. M., Clarke, A. E., Goldman, D. P., and Gluck, M. E. 1992. *Federal and Private Roles in the Development and Provision of Alglucerase Therapy for Gaucher Disease.* Washington, D.C.: U.S. Government Printing Office.

Institute of Medicine. 1985. *Assessing Medical Technologies.* Washington, D.C.: National Academy Press.

Institute of Medicine. 1988. *Medical Technology Assessment Directory.* Washington, D.C.: National Academy Press.

McGivney, W. T. 1992. Proposal for assuring technology competency and leadership in medicine. *Journal of the National Cancer Institute* 84:742-744.

McGivney, W. T., and Hendee, W. R. 1988. Technology assessment in medicine: The role of the American Medical Association. *Journal of the American Medical Association* 112:1181-1185.

McGuire, P. 1990. Kaiser Permanente's New Technologies Committee: An approach to assessing technology. *Quality Review Bulletin* 16:240-242.

Relman, A. S. 1980. Assessment of medical practices. *New England Journal of Medicine* 303:153-154.

Sox, H. C., Jr., ed. 1987. *Common Diagnostic Tests: Use and Interpretation.* Philadelphia: American College of Physicians.

Yarbro, J. W., and Mortenson, L. E. 1985. The need for diagnosis-related group 471. *Journal of the American Medical Association* 253:684-685.

14

Health Care Reform: Some Reflections on Technology

SUSAN BARTLETT FOOTE

Coverage and adoption decisions about medical technology fundamentally affect the pace of innovation in medicine. The papers in this volume discuss how these decisions are presently made by a variety of public and private payers. But there is a broader context for those decisions. There are, for example, enormous implications for medical technology in the current movement to reform the delivery of health care in the United States. Indeed, just as innovation is a dynamic process, so too is the health policy environment. Health care reform was a major issue throughout the course of the 1992 presidential campaign and President Clinton has made health care reform a cornerstone of his administration's policy agenda. This paper provides (1) a discussion of the legislative background for reform, (2) a model for analyzing the implications of health care reform proposals on decisionmaking about medical technologies, and (3) some reflections on medical technology policy.

LEGISLATIVE BACKGROUND

The legislative process over the last few years has provided an illuminating lesson on how issues emerge on the national agenda. Although health policy experts have long debated issues of access, cost, and quality, until recently comprehensive health care reform was only sporadically addressed in Congress. True, there has been some activity in the Senate, chiefly on Medicare and Medicaid policy in the Finance Committee and on public health issues in the Labor and Human Resources Committee. Similarly, in the House, the Ways and Means Committee and the Energy and Commerce Committee have also addressed these issues. But these efforts were discrete, relatively modest events.

From 1989 to 1990, a major breakthrough occurred. The bipartisan Pepper Commission (named after its first chair, Representative Claude Pepper), recommended legislation to ensure that all Americans had coverage for health care and long term care. The Commission's final report, released in September of 1990, made quite detailed recommendations about access issues, but gave few specifics on how to finance its recommendations. Because of the flaws in identifying financing mechanisms, the commissioners were divided in their support for the recommendations (Pepper Commission, 1990).

While Congress mulled over the problems of access and financing, health care remained in the minds of the American public. The special election in Pennsylvania to fill the Senate seat of the deceased Senator John Heinz confirmed that health care remained a pressing public concern. The success of Democrat Harris Wofford, who ran a campaign focused on the need for health care reform, convinced politicians that the issue of health care had to be addressed. A spate of legislative proposals quickly followed, joining many that were already under consideration.

In response to the Wofford victory, a group of Senate Republicans quickly introduced a reform package that a task force of their party had been discussing for many months (S. 1936). House Republicans produced a somewhat similar proposal later in the summer (H.R. 5325).

There was considerable diversity among the Democratic health care reform plans in Congress. Democratic bills ranged from a single-payer Canadian-style system (Wellstone, S. 3207) to the Conservative Democratic Forum's managed competition, market-based model (H.R. 5936). Perhaps in consequence, few plans drew more than a handful of cosponsors in either chamber. Even the Democratic leadership proposal, commonly known as "pay-or-play" and drafted by key Democratic leaders (Senators Edward Kennedy, George Mitchell, Jay Rockefeller, Donald Riegle), failed to draw more than nine cosponsors (S. 1227).

The presidential candidates also weighed in. President Bush gave what was billed as a major health address in the early spring of 1992, circulated a white paper entitled "The President's Comprehensive Health Reform Program," which contained his market-based reforms, and introduced some of his proposals in legislative form soon thereafter (President's Program, 1992). The Democratic presidential nominee, Governor Bill Clinton, also presented a plan. In defining fundamental reform, Mr. Clinton called for "an appropriate and revised governmental role with a reliance on the private sector" (Clinton, 1992).

Few of these early plans, however, whether Democratic or Republican, came to terms with the intractable issue of financing. Not until June of 1992 did bills with clear and explicit cost-containment appear. In the controversial StarkGephart proposal, the Health Care Cost Reduction Act (H.R. 5502), a national health budget (or global budget) would be established to control spending. States could impose cost-containment programs if they came in under the projected budget. Otherwise the federal government would set maximum rates for hospi tal, physician, pharmaceutical, and other services. In the same month, the Dingell-Waxman "Health Choice" plan was introduced. It proposed to control spending by relying on overall limits on expenditure growth (or "inflation") that would be overseen by a quasi-public (Federal Reserve-type) board with representation from consumers and providers (H.R. 5514). Despite the rash of legislative activity, no major health care reform passed in the 102nd Congress before it adjourned in October of 1992. Why?

The Democratic majority in Congress remained deeply divided philosophically on how to create a reform proposal. Unable to pass comprehensive reform, some Democrats resisted efforts to address specific problems in health care, such as the small group insurance market. Although the Senate managed to pass the bipartisan Bentsen-Durenberger bill to reform the insurance market for small employers (S. 1872) twice, the proposal never emerged from the conference committee.

President Clinton put health care reform at the top of his agenda during the transition period following the election. His selection of First Lady Hillary Rodham Clinton to supervise the effort symbolized his personal commitment to reform. Throughout the spring and summer of 1993, hundreds of members of a White House Task Force put together volumes of option papers for the administration. By the fall, the president and his administration began to market his plan in earnest. In addition to the president's proposal, the supporters of a Canadian-style plan reintroduced their bill, and the conservative Democrats and moderate Republicans supported market-based reform plans.

Immediately before the Christmas recess, a series of major bills was introduced. Prominent among them was Clinton's Health Security Act (S. 1757), introduced on November 22, 1993. Primary competitors included the Managed Competition Act, introduced by Representatives Cooper and Grandy in the House (H.R. 3222) and Senators Breaux and Durenberger in the Senate (S. 1579), and the Senate Republican task force's Health Equity and Access Reform Today (HEART) Act of 1993, led by John Chafee (S. 1770) and sponsored in the House by Representative Thomas (H.R. 3704). Nineteen ninety-four will be the year in which these approaches are debated and voted upon.

AN ANALYTIC MODEL

The key issue that distinguishes various approaches to health care reform is the role of government in the newly designed system. A public regulator model concentrates health care policy decisions in the hands of government. These policy decisions could include the setting and enforcing of global budgets, determining prices for services, and allocating buying responsibility to public agencies.

The most extreme version of the public regulator model is a Canadian-style system. In it, government becomes the single payer and every citizen is a partici pant in the public program. In contrast, the private regulator model relies on the private sector to finance and deliver health care. Government retains two roles. First, it sets the rules for the marketplace through such measures as insurance reforms to guarantee policy issuance (e.g., elimination of experience rating) and portability, mandated disclosure of information on cost and quality, and assistance for individual purchasing decisions through the certification of private-sector group purchasing arrangements.

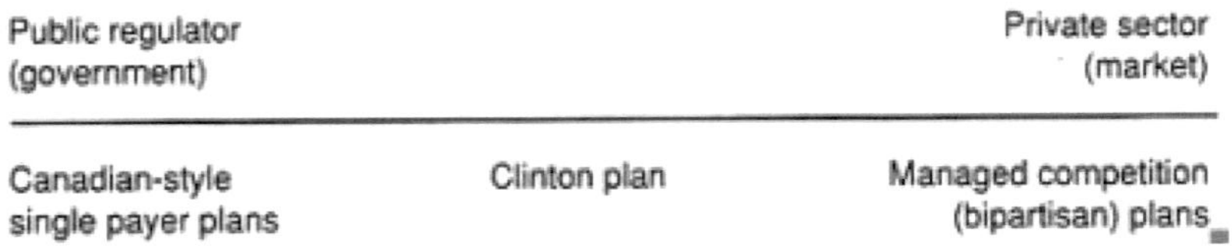

FIGURE 14-1 Health care reform spectrum: Government versus the market models. The figure shows how the various health care plans discussed in the paper fall within the range of public and private models.

Second, government can also guarantee financial access for those who cannot afford to purchase health care. In these market-based proposals, government provides vouchers or other forms of cash assistance and eligible individuals purchase health plans through purchasing groups. The Jackson Hole Group, a loose collection of health policy experts and health care providers, inspired the "managed competition" model that is premised on this limited role for government (Enthoven and Kronick, 1989).

The president's reform plan, which circulated in health policy circles in the fall of 1993, tried to merge the market-based approach of managed competition with some of the tools of government control. The bill included references to a competitive marketplace, but also added global budgets and premium price controls, state-run monopolistic purchasing groups (called health alliances), and regulatory powers in the hands of a National Health Board and the states.

IMPLICATIONS FOR MEDICAL TECHNOLOGY POLICY

In the early stages of the debate on reform, medical technology issues have taken a back seat to system reform. This situation stems from the erroneous premise that medical technology is separate from health care services. Technology is often perceived as an independent, cost-raising feature, a problem that one would turn to after the fundamental work of health care reform has been done. But medical technology, of course, is not separate from health care: it *is* health care. Health care reform plans must consider how the interrelationships of technology and the provision of health services will affect the form of the health care system.

At a minimum, the approach to medical technology must be consistent with the overall philosophy of health care reform. Ideally, it will try to anticipate the longer-term effects of policies affecting technology on the health care system as a whole. For example, some supporters of a market-based model of health care reform have assumed that a federal regulatory board should control technology. This assumption epitomizes the erroneous view of technology as separate from health care services and is furthermore inconsistent with a market approach. It is hard to see how competition could thrive if government regulated all the tools of the trade.

Some advocates of a government model also assume that a public regulator will control most of the decisions made about health care services. Among these decisions are when and how a technology becomes available and the price that can be charged for it (Wellstone-McDermott American Health Security Act of 1993). These approaches illustrate a strong distrust of the private sector, and that attitude spills over into technology decisions at all levels.

The managed competition model will likely be the starting place for discussions of technology policy in health care reform. Managed competition rests on a careful mix of market forces and government direction. The challenge is to design a system that ensures the proper balance between government and the private sector. How can that balance be struck? The analysis is made easier by using a categorization developed by Blumenthal in which medical technology issues can be divided into three distinct categories: (1) knowledge development, such as clinical trials, analyses of cost effectiveness, and quality of life assessments, (2) knowledge processing, such as systems for gathering, validating, interpreting, and disseminating information, and (3) decisionmaking, which includes questions about who has the power to make decisions on coverage and payment for the use of a particular technology (Blumenthal, 1983).

The roles of government and the private sector vary in each of these three categories. For example, start first with the focus of this volume: coverage and adoption decisionmaking. In a managed competition model, the health plans are the appropriate locus of decisionmaking. Each health plan will determine which specific procedures are appropriate to treat the conditions of individual enrollees. However, plans must be able to articulate defensible, scientific principles for their decision to exclude a new technology.

Health plans are in the best position to respond to consumers and their decisions are more accessible to them. Decentralization allows for greater experimentation and diversity, which will result in data that inform further developments and improvements. Skeptics may argue that the economic incentives in health plans will lead to decisions to deny coverage (and save money) at the expense of patients' health. In response, it can be argued that government, particularly when it is the payer, is in no position to be more generous. The experience of technology assessment for Medicare beneficiaries is a telling case in point.

To a certain extent, then, one must decide who to trust—government or the market—a decision that divides the health care reform debate. How one answers that question depends upon one's personal values and experience. Uwe Reinhardt (1989) has commented that, in general, Americans tend to trust the private sector more than government and tend to forgive mistakes more readily when they occur on the private side.

Even in market-based models, there remains a critical role for government in technology policy. Government can play a role in assisting decisionmaking. The National Health Board, or whatever central body is established, could provide a safety valve for challenges to coverage decisions made by private sector health plans. Thus, the board could issue explicit, uniform decisions based on scientific, expert judgments if there were disruptive and contentious variations from plan to plan or if new, expensive, and highly beneficial technologies were being excluded on cost grounds alone.

Information is key to the success of any market-based managed competition model. This requires knowledge development. The current public and private efforts in technology assessment and effectiveness research—the knowledge development stage—are too decentralized and disorganized to provide the information that health care providers and patients need. When a practitioner seeks information needed to make an important decision, most of the time the necessary information is simply not available. We cannot improve the quality of care, or potentially reduce the inappropriate use of services, unless we first generate knowledge.

Government can play an important role in facilitating the development of knowledge about health care technologies. It can fund and direct clinical trials, identify areas where additional research is necessary, and coordinate public- and private-sector cooperation. Many health care plans have developed sophisticated technology assessment programs. These private-sector activities should be promoted and supported. Unfortunately, to date the federal government's track record in supporting technology assessment activities has been mixed. It has generally been reluctant to invest in expenses associated with information development. In fact, the politics of government's technology assessment efforts are sobering (Foote, 1987; Garber, this volume).

Thus, medical technology policy in health care reform plans must include efforts to reorganize the federal government's many disparate sources of knowledge development—including the National Institutes of Health, the Food and Drug Administration, the Agency for Health Care Policy and Research, the National Center for Health Statistics, and the Office of Research and Demonstrations at the Health Care Financing Administration.

Finally, government can also play a role in knowledge processing. Information about the efficacy, effectiveness, and outcomes of health care services will help improve decisionmaking at all levels. This activity would require a highly sophisticated ability to acquire and analyze large databases. Government has demonstrated some expertise in this regard—processing millions upon millions of Medicare claims, for example. It has also undertaken new efforts to disseminate this information to providers and patients. It is essential that the government maintains, and perhaps expands, its contribution to the planning and implementation of knowledge processing activities.

We must ensure that a dynamic and innovative medical technology industry will continue to thrive no matter how the health care system changes. The industry cannot thrive if we do not understand its contribution to the cost and the quality of health care. We cannot ignore basic issues of technology coverage and payment that are essential to the design of reform.

The design of health care tools and institutions will necessarily depend upon the underlying philosophy of the health care reform plan that is adopted. It is likely that a mix of government and private-sector markets will emerge. As we move closer to adopting a reform plan, it is essential that we carefully consider the desired formulation of this mix. In 1934, Lewis Mumford described the challenge that we face today:

> The gains of technics are never registered automatically in society; they require equally adroit inventions and adaptations in politics; . . . the machine itself makes no demands and holds out no promises: it is the human spirit that makes demands and keeps promises.

We must be as adroit inventing political and economic structures as we have been in producing technological gains.

REFERENCES

Blumenthal, D. 1983. Federal policy toward health care technology: The case of the National Center. *Milbank Memorial Fund Quarterly/Health and Society* 61:584613.

Clinton, B. 1992. The Clinton health care plan. *New England Journal of Medicine* 327:804-806.

Enthoven, A., and Kronick, R. 1989. A consumer-choice plan for the 1990s: Universal health insurance in a system designed to promote quality and economy. *New England Journal of Medicine* 320:29-37, 94-101.

Foote, S.B. 1987. Assessing medical technology assessment: Past, present and future. *The Milbank Quarterly* 65:59-80.

Mumford, Lewis. 1934. *Technics and Civilization.* New York: Harcourt, Brace, Jovanovich.

Reinhardt, U. 1989. Respondent: What can Americans learn from Europeans? *Health Care Financial Review* (annual supplement): 97-104.

The Pepper Commission: U.S. Bipartisan Commission on Comprehensive Health Care. 1990. *A Call for Action: Final Report.* Washington, D.C.: Government Printing Office.

The President's Comprehensive Reform Program. February 6, 1992.

APPENDIXES

APPENDIX A

Workshop Agenda

IMPROVING THE TRANSLATION OF RESEARCH FINDINGS INTO CLINICAL PRACTICE: WORKSHOP IV

Examining Coverage and Adoption Decisions About Medical Technologies

Friday, September 18, 1992

8:30 a.m.	Registration and Continental Breakfast
9:00	**Welcome and Opening Remarks** Kenneth Shine, President, Institute of Medicine

SESSION I. SETTING THE STAGE

Moderator: Gerald Laubach, Chair, Committee on Technological Innovation in Medicine

9:15	**The Nature of Technological Change: Incentives Matter!** Burton Weisbrod, Northwestern University
9:45	Discussion

SESSION II. PROVIDER DECISIONMAKING

Moderator: Richard Nesson, Brigham and Women's Hospital

10:00	**An Overview of Coverage and Adoption Decisionmaking by Payers and Providers** Bryan Luce and Ruth Brown, Battelle

10:30 **Role of the Hospital in the Acquisition of Technology** Gerard Anderson and Earl Steinberg, Johns Hopkins University

11:00 Break

11:15 **Physicians' Decisions Regarding the Acquisition of Technology** Mark Fendrick and Sanford Schwartz, University of Pennsylvania

11:45 Discussion

12:30 Lunch

SESSION III. THIRD PARTY PAYER COVERAGE DECISIONS

Moderator: Michael Soper, CIGNA

1:45 **The Experience of Blue Cross and Blue Shield Association** Susan Gleeson, Blue Cross and Blue Shield Association

2:15 **Decisionmaking at the Health Care Financing Administration** Kathleen Buto, Health Care Financing Administration

2:45 **Current and Future Approaches to Coverage in a Group Model Health Maintenance Organization** Paul Lairson, Kaiser Permanente

3:15 Break

3:30 **High Dose Chemotherapy-Autologous Bone Marrow Transplantation: A Model for Health Care Decisionmaking?** William McGivney, AEtna Health Plans

4:00 **Legal Implications of Experimental Exclusions** Lee Newcomer, United Health Care

4:30 Discussion

5:30 Adjournment and Reception

6:00 **Reception Speech: Fishbowl Medicine Versus Muddling Through** Uwe Reinhardt, Princeton University

Saturday, September 19, 1992

8:00 a.m.	Continental Breakfast

SESSION IV. INCREASING THE RATIONALITY OF COVERAGE DECISIONMAKING

Moderator: Uwe Reinhardt, Princeton University

8:45	**Strengthening the Connection Between Evaluative Research and Coverage Decisionmaking** Lucian Leape, Harvard School of Public Health
9:15	**Manufacturers' Responses to the Increased Demand for Outcomes Research** Ann Marshall, Abbott Laboratories
9:45	Discussion
10:15	Break
10:30	**Paying for Evaluative Research** Alan Garber, Palo Alto Veterans Administration Medical Center and Stanford University
11:00	**Health Care Reform: Implications for Decisionmaking** Susan Bartlett Foote, Staff, U.S. Senate
11:30	**Panel Discussion:** Lucian Leape, Harvard School of Public Health Ann Marshall, Abbott Laboratories Alan Garber, Stanford University Susan Bartlett Foote, Staff, U.S. Senate
12:00	Discussion
12:30	**Summary of the Conference and Adjournment** Uwe Reinhardt, Princeton University

APPENDIX B

Contributors

GERARD F. ANDERSON is the director of the Center for Hospital Finance and Management, Johns Hopkins Medical Institutions, co-director of the Program for Medical Technology and Practice Assessment, and an associate professor of health policy and management, Johns Hopkins University. He teaches graduate level courses in international health, statistics, and health care financing in the School of Hygiene and Public Health. Dr. Anderson is currently conducting research on comparative insurance systems in developing countries, medical education, hospital payment reform, technology diffusion, capital, and capitated systems.

He has published over 60 articles in the New England Journal of Medicine, Journal of the American Medical Association, Inquiry, Health Affairs, Medical Care, Health Care Financing Review, Review of Economics and Statistics, Southern Economic Journal and many other journals. Dr. Anderson has recently completed two books on health care payment policy. One book, published by the Johns Hopkins University Press, examines how academic medical centers are being affected by changes in the competitive environment and how they must alter their behavior to cope with changes in the financing for uncompensated care, graduate medical education, biomedical research, and patient care services. A second book, also published by the Johns Hopkins University Press, describes and analyses the impact of the myriad of public and private cost containment efforts launched over the past 15 years and sets forth long range policy proposals for the future.

Prior to coming to Johns Hopkins in 1983, Dr. Anderson held various positions in the Office of the Secretary, U.S. Department of Health and Human Ser vices. He worked primarily on health care financing issues. One of his major activities was the development of major aspects of the Medicare Prospective Payment legislation.

RUTH E. BROWN is a research associate with Battelle's Medical Technology and Policy Research Center, Washington, D.C. office. She holds master's degrees in microbiology and health policy and planning and has had more than 14 years experience in the biomedical/health fields. At Battelle, she has been the principal investigator for several projects and has had considerable experience in managing clinical studies. She has participated in studies of chronic mental disease outcomes and evaluations of quality of life for AIDS, cancer and renal dialysis patients. She has directed studies of cost-effectiveness to prevent such diseases as Hepatitis B and childhood diseases and directed health policy projects related to reimbursement criteria for off-label and immunosuppressive drugs, developing options for reducing the volume of unnecessary services provided to Medicare beneficiaries, and analyzing the utilization of technology assessment in decisionmaking by health care providers and payers. She is co-author of papers appearing in *Hospital and Community Psychiatry, Quality Review Bulletin, Quality of Life Research, Journal of Clinical Epidemiology, Morbidity and Mortality Weekly Report,* and *Post Marketing Surveillance.* Before coming to Battelle, Ms. Brown was a researcher at the Walter Reed Army Institute of Research.

KATHLEEN A. BUTO, in her current position, directs the policy development bureau of the Health Care Financing Administration. Her organization's responsibilities span a wide range of Medicare coverage, payment, and eligibility policy issues. These include developing Prospective Payment System rates for hospitals, physician fee schedules, Medicare coverage rules for technologies and procedures, and conditions of participation for hospitals, nursing homes and home health agencies. Ms. Buto has held positions in the Health Care Financing Administration since 1982. From 1976-1982, she served on the immediate staff of three Secretaries of the Department of Health and Human Services and with the Public Health Service's Review Panel on New Drug Evaluation. She holds a B.A. in American Studies from Douglass College and an M.P.A. from Harvard University.

HOLLY V. DAWKINS is a research assistant in the Divisions of Health Care Services and of Biobehavioral Sciences and Mental Disorders at the Institute of Medicine. Since joining the Institute of Medicine in June 1988, she has worked on over a dozen IOM projects, ranging from the IOM program on technological innovation in medicine to two studies evaluating the development and use of clinical practice guidelines. Current studies she is working on address substance abuse and mental health issues in federal AIDS research; the Health Care Financing Administration's evaluation of its peer review organization program; and preventing nicotine dependency in children and youths. In 1991, she received the Institute of Medicine staff award for her work on the Institute of Medicine study to evaluate the artificial heart program of the National Heart, Lung, and Blood Institute. Holly earned her A.B. with honors in English from Brown University in 1986.

A. MARK FENDRICK is an assistant professor of internal medicine and an assistant professor of health services management and policy at the University of Michigan. Dr. Fendrick's research focuses on the economic assessment of medical interventions with special attention to the study of the diffusion of emerging technologies. He completed his bachelor's degree in health economics and chemistry with highest honors from the University of Pennsylvania and received his medical education at Harvard University. He interrupted medical school for one year to be a Charles A. Dana Foundation research scholar at the University of Pennsylvania School of Medicine, where he received training in clinical research methodology, computer sciences, and health care policy. Dr. Fendrick completed his residency in internal medicine at the Hospital of the University of Pennsylvania. Immediately following his residency, Dr. Fendrick spent a year as a visiting scholar divided between the Swedish Council for Medical Technology Assessment and the École Polytechnique in Paris, where he studied issues related to the diffusion and policy impact of medical innovation. Upon return, Dr. Fendrick spent two years as a Robert Wood Johnson Clinical Scholar, where he completed his postgraduate training in health services research, medical technology diffusion, and physician decisionmaking.

SUSAN BARTLETT FOOTE was formerly an associate professor of business and public policy at the Walter A. Haas School of Business, University of California, Berkeley. She is now senior health policy advisor to Senator Dave Durenberger (R-MN); Senator Durenberger serves both on the Senate Finance and Senator Labor Committees. Ms. Foote has responsibility for issues of health reform and medical technology that are within the committees' jurisdiction. She has written widely in the field of safety regulation and business-government relations, with a special emphasis on medical devices. Ms. Foote's work has appeared in the *Journal of Health Policy, Politics and Law, Milbank Quarterly,* and numerous law and business journals. Her book on the influence of public policy on medical device innovation, *Managing the Medical Arms Race,* was published by the University of California Press in 1992. Ms. Foote is a member of the Institute of Medicine (IOM) Committee on Technological Innovation in Medicine and served on the IOM Forum on Drug Development. She served as a consumer representative for the Office of Device Evaluation at the Food and Drug Administration and contributed to reports of the Office of Technology Assessment of the U.S. Congress. She holds a J.D. degree from Boalt Hall, Univer sity of California, Berkeley. In 1990-1991, she was a Robert Wood Johnson health policy fellow working on issues of medical technology in the U.S. Senate.

ALAN M. GARBER is an associate professor in the Departments of Medicine, Economics, and Health Research and Policy at Stanford University. He is also a staff physician and health services research and development senior research associate of the Department of Veterans Affairs, and research associate and director, Health Care Program, of the National Bureau of Economic Research, Inc. (NBER). He graduated from Harvard College *summa cum laude,* and received his Ph.D. in economics from Harvard and an M.D. with research honors from Stanford. His fellowships and awards include a National Science Foundation Graduate Fellowship, Christopher Walker Research Fellowship, John Harvard Scholarship, Henry J. Kaiser Family Foundation Faculty Scholarship in General Internal Medicine, and the Young Investigator Award of the Association for Health Services Research. He has served as a consultant to the Institute of Medicine, the Office of Technology Assessment, and the Clinical Efficacy Assessment Project of the American College of Physicians, and is a member of the Blue Cross and Blue Shield Association Medical Advisory Panel. He is a fellow of the American College of Physicians and a National Councillor of the American Federation for Clinical Research.

Dr. Garber's research is directed toward methods for improving health care while limiting its costs. It includes two complementary areas: developing methods for determining the cost-effectiveness of health interventions and structuring incentives to ensure that cost-effective care is actually delivered. His ongoing research includes both methodological and applied work in cost-effectiveness analysis in health care, studies of the role of financial incentives in the utilization of hospital and nursing home care among the elderly, projections of health expenditures, and international comparisons of health care financing and health outcomes.

ANNETINE C. GELIJNS is associate director, The Habif Center for Surgical Studies, and assistant professor, the Department of Surgery and the School of Public Health, Columbia University. Prior to joining the Columbia faculty, Dr. Gelijns was director of the Program on Technological Innovation in Medicine at the Institute of Medicine (IOM) and editor of the series *Medical Innovation at the Crossroads.*

Before joining the IOM, she was senior researcher for the Project on Future Health Care Technology, in The Hague, The Netherlands, which was cosponsored by the European office of the World Health Organization (WHO) and the Dutch government. From 1983 to 1985, Dr. Gelijns worked for the Steering Committee on Future Health Scenarios, where she helped develop models for long-term health planning in the areas of cancer, cardiovascular disease, and aging; she also had a joint appointment to the Staff Bureau for Health Policy Development, Department of Health, the Netherlands.

Dr. Gelijns has been a consultant to various national and international organizations, including the WHO and the Organization for Economic Cooperation and Development. She is an officer of the board of the International Society on Technology Assessment in Health Care. Her research focuses on the factors shaping the rate and direction of medical innovation, as well as on the economic assessment of surgical interventions. She received the LL.M. degree from the University of Leyden and her Ph.D. from the University of Amsterdam.

SUSAN GLEESON is the executive director of Medical and Quality Management for the Blue Cross and Blue Shield (BCBS) Association. In this capacity Ms. Gleeson is responsible for two technology evaluation programs: the Medical Necessity Program and the Technology Evaluation and Coverage Program. Both programs determine the appropriate uses of technologies. Program information is used by Blue Cross and Blue Shield Plans for coverage decisions, utilization review activities, and monitoring quality.

Ms. Gleeson is director of the Association's recently created Center for Quality Health Care. In this capacity she is responsible for coordinating the development of programs that support BCBS Plans' activities to assess, monitor, and promote quality care for their subscribers. The Center also sponsors demonstration projects to evaluate new quality management approaches.

Ms. Gleeson joined the Association in 1977 and she has been responsible for technology management programs since 1980. Prior to joining the Association, Ms. Gleeson was active in health care delivery and administration.

PAUL D. LAIRSON is the former central office physician liaison of the Permanente Medical Groups; he had held that position since October 1981. Dr. Lairson received both his B.A. and M.D. degrees from the University of Michigan. He joined Kaiser Permanente in 1966 as an internist in the Northwest Region, later holding positions of medical director of the extended care facility, director of a medical office, and associate regional medical director. From 1975 to 1977, Dr. Lairson served as medical director of the Georgetown University Community Health Plan. In 1978, he helped organize the Kaiser/Prudential Health Plan and the Permanente Medical Association of Texas in Dallas, and the next year became the medical director there. In 1981, he moved to Oakland as the medical advisor to Kaiser Permanente Advisory Services and physician liaison in the Central Office.

Dr. Lairson served as the liaison between the medical directors and the central office and was the director of the Permanente Medical Groups Interregional Services. He also served as chair of the Interregional New Technologies Committee, Garfield Memorial Fund Committee, Interregional AIDS Committee, In terregional Committee on Aging, and Interregional Quality Assurance Committee.

GERALD D. LAUBACH holds a B.A. from the University of Pennsylvania and a Ph.D. in organic chemistry from the Massachusetts Institute of Technology. He is formerly president of Pfizer, Inc., and chair of the IOM Committee on Technological Innovation in Medicine. Dr. Laubach is a research chemist by training and served as a laboratory scientist in his early years at Pfizer. He is a member of the Institute of Medicine and the National Academy of Engineering, and served on the now disbanded IOM Council on Health Care Technology. His current activities also include membership on the executive committee of the Council on Competitiveness (successor group to the President's Commission on Industrial Competitiveness), the board of the Food and Drug Law Institute, the Corporation of the Rockefeller University Council, the Carnegie Institution of Washington, the National Committee for Quality Health Care, the Medical Center Advisory Board, the New York Hospital-Cornell Medical Center, and the Corporation Committee for Sponsored Research at the Massachusetts Institute of Technology; he is a director of CIGNA Corporation of Philadelphia and the Millpore Corporation of Bedford, Massachusetts. Previously, Dr. Laubach served as chair of the Pharmaceutical Manufacturers Association from 1977 to 1978 and as a board member until April 1989. He has received honorary doctorates in humane letters from the City University of New York, in law from Connecticut College, and in science from Hofstra University.

LUCIAN L. LEAPE is a graduate of Cornell University and Harvard Medical School. Following his residencies in surgery at the Massachusetts General Hospital and pediatric surgery at Boston Childrens Hospital, he spent a year as a pediatric surgical registrar at the Alder Hey Hospital in England. He then joined the faculty of the University of Kansas School of Medicine, where he was appointed a Markle Scholar. In 1973, Dr. Leape was appointed professor of surgery at Tufts University School of Medicine and chief of pediatric surgery at the New England Medical Center Hospital. In 1986-87, he spent a year as a Pew health policy fellow at the RAND/UCLA Center for Health Policy Study, and then joined the faculty of the Harvard School of Public Health, where he is currently lecturer on health policy in the Department of Health Policy and Management. He is also a consultant at RAND.

While an academic surgeon, Dr. Leape pursued research interests in burns, lye injury, parenteral nutrition, gastroesophageal reflux, Wilms' tumor, and laparoscopy in children. He chaired the organizing committee that founded the American Pediatric Surgical Association, and organized the Kiwanis Pediatric Trauma Center at New England Medical Center. Recent work has focused on unnecessary surgery, the assessment of quality of health care, development of practice guidelines, and the prevention of injury. At RAND, he has been co-PI of the RAND/Academic Medical Center Consortium Appropriateness Initiative. At Harvard, he has participated in the medical practice study of malpractice and the resource based relative value study.

Dr. Leape is a member of Alpha Omega Alpha, Sigma Xi, and numerous professional societies. He is the author of over 100 original papers, 25 book chapters, and a textbook of pediatric surgery. He recently served on the AHCPR Health Services Research Review Committee and is a member of the Institute of Medicine Committee on Technological Innovation in Medicine.

BRYAN R. LUCE is a senior research scientist and director of Battelle's Center for Public Health Research and Evaluations (CPHRE) at Arlington, Virginia. As director, Dr. Luce is responsible for numerous research projects for both government and industrial clients and is principal investigator for a large multi-year economic research support contract with the Centers for Disease Control and a research center for the Health Care Financing Administration, as well as a number of other health policy and cost-effectiveness studies. He is also responsible for the MEDTAP Europe office located in London. Before coming to Battelle, Dr. Luce was director of the Office of Research and Demonstration, Health Care Financing Administration. Earlier, he worked as senior analyst in the Office of Technology Assessment of the U.S. Congress. Dr. Luce has co-authored three textbooks in health economic methodology and technology assessment, and has published articles in a number of scientific health-related journals. Dr. Luce has adjunct appointments with Georgetown University Medical School and the George Washington University. He is also a lieutenant colonel in the Medical Service Corps, U.S. Army Reserves. He did his undergraduate and master's training at the Universities of Vermont and Massachusetts and his doctoral training at the University of California, Los Angeles.

ANN K. M. MARSHALL is director, Product Planning, Abbott International. In this capacity, she is responsible for commercial and strategic assessment of Abbott's developmental products for major overseas markets. Previously, Ms. Marshall was manager, Corporate Strategic Planning, at Abbott Laboratories, a role in which she managed a range of strategic issues and assessed business and technology acquisition opportunities. Prior to joining Abbott, Ms. Marshall was a management consultant at KPMG Peat Marwick, where she specialized in strategic planning and financial management consulting. Before that, she was a faculty lecturer at the University of Michigan, as well as director and founder of REALM, Inc., a diversified educational services firm. Ms. Marshall did her undergraduate training at Syracuse University and the University of London, U.K. She received her Ph.D. in philosophy and her M.B.A., concentrating in finance and corporate strategy, from the University of Michigan.

WILLIAM T. McGIVNEY is vice president, Clinical Evaluation and Research, for AEtna Health Plans. This unit is responsible for evaluating medical technologies, developing clinical guidelines, and establishing coverage policy. Prior to joining AEtna in June of 1991, Bill spent 10 years with the American Medical Association, most recently serving as director of the Division of Health Care Technology.

Bill received his Ph.D. in pharmacology from the University of North Carolina Medical School and then completed a postdoctoral fellowship in the Department of Psychiatry at Harvard Medical School. He is a nationally recognized expert in the area of drug and device regulation and coverage and reimbursement policy. In 1989, he was recognized for this expertise and his contributions to drug and device policy development with the Food and Drug Administration Commissioner's Medal of Appreciation. Bill has served on numerous national committees including the board of directors of the United Network for Organ Transplantation, the nation's transplant policy board.

LEE N. NEWCOMER is vice president, Health Services Operations, for United Health Care Corporation. His responsibilities for the company include development of technology assessments and medical guidelines, oversight of medical policy for the company's health plans and specialty companies, and assisting with health services research within the organization. Dr. Newcomer received his medical degree in 1976 from the University of Nebraska College of Medicine. He completed a residency in internal medicine at the same institution in 1979. He was a fellow in medical oncology at Yale University until 1981. Dr. Newcomer practiced as a medical oncologist for nine years and he is board certified in both internal medicine and medical oncology. Following completion of a master's degree in health administration from the University of Wisconsin in 1990 he joined United Health Care Corporation as their national medical director in 1991. Dr. Newcomer has published several articles about medical policy and medical oncology in the medical literature and the lay press.

DOUGLAS K. OWENS is a health services research and development service research associate at the Department of Veterans Affairs Medical Center, Palo Alto, and an assistant professor of medicine and an assistant professor of health research and policy at Stanford University. He received a bachelor of science in biology from Stanford University in 1978, and subsequently attended medical school at the University of California, San Francisco. He completed residency training in internal medicine at the University of Pennsylvania, followed by a postdoctoral research fellowship in Health Care Research and Health Policy at Stanford University. In 1991 he received a master of science degree in health services research from Stanford.

Dr. Owens is interested in technology assessment and the application of decision theory to clinical and health policy problems. His research focuses on assessment of diagnostic and screening strategies, as well as related policy ques tions. He has a particular interest in policy questions related to disease caused by the human immunodeficiency virus, and is currently studying screening and other interventions designed to reduce transmission of HIV infection. He also is developing methods for producing normative model-based practice and screening guidelines.

J. SANFORD SCHWARTZ is associate professor of medicine and senior scholar in clinical epidemiology in the School of Medicine, associate professor of health care systems in the Wharton School, Robert D. Eilers professor of health management and economics, and executive director of the Leonard Davis Institute, the University of Pennsylvania's multidisciplinary center for health policy and health services research. Sandy graduated from the University of Rochester with an A.B. in history and received his M.D. degree from the University of Pennsylvania. Following a residency in internal medicine at the Hospital of the University of Pennsylvania, he was a Robert Wood Johnson Foundation clinical scholar, during which he completed the M.B.A. program in health care administration at the Wharton School of the University of Pennsylvania and obtained additional formal training in biostatistics, epidemiology, legal aspects of health care, and public policy of health care at the Schools of Law and Public Policy at the University of Pennsylvania.

Following completion of his fellowship in 1977, Sandy joined the faculty in the School of Medicine at the University of Pennsylvania. The focus of Sandy's research has been the evaluation of medical practices and medical decisionmaking, including evaluating the trade-offs among cost, quality, and outcomes in health care, and optimizing the value of clinical information. His work in these areas has been widely published in clinical and health services research journals, as well as in text- and other books. Sandy has received fellowship awards from the U.S. Public Health Service, the Hospital and Research Educational Trust, the American College of Physicians, and the W.K. Kellogg Foundation. His research has been supported by the National Center for Health Services Research, Agency for Health Care Policy and Research, National Institutes of Health, National Library of Medicine, Centers for Disease Control, Health Care Financing Administration, Henry J. Kaiser Family Foundation, John A. Hartford Foundation, Robert Wood Johnson Foundation, W.K. Kellogg Foundation, and several pharmaceutical and medical device manufacturers. In 1981, Sandy developed and then served as the first director of the American College of Physicians' Clinical Efficacy Assessment Project.

He has been an advisor and consultant to a wide variety of government and private sector groups, including the Centers for Disease Control, Department of Defense, Health Care Financing Administration, Institute of Medicine, National Institutes of Health, U.S. Congress Office of Technology Assessment, U.S. Preventive Services Task Force, Veterans Administration, World Health Organization, Blue Cross and Blue Shield Associations of America, the John A. Hartford,

Henry J. Kaiser, Robert Wood Johnson and W.K. Kellogg Foundations, and a broad range of pharmaceutical, medical technology and health care delivery corporations. Sandy is a member of the Health Services Research Study Section of the Agency for Health Care Policy and Research, the editorial board of the *Journal of General Internal Medicine,* and a former member of the editorial board of *Medical DecisionMaking.* Sandy has held a variety of leadership positions in academic and research societies. He is past president and member of the board of trustees and former Eastern section chair of the American Federation for Clinical Research, a member of the Council of Academic Societies of the Association of American Medical Colleges, chair of the Technology Assessment Committee of the Society for General Internal Medicine, and former president of the Society for Medical DecisionMaking.

EARL P. STEINBERG is professor of medicine at the Johns Hopkins School of Medicine with a joint faculty appointment in the Department of Health Policy and Management at the Johns Hopkins School of Hygiene and Public Health. Dr. Steinberg is also director of the Johns Hopkins Program for Medical Technology and Practice Assessment, a member of National Blue Cross/Blue Shield's Medical Advisory Panel, and a member of the federal Physician Payment Review Commission. His research focuses on technology assessment, the cost and effectiveness of alternative patterns of medical practice, evaluation of the quality of medical care, and the clinical and economic impacts of health care payment innovations.

Dr. Steinberg received his A.B. degree from Harvard College, his M.D. from Harvard Medical School, and a master of public policy degree from the Kennedy School of Government at Harvard. His residency training in internal medicine was performed at the Massachusetts General Hospital.

Dr. Steinberg has received numerous awards, including the A.B. degree *summa cum laude.* In July 1984, Dr. Steinberg received a Henry J. Kaiser Family Foundation faculty scholar award in general internal medicine, an award given "to support exceptionally talented young faculty in general internal medicine," and in 1988 Dr. Steinberg received the Outstanding Young Investigator Award from the Association for Health Services Research.

BURTON A. WEISBROD is Johns Evans professor of economics and director of Northwestern University's Center for Urban Affairs and Policy Research. He was, until July, 1990, Evjue-Bascom professor of economics at the University of Wisconsin, where he had been on the faculty since 1964, and where he had founded and directed the Center for Health Economics and Law. He was born in Chicago, receiving his undergraduate degree in management from the University of Illinois, and his M.A. and Ph.D. degrees in economics from Northwestern University. Professor Weisbrod has held visiting faculty appointments at Brandeis, Harvard, Princeton, and Yale Universities, and abroad at the Australian

National University and the University Autonoma de Madrid, in addition to being a senior staff member of the Council of Economic Advisers to Presidents John F. Kennedy and Lyndon B. Johnson.

Professor Weisbrod's elected positions include: fellow of the American Association for the Advancement of Science, member of the Institute of Medicine of the National Academy of Sciences, member of the executive committee of the American Economic Association and president of the Midwest Economic Association. He is the author or co-author of 9 books, editor of 4, and author of more than 100 articles in professional journals and books. His research has focused on public policy analysis in the areas of economics of education, health, medical research, manpower, public interest law, the military draft, benefit-cost analysis and, most recently, philanthropy, voluntarism, and the nonprofit sector. In addition to consulting widely for governments, foundations, nonprofit organizations, and private firms in the United States, Europe, and Asia, Professor Weisbrod has also served on numerous national and international study and conference committees, and has been on the editorial boards of six journals. His biography is listed in such publications as *Who's Who in Science, Who's Who in U.S. Writers, Editors and Poets, Who's Who in America,* and *Who's Who in the World.*

Index